JANE AUSTEN AND THE CLERGY

JANE AUSTEN
AND THE CLERGY

IRENE COLLINS

THE HAMBLEDON PRESS

LONDON   AND   RIO GRANDE

Published by The Hambledon Press 1993
102 Gloucester Avenue, London NW1 8HX (U.K.)
P.O. Box 162, Rio Grande, Ohio 45674 (U.S.A.)

ISBN 1 85285 114 7

A description of this book is available from
the British Library and from the Library of Congress

Typeset by York House Typographic Ltd
Printed on acid-free paper and bound in Great
Britain by Cambridge University Press

Contents

Illustrations

Between Pages 82 and 83

Acknowledgements

The author and publisher are grateful to the following for permission to reproduce illustrations: Bath City Library, p. 178, pl. 11; The British Library, pp. 23, 146; The Jane Austen Memorial Trust, Chawton, p. 53, pls 4, 5, 6; The Knight Family, pl. 10; Manchester Central Library, pls 7, 12, 13; The National Portrait Gallery, pls 3, 14, 15, 16, 17, 18; The Parochial Church Council of St Nicholas's Church, Steventon, pl. 2; Dr Williams's Library, pp. 142, 170, 183.

Preface

Jane Austen's novels hold a unique place in the affections of the reading public on account of their portrayals of life among the gentry of England on their country estates at the beginning of the nineteenth century. The atmosphere is created so unobtrusively, with never a hint of a description dragged in for the sake of 'local colour', that it is easy to assume that the author was writing about her own lifestyle.

This is not quite true. Jane Austen, both during her early life at Steventon and later at Chawton, was on visiting terms with the local gentry: but visiting is not living. She depended a good deal on observation, and in the early stages of her novel-writing she was not above making the occasional gaffe. She realized herself, on reading the newly-published *Pride and Prejudice*, that she had slipped up over the fashion in eating habits among the gentry: since dinner was taken late in the evening instead of at the customary hour of 3 or 4 p.m., and 'suppers' were no longer served, Mrs Bennet ought not to have been expecting Mr Darcy and Mr Bingley to stay for such refreshment at Longbourn. 'But I suppose it was the remains of Mrs Bennet's old Meryton habits', Jane wrote ruefully to Cassandra (Mrs Bennet having lived in humbler circumstances before her marriage).[1]

Jane's niece Fanny Knight thought that her aunt owed most of her knowledge of country house life to the visits she paid to her brother Edward and his wife Elizabeth (daughter of Sir Brook Bridges) after Edward inherited the elegant Georgian mansion of Godmersham Park from his adoptive father Thomas Knight. Some years after Jane Austen's death, Fanny wrote in an undated letter to a younger relative, with reference to both Jane and her sister Cassandra:

They were not rich & the people around with whom they chiefly mixed, were not at all high bred, or in short anything more than *mediocre* & they of course tho' superior in *mental powers* and *cultivation* were on the same level as far as *refinement* goes – but I think in later life their intercourse with Mrs Knight (who was very fond of & kind to them) improved them both & Aunt Jane was too clever not to put aside all possible signs of 'common-ness' (if such an expression is allowable) & teach herself to be more refined, at least in intercourse with people in general. Both the Aunts (Cass. & Jane) were brought up in the most complete ignorance of the World & its ways (I mean as to fashion &c) & if it had not been for Papa's marriage which brought them into Kent, & the kindness of Mrs Knight who used often to have one or other of the sisters staying with her, they would have been, tho' not less clever and agreeable in themselves, very much below par as to good Society and its ways.[2]

This was not entirely true either, but the general impression of Jane Austen as not quite a member of the gentry class is fair enough.

The life in which she felt thoroughly at home was that of the country clergy. Biographers usually mention as important the fact that her father, two of her brothers and four of her cousins were clergymen, but none so far has demonstrated the extent to which she was involved in their situation and way of thinking. This book is the first attempt to do so, and hence to bring us nearer to the true Jane Austen. Without suggesting that knowledge of an author's life necessarily helps us to understand that author's work, the biography of a person as important as Jane Austen in the cultural life of the nation both past and present must always be significant.

Nor is the history of the church during Jane Austen's lifetime well known. Such attention as it has been given has been concentrated on the Evangelical movement to the detriment of the mainstream of the Anglican church, which is generally remembered only for its failings. Not only are histories of the subject rare: there is a paucity of source material due, it has been suggested, to the fact that the Victorian clergy were ashamed of their predecessors and had no wish to investigate or publicize their activities.[3] Another purpose of this book, therefore, is to use the information we can obtain from a study of Jane Austen's life and novels to help fill the gap. Parsons' daughters were thick on the ground at the time, but few have left as many of their own writings or been honoured with as many reminiscences by friends and relatives as she has. The evidence provided by this material is worthy of at least as much attention as the journals of the handful of contemporary parsons – James Woodforde, William Jones, John Skinner, Benjamin Newton and a few others – much quoted by historians.

Grateful as one is for the novels Jane Austen wrote during her all too brief life, there is room for a slight feeling of regret that she did not take seriously the suggestion once made to her that she should devote a novel to depicting the lifestyle of a contemporary clergyman. Edmund Bertram hardly counts: although he is a central character in *Mansfield Park* he is a mere ordinand rather then a fully-fledged parson for most of the book. Fortunately, clergy at the time were so ubiquitously involved in the activities of the gentry that Jane Austen could not avoid bringing considerable numbers of them into her stories of country house life. The fact that they are brought in more in their capacity as lovers, husbands and neighbours than in their role as pastors is significant in itself.

Two of her best-known clergy characters, Mr Collins of *Pride and Prejudice* and Mr Elton of *Emma,* are so ruthlessly pilloried for their faults that they have been cited again and again by historians seeking to criticize churchmen of the period. That they were not mere caricatures, but were meant to be taken seriously, is evidenced by the dismay expressed by some of Jane Austen's acquaintance that she should be portraying such clergymen at a time when the church had a particular need to be seen in a good light. Yet it was possible even at the time for Jane Austen's mother (the daughter, widow and mother of clergymen) to enjoy Mr Collins, and for her future nephew-in-law Ben Lefroy (son and brother of clergymen, and shortly to be ordained himself) to describe Mr Elton and his vulgar wife as singularly well-drawn, without either of these witnesses feeling that the church as a whole was being undermined.[4] Presumably they believed, with Edmund Bertram, that the majority of clergy were not guilty of the gross errors patent in a few, and attributed by their critics to the whole body. One of the interesting things that we can learn from a study of Jane Austen's life and writing is how it came about that an intelligent and devout Christian could love and respect the Anglican church of her day. Although it was not as corrupt as some historians have supposed, it remained to a large extent in the condition which had prompted Gibbon to accuse it of enjoying 'fat slumbers'.

As sources for this study, Jane Austen's novels have been valued equally with her letters. This would once have been a common practice. Macaulay was in the habit of drawing heavily on novels for information concerning the social conditions of earlier times. In this, as in much else, he greatly influenced succeeding generations: in 1939 it was still possible for G.M. Young, in what became a celebrated essay on Victorian England, to refer to characters in the novels of Dickens and Disraeli as though they were real people, and to quote Thomas Hardy and Rider Haggard as 'observers of unquestioned competence' on matters of social change.[5] In more recent years, the growing emphasis on archival research and demographic techniques has made historians reluctant to

follow suit, but the practice can reasonably be revived in the case of Jane
Austen's portraits of clergymen for a number of reasons. One is that
they were introduced casually, as though all her readers would recognize at once the type of person and situation she had in mind – a
criterion which even Peter Laslett, the severest critic of literary sources,
has accepted as the surest guide to reliability.[6] Her characters were
regarded by contemporaries as realistic: they were sometimes criticized
as being too dull to have been put into novels but never as untrue. Their
apparent realism was such that some of her acquaintances claimed to see
themselves portrayed in the more attractive characters – claims which
she always vigorously denied. She was too proud of her inventions, she
said, to have copied them from anybody. Like most authors she wished
to distance herself from her characters in order to give them wider
significance. Unlike many others, she did not seek to achieve this effect
by setting her stories in times past – during her own childhood or in
some historical period. She liked to think that they were up-to-date. It
was with some anxiety that she considered submitting again for publication the novel ultimately called *Northanger Abbey*, whose original version
had been 'sat on' so long by the publisher to whom it was first sent that
one of its major themes, the craze for Gothick novels, was past its heyday.

Of course there are problems. It has to be borne in mind that although
Jane Austen's novels were not as pointedly didactic as, say, George
Eliot's, they were nevertheless written with a moralizing purpose at least
partly in mind. This, however, makes them no more difficult to use for
historical purposes than tracts for the times such as Wilberforce's
Practical View or William Payne Knight's vituperative poem *The Landscape*. Equally it has to be remembered that Jane Austen as narrator
employed a number of different 'voices' in her novels. When she is
expressing the views of the hero or heroine and when her own is a
matter for the historian's judgement.

   If novels require caution, however, so do letters, which have never
been rejected as historical sources to the same extent. Jane Austen's
letters have been a disappointment to many readers because they are
mostly concerned with family chit-chat and include few comments on
the times. From the historian's point of view they have the advantage
that they were not written with any thought or prospect of subsequent
publication. Most of those which have survived were addressed to her
sister Cassandra, with whom she had an intimate relationship that
demanded from her no pretences other than those she chose to adopt

for fun. Like her novels, they contain a rich vein of burlesque which has to be taken into account.

In view of the somewhat unusual nature of this study, I should like to conclude by thanking the many members of the Historical Association who at one time or another have listened to my lectures on Jane Austen's contributions to history, and by their appreciation and comments have encouraged me to persevere with my ideas; also my former colleague Margaret Gibson for her energetic support.

Chapter 1

Jane Austen's Clerical Connections

In 1815 the Rev. James Stanier Clarke, librarian to the Prince Regent, conceived the idea that Jane Austen, whom he had met when she was staying with her brother in London, should devote one of her excellent novels to depicting the character and lifestyle or an English clergyman of the day.[1] He had in mind someone more distinguished than Mr Collins of *Pride and Prejudice* and Mr Elton of *Emma*, mere country parsons both; someone, indeed, more like himself – a clergyman who divided his time between the metropolis and the country, devoting his time to literature but remaining, withal, gentle and unworldly, 'no man's Enemy but his own'. Jane Austen protested her inability to oblige, but Clarke, nothing daunted, warmed to his theme. 'Do let us have an English Clergyman after *your* fancy', he urged:

> Much novelty may be introduced – shew dear Madam what good would be done if Tythes were taken away entirely, and describe him burying his own mother – as I did – because the High Priest of the Parish in which she died did not pay her remains the respect he ought to do . . . Carry your Clergyman to Sea as the Friend of some distinguished Naval Character about the court . . .

Clarke was by all accounts a bit of an ass and Jane could not resist incorporating some of his wilder notions into the plan of a novel she was supposed to be writing – a novel in which the main character, an elderly clergyman who had 'lived much in the World', occupied the greater part of the first volume relating his extraordinary experiences to his daughter, and after many further adventures expired at the end of the second volume 'in a fine burst of Literary Enthusiasm, intermingled with Invectives against Holders of Tythes'.[2] She nevertheless felt herself indebted to Clarke in various ways. He had shown her around Carlton

House, offered her the use of his library and his apartments in Golden Square should she need them when he was away, and arranged for her to dedicate *Emma*, with permission, to the Prince Regent. In any case, she believed, like Mr Woodhouse, in giving people the respect due to their position. Her comedy at Mr Clarke's expense was therefore reserved for her family's enjoyment, and her reply to the gentleman himself was firm but courteous. 'I am quite honoured by your thinking me capable of drawing such a clergyman as you gave the sketch of', she wrote:

> But I assure you I am *not*. The comic part of the character I might be equal to, but not the good, the enthusiastic, the literary. Such a man's conversation must at times be on subjects of science and philosophy, of which I know nothing; or at least must be occasionally abundant in quotations and allusions which a woman who, like me, knows only her own mother tongue, and has read very little in that, would be totally without the power of giving. A classical education, or at any rate a very extensive acquaintance with English literature, ancient and modern, appears to me quite indispensable for the person who would do justice to your clergyman; and I think I may boast myself to be, with all possible vanity, the most unlearned and uninformed a female who ever dared to be an authoress.

Clarke's bumptiousness has cost him some rough handling by posterity, but his idea that Jane Austen might write a novel about a clergyman was not wholly without sense. Clergy had already appeared in secondary roles in all her novels, and were to do so again in *Persuasion*, the only further novel she was to live to complete. Admittedly, none was a high flyer, although Dr Grant was sophisticated enough to occasion no surprise when he was translated to a stall in Westminster Abbey at the end of *Mansfield Park*, and Henry Tilney was capable of conversation brilliant enough for Lord David Cecil to think that he might have been modelled on the Rev. Sydney Smith, the cleverest talker of that age.[3] Jane Austen may not have thought herself capable of simulating the interests of a truly learned cleric, but on the ins and outs of clerical life in an ordinary parish few people can have been better informed. The briefest account of her own life is sufficient to show that clergymen had played an important part in it from the beginning.

When Jane was born, in December 1775, her father had already spent fourteen years as rector of the parish of Steventon, on the northern border of Hampshire. He owed his preferment to the grace and favour of a second cousin, Thomas Knight I, whose extensive lands in Hampshire and in Kent provided livings for more than one relative and friend. George Austen was grateful for his good fortune and never moved from his little parish, other than on short visits to relatives, until he retired to Bath in 1801. Thus it came about that Jane, who never married, spent almost all of the first twenty-five years of her life in a country parsonage.

Mrs Austen, as the daughter and niece of more affluently placed clergymen in Oxfordshire, was less enamoured of the restricted surroundings at Steventon, but she accepted them cheerfully enough whilst engaged in bringing up a moderately large family. There were eight children in all: James, George, Edward, Henry, and Cassandra, born ten, nine, eight, four and two years before Jane; Frank, only one year older than Jane; and Charles, 'our own particular little brother' as his sisters called him, born four years later.[4] Their father was a good-tempered man, not too repressive of the young: life at the parsonage was, as far as he could make it, relaxed and happy. As Jane grew up, the other members of the family were seldom all at home together. George, who was mentally retarded, never lived at the parsonage after his infancy. Edward from an early age spent a part of each year with his wealthy uncle, Thomas Knight II, who eventually adopted him. The other boys gradually went away to take up careers. Jane was devoted to her father and loved her one and only sister dearly, but it was her brothers who provided her with interest and excitement. She always looked forward to their return home for the holidays.

In gentry and professional families the size of the Austens it was taken for granted that one or two of the sons would enter the church. Opportunities elsewhere were not numerous, the lay professions having only just begun to organize themselves.[5] Of the four Digweed brothers at Steventon Manor, playmates of the Austen boys, James was destined for ordination; the Rev. I.P. George Lefroy in the neighbouring parish of Ashe produced two clergymen from among his four sons; the Terrys of nearby Dummer were unusual in producing only one ordinand out of their numerous progeny. George Austen sent both James and Henry to Oxford with clerical careers in mind, leaving Frank and Charles to go to sea. Frank might have been a better choice for a clergyman than Henry, for he became a deeply religious man whereas Henry was something of a fly-by-night. By the time Henry graduated war was being waged against revolutionary France and he decided to enter the militia rather than the church. James, however, had been duly ordained deacon on 10 December 1787, a few days before Jane's twelfth birthday. He was always the most studious of the Austen brothers, happy to guide his younger sister in her reading. During vacations from Oxford he had been content to write prologues for the amateur theatricals performed in his father's old tithe barn, leaving Henry to play opposite their lively cousin

Eliza in the leading roles. When war came he purchased a naval chaplaincy, with no intention of making it into anything other than a sinecure.[6]

Jane admired her eldest brother enormously. She did not imagine that ordination and a curacy at nearby Stoke Charity would alter their relationship, for the duties were little more than nominal: he could retain a Fellowship at Oxford with nothing more than a brief visit to the parish during the vacations. Far from abandoning his literary interests, he had embarked on something of a literary career at Oxford, editing a satirical journal entitled *The Loiterer* and writing a good many of its articles himself. Knowing that further theatricals were pending for the holidays, Jane composed a dramatic piece entitled *The Visit* and dedicated it to James, hoping that it would 'afford some amusement to so respectable a Curate'.[7] When the summer of 1790 came, however, James obtained a curacy at Overton, and life took a different turning for him. There were real duties to be performed in the new parish, including taking services at Laverstoke; and there the susceptible young clergyman met and courted Anne, daughter of General Mathew, tenant of the manor house, marrying her in 1792. Resigning his Fellowship perforce, he needed somewhere to live; and like many a young man before and since he turned to his father to provide. The latter came to the rescue by accommodating the couple in his spare parsonage house at Deane.

George Austen had become rector of the neighbouring parish of Deane in 1773, the presentation to the living having been purchased for his benefit by his well-to-do uncle, Francis Austen, a barrister at Sevenoaks. Deane was adjacent to Steventon and for nearly twenty years George Austen looked after both parishes himself and made a little extra money by letting out Deane parsonage to friends. By 1792, with his sons more of less off his hands, he was prepared to forgo the rent on the parsonage and install James as his resident curate.

It is reasonable to assume that there was much coming and going between the two households, since they were only a mile and a half apart. Jane's affection for her brother and her concern for his welfare soon took on a new importance, for to everybody's sorrow Anne Mathew died suddenly in 1795. James was then glad to be able to send his little daughter Anna to Steventon to live with her grandparents and her two aunts, whom she liked and trusted. James rode over every day, a practice he continued even when he had married again and taken Anna back to Deane. Sometimes he would turn up in his mother's kitchen before breakfast and appear again in the course of the same day.[8]

The only drawback to James's installation at Deane was that the previous occupants of the parsonage had to be asked to leave. For the past three years the house had been let to Mrs Martha Lloyd, widow of a clergyman friend of George Austen, who lived there with her two unmarried daughters, Martha and Mary. The two young ladies became great friends of Jane and Cassandra. Jane was especially fond of Martha and continued to visit her when she moved with her mother and sister to Ibthorpe, some fifteen miles away. The distance was always an excuse for a fairly long stay. There being no church at Ibthorpe, the two friends usually walked a mile or so on Sundays to attend services at Hurstbourne Tarrant, where the four gossipy daughters of the Rev. Peter Debary fell upon them as though they were visitors from another planet. Their brother Peter, who was the same age as James Austen, was ordained and serving as a curate in the vicinity. Jane could not bear him – when he once, at a later date, called on her and her mother at Southampton, she could hardly wait to get rid of him.[9] James, however, got on well with Peter and kept in touch with him when he eventually settled in a parish at Eversley. James had by then married Mary Lloyd as his second wife, and Mary was more in tune with the Debarys than Martha and Jane had ever been. In consequence 'the endless Debaries', as Jane called them, seemed to turn up everywhere and she was always bumping into them. The eldest Miss Debary acted as nurse for Mary when her children were born.[10]

There was a third Lloyd sister, Eliza, who had married her cousin the Rev. Fulwar Craven Fowle. It is not known for certain whether Jane ever visited Eliza and Fulwar in their first parsonage in Gloucestershire, but it is likely that she did. The Austens were on very friendly terms with the Fowles and connected with them in more ways than one. When George Austen was preparing his own sons for university, he took in Fulwar Fowle and his brother Tom as boarding pupils, along with a few other boys from the neighbourhood. Both were destined for the church. There were four Fowle brothers altogether, sons of the Rev. Thomas Fowle of Kintbury, an old friend of George Austen. James Austen retained fond memories of visits to 'the village Parson's cheerful family'. and wrote of them long afterwards in nostalgic verse.[11] Of the four 'manly boys' he most admired the forceful Fulwar, who was a year older than himself; Jane and Cassandra were happier with the gentler Tom, who came along later. It was Tom who is known to have taken part in the amateur theatricals at Steventon, pronouncing on one occasion the inappropriate epilogue James had written to a seering melodrama: 'Halloo, good gentlefolk! What! none asleep?'[12] Cassandra in due course became engaged to Tom and was waiting for him to acquire a living

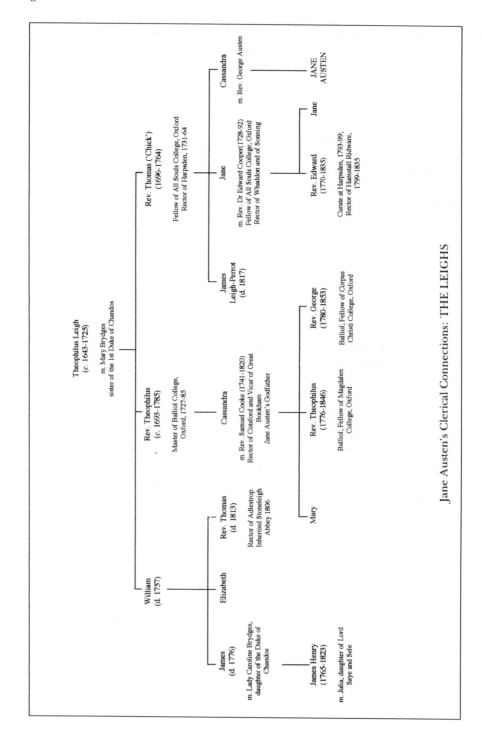

Jane Austen's Clerical Connections: THE LEIGHS

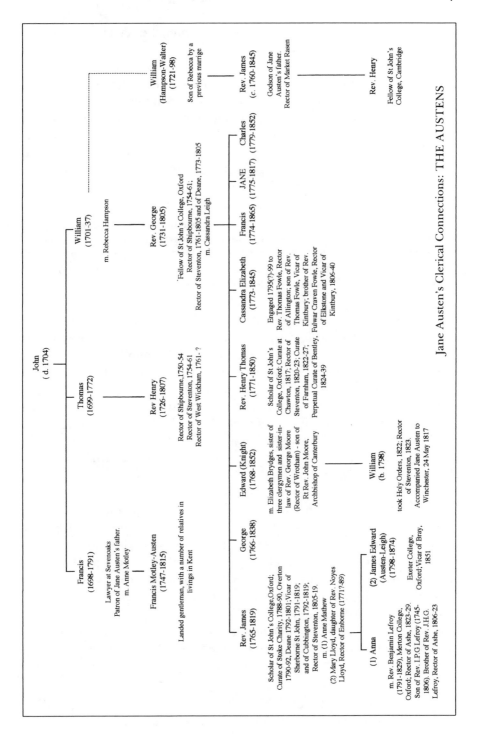

John
(d. 1704)

William
(1701-37)

m. Rebecca Hampson

William
(Hampson-Walter)
(1721-98)

Son of Rebecca by a
previous marrige

Francis
(1698-1791)

Lawyer at Sevenoaks
Patron of Jane Austen's father.
m. Anne Motley

Thomas
(1699-1772)

Rev Henry
(1726-1807)

Rector of Shipbourne,1750-54
Rector of Steventon, 1754-61
Rector of West Wickham, 1761-?

Rev. George
(1731-1805)

'Fellow of St John's College, Oxford
Rector of Shipbourne, 1754-61;
Rector of Steventon, 1761-1805 and of Deane, 1773-1805
m. Cassandra Leigh

Rev. James
(c. 1760-1845)

Godson of Jane
Austen's father.
Rector of Market Rasen

Francis Motley-Austen
(1747-1815)

Landed gentleman, with a number of relatives in
livings in Kent

Rev. James
(1765-1819)

Scholar of St John's College,Oxford;
Curate of Stoke Charity, 1788-90, Overton
1790-92, Deane 1792-1801;Vicar of
Sherborne St John, 1791-1819;
and of Cubbington, 1792-1819,
Rector of Steventon, 1805-19.
m. (1) Anne Mathew
(2) Mary Lloyd, daughter of Rev. Noyes
Lloyd, Rector of Enborne (1771?-89)

George
(1766-1838)

Edward (Knight)
(1768-1852)

m. Elizabeth Brydges, sister of
three clergymen and sister-in-
law of Rev. George Moore
(Rector of Wrotham) - son of
Rt Rev. John Moore,
Archbishop of Canterbury

Rev. Henry Thomas
(1771-1850)

Scholar of St John's
College, Oxford; Curate at
Chawton, 1817; Rector of
Steventon, 1820-23; Curate
of Farnham, 1822-27;
Perpetual Curate of Bentley,
1824-39

Cassandra Elizabeth
(1773-1845)

Engaged 1795(?)-99 to
Rev. Thomas Fowle, Rector
of Allington; son of Rev.
Thomas Fowle, Vicar of
Kintbury; brother of Rev.
Fulwar Craven Fowle, Rector
of Elkstone and Vicar of
Kintbury, 1806-40

Francis
(1774-1865)

JANE
(1775-1817)

Charles
(1779-1852)

(1) Anna

m. Rev. Benjamin Lefroy
(1791-1829), Merton College,
Oxford; Rector of Ashe, 1823-29.
Son of Rev. I.P.G Lefroy (1745-
1806). Brother of Rev. J.H.G.
Lefroy, Rector of Ashe, 1806-23

(2) James Edward
(Austen-Leigh)
(1798-1874)

Exeter College,
Oxford; Vicar of Bray,
1851

William
(b. 1798)

took Holy Orders, 1822; Rector
of Steventon, 1823.
Accompanied Jane Austen to
Winchester, 24 May 1817

Rev. Henry

Fellow of St John's
College, Cambridge

Jane Austen's Clerical Connections: THE AUSTENS

when he died tragically at the age of thirty-one. She remained a spinster for the rest of her long life.

Jane herself was attracted to several young men during her early womanhood at Steventon but the only one who came anywhere near to seeking her hand in marriage was the Rev. Samuel Blackall, a young clergyman from Cambridge whom she met visiting in the neighbour-hood. He was a pompous fellow, fond of discoursing on the subject of the ideal wife, and Jane was not really sorry when he cried off. Years later, when she heard that he had got married at last to a Miss Lewis of Clifton, she wrote to her brother Frank, who had also known him:

> I should very much like to know what sort of a Woman she is. He was a piece of Perfection, noisy Perfection himself which I always recollect with regard . . . I would wish Miss Lewis to be of a silent turn & rather ignorant, but naturally intelligent & wishing to learn; – fond of cold veal pies, green tea in the afternoon, & a green window blind at night.[13]

During Jane's last few years at Steventon parsonage, references to neighbouring clergy flit across the pages of the letters she wrote to Cassandra whenever the latter was away from home. Some refer to acquaintances made at the home of Mrs Lefroy, wife of the rector of Ashe, a lively and hospitable lady who was Jane's adored friend during her adolescence. Only once is there a mention of a church service: 'Harry St John is in Orders, has done duty at Ashe, and performs very well', we read in a letter of 17 November 1798.[14] Otherwise, clergy appear only in a social capacity: the charming Benjamin Portal of the handsome eyes calling to enquire if Cassandra would be home in time for the Ashe ball; James Digweed coming to collect his brother's licence to share with Mr Austen the right to shoot over the manor; Henry Rice making love to Lucy Lefroy at Mr Holder's dinner party; Tom Chute of The Vyne, not yet ordained but shortly to be so, playing cards with Mr Lefroy at Ashe Park; Charles Powlett, curate at Winslade, trying to steal a kiss from Jane, and on another occasion giving a rowdy party to the disturbance of all his neighbours.[15] The clear impression is that Jane took clergymen for granted and judged them as she found them, expecting them to be neither better nor worse than other men. They formed an integral part of the social scene which she was to be sorry to leave.

Mr Austen's decision to retire from Steventon in 1801 came as a shock to Jane, although there were obvious reasons why he should have made it.

He was approaching seventy. He had little in the way of private fortune and pensions were unheard of, but he could retire from active ministry without actually resigning the living: he could leave James in charge and pay him a stipend, retaining a suitable income for himself. The choice of Bath was also a fairly obvious one. He and his wife had married there; they knew it well. The spa was no longer a social centre for the fashionable world but had become more residential and had acquired a reputation as a health resort and as a suitable retreat for the elderly. There were plenty of doctors on hand. Mrs Austen, who had become something of a hypochondriac since her children had grown up, was pleased at the idea of being near her brother, James Leigh-Perrot, who spent half his time in Bath on account of a gouty foot.

Jane and Cassandra were both away from home when the decision was made. Jane had found considerable amusement in Bath on the occasions when she visited it in the company of her uncle or her brother Edward, but as a place to live in she was less happy with it. She was depressed by the damp weather, the jerry-built houses and the prices in the shops; and she greatly disliked the private parties which were gradually replacing public assemblies as the accepted mode. She had no love for her aunt Leigh-Perrot and no wish to see more of her. However, neither she nor Cassandra had any choice but to accompany their parents. Jane was twenty-five and Cassandra twenty-eight. They were both unmarried and their brothers could not have been expected to want them.

Jane found some compensation for the loss of Steventon in the prospect of holidays by the sea.[16] Her parents had already talked of indulging in this novel practice, but it is unlikely that they would have done so had Mr Austen remained in harness. Even when he retired they needed an added inducement, which came in the form of a pressing invitation from Richard Buller, one of George Austen's former pupils, to visit him in his vicarage at Colyton in East Devon. Buller had been a guest at Steventon parsonage at least once since his schooldays and now that he was married he was eager to return the hospitality. Jane was not keen on the idea of visiting a newly-married couple, whom she was afraid would show an embarrassing degree of affection for each other, but she was touched by Buller's solicitous enquiries after the family. She eventually decided in favour of the scheme when she realized that it might enable her at last to see Dawlish, a place people talked of endlessly. In the event the four of them – Jane, Cassandra and their parents – spent the latter part of the summer of 1801 not at Dawlish itself but at Sidmouth, on the same side of the river as Colyton. The visit passed off well, Buller having shown the good sense not to address his wife in embarrassingly affectionate terms. Jane thereafter kept up a friendly correspondence with him.[17] There may have been another visit to the vicarage in 1804, but the relationship was destined to come to an end soon after. To Jane's genuine concern, Buller appeared in Bath in 1805 looking distinctly ill and seeking treatment. He had always been of 'a billious habit', she remembered; but this time she feared the worst. He died the following year, aged thirty.

Among welcome visitors to Bath were Jane's godfather the Rev. Samuel Cooke, vicar of Great Bookham in Surrey, and his wife Cassandra, who was Mrs Austen's cousin. Jane was glad to have their daughter Mary to accompany her on long walks, and she was favourably impressed, too, by their clergyman son George when he and some friends joined her and Mary on a stroll around Sydney Gardens. 'My cousin George was very kind', she reported,

> & talked sense to me every now & then in the intervals of his more animated fooleries with Miss Bendish, who is very young & rather handsome . . . There was a monstrous deal of stupid quizzing, & commonplace nonsense talked, but scarcely any wit; – all that border'd on it, or on sense came from my Cousin George, whom altogether I like very well.

She was less enamoured of George's brother, the Rev. Theophilus Cooke, whom she later met in London and who seemed to her to be full of 'nothing-meaning, harmless, heartless Civility'.[18]

Try as she might, she could not like Bath, which became more and more intolerable after January 1805 when Mr Austen died and the three ladies could not see their way to supporting a reasonable standard of living in the town. Even Mrs Austen became anxious to get away. For a while there seemed to be nowhere to go, but a solution was found when in July 1806 Frank, the elder of the two sailor brothers, married and proposed to set up home at Southampton. His mother and sisters arranged to join him there, share household expenses and provide companionship for his wife during his spells of service at sea. Whilst Frank was finding suitable accommodation, Mrs Austen decided to visit her relations in Gloucestershire, taking Jane and Cassandra with her. She was proud of her descent from the younger branch of the Leigh family, which had owned Adlestrop Park since the Reformation. Most of the house built by her great grandfather had been pulled down in the 1750s and replaced by a Gothic structure whose exquisite south-west front was the admiration of the county.[19] It was occupied by a half-cousin, James Henry Leigh, whose wife Julia was a daughter of Lord

Saye and Sele. Mrs Austen seems to have regarded the couple as a little above her touch; however, at the rectory alongside lived her widower cousin, the Rev. Thomas Leigh, and his sister Elizabeth. It was to these that she now repaired.

Jane and Cassandra had visited Adlestrop ten years earlier. Jane was fond of Elizabeth Leigh, who was Cassandra's godmother; but her feeling for the Rev. Thomas Leigh was less certain. In his younger days he had been in the habit of calling at Steventon on his way to London and had usually given the Austen boys a little present of money when he left.[20] Jane had not come in for these attentions but she had always heard Mr Leigh spoken of in the family as a good and kind person. This was probably how she had thought of him until her attitude was clouded by the situation which met them on their arrival at Adlestrop.[21]

The Rev. Thomas Leigh had recently heard some amazing news. On 2 July 1806 the last representative of the elder branch of the Leigh family, the Honourable Mary Leigh, had died at the ancestral home of Stoneleigh Abbey in Staffordshire. In her will she had stipulated that the mansion and its huge estate should revert to the Adlestrop Leighs – to the Rev. Thomas Leigh for his life, then to James Leigh-Perrot (Mrs Austen's brother) for his life, and finally to James Henry Leigh of Adlestrop Park. The first two were childless old men. Nobody supposed that they would show much interest in the legacy or that the forty-year-old James Henry Leigh would be long in succeeding. Indeed, the Leigh family lawyer imagined that the two older legatees would relinquish their claims at once for suitable financial compensation. The Rev. Thomas Leigh, however, had other ideas. He was evidently tired of being regarded as the poor relation and was determined to enjoy a few years of consequence. He had already paid one visit to Stoneleigh but had been obliged to return to London to establish his claim with the lawyers. He was now so keen to secure possession that as soon as Mrs Austen and her daughters arrived at Adlestrop he set out for Staffordshire, taking them with him.[22]

Mrs Austen had no doubt heard of her cousin's good fortune before she left Bath and could be excused for thinking that, if she reminded him of her existence at this critical juncture (when he was doubtless making a new will), he might do something for her and the girls. Her main hope, however, was centred upon the second heir, James Leigh-Perrot, the very brother whose presence in Bath had induced her to take up residence in the town. Her expectations rubbed off on Jane, who increasingly regarded both gentlemen in the light of a possible legacy. Without wishing the Rev. Thomas Leigh any harm, she could not help looking forward to his death. He had apparently obtained a new lease of life, however, and was to be seen posting up and down the country between Adlestrop, Stoneleigh and London in a manner which convinced Henry Austen that he would live for ever.[23] He also displayed an alarming desire to embark on expensive landscape gardening schemes. Meanwhile James Leigh-Perrot was negotiating to sell out his claim to the inheritance. Jane could never understand why this should be to his advantage: to her it was a 'vile compromise'. 'Indeed, I do not know where we are to get our Legacy,' she wrote in June 1808, 'but we will keep a sharp look-out.'[24] Not until 1813 was she able to report that 'Mr Tho[s] Leigh – the respectable, worthy, clever, agreeable Mr Tho. Leigh' had finally died at the age of seventy-nine. He left his relatives nothing. Uncle Leigh-Perrot died in 1817 and left them very little more – a disappointment which Jane was to find difficult to accept, coming as it did when she was desperately ill from the disease that was soon to kill her.[25]

Fortunately the visit to Stoneleigh Abbey had its own rewards, for Jane was to make good use of it in her fiction. The ladies were astonished at the sheer size of the mansion, as well as at the sudden contrast between the older portions and the new Palladian range. Mrs Austen had imagined that the Abbey would be surrounded by 'dark rookeries and dismal yew trees', and was obliged to confess that it was nothing of the kind; but she was always afraid of getting lost in the maze of corridors and she found the state bedroom with its high, dark, crimson velvet bed 'an alarming apartment, just fit for a heroine'. The Rev. Thomas Leigh introduced a strict regimen of prayers morning and evening in the private chapel, which was draped in black on account of the death of the previous owner. This was Jane's first experience of a private chapel, although she had probably heard about the famous one at The Vyne from Tom Chute. At Stoneleigh, visitors normally entered the chapel from the first floor of the house, by a door leading into the gallery, and left it by descending into the nave where another door led straight into the garden. This lay-out provided Jane with a model for the chapel she was to describe at Sotherton Court and hence with a setting for a crucial episode in *Mansfield Park*.[26]

Having arrived in Staffordshire it would have been churlish of Mrs Austen not to visit her nephew, the Rev. Edward Cooper, at his rectory at Hamstall Ridware. He had been asking her to do so for years but she had never gone. In the old days, when the families were growing up, Edward and his sister had frequently spent a part of their holidays at Steventon parsonage. Later, when Edward was ordained and installed as a curate at Harpsden, Mrs Austen had been glad enough to take the girls to visit him in the parish which had been her own girlhood home. The trouble was that Edward had become a pompous and insensitive man. Jane was probably not alone in her reluctance to visit him, especially as he was now proudly ensconced in a different parish with which her family had no connection. However, they went and the visit passed off successfully, except that Jane afterwards succumbed to whooping-cough which she caught from one of Edward's numerous children. She also developed something of a dislike for the eldest boy, who apparently took after his father.[27]

Arriving at Southampton in October 1806, the three were obliged for a while to join Frank and his wife in furnished lodgings. They were so glad to escape from Bath that they were more than willing to put up with a few domestic inconveniences, although these were to create unforeseen problems. One of the advantages they had anticipated on returning to Hampshire was that they would be able once more to receive regular visits from James – not one or twice a day, as in the old times at Steventon, but perhaps once a week. He did indeed come to see them frequently, though not regularly; he tended, rather, to turn up without warning whenever it suited him. Jane always looked forward to his visits, but they sometimes proved to be a disappointment. 'I am sorry & angry that his Visits should not give one more pleasure', she wrote.

> The company of so good & clever a Man ought to be gratifying in itself; – but . . . his time here is spent I think in walking about the House & banging the doors, or ringing the bell for a glass of water.

In her letters to Cassandra she accused James's wife Mary of making him crotchety and morose but this was probably unfair. His younger brother Frank was accustomed to cramped conditions on board ship and had learnt to occupy himself in knotting fringes, cutting out patchwork and turning silver; James, by contrast, had no indoor pursuits other than his books and when he was cut off from these he found it hard to keep still. He was happier when the family rented an apartment in a big old house in Castle Square, where there was an attractive garden with a terrace walk on part of the old city wall and he could stroll with his sisters in the fresh air.[28]

In 1808 James and his wife accompanied Jane on a visit to Edward and his family at Godmersham.[29] The widow of Thomas Knight II had resigned the elegant Georgian house and its considerable estate to Edward in 1798 and Jane had been there at least once before, but it was the first time James and Mary had seen it. They were both 'much struck by the beauty of the place'. The two brothers spent most of the day riding round the farm and exploring the countryside, returning in time to stroll with Jane through the plantations. James made several excursions to Canterbury, where one of his old Oxford tutors, Dr Marlow, occupied a prebendal stall.[30] On at least one Sunday, James took services at Godmersham church. After dinner, which was at a fashionably late hour, he read aloud to the assembled company, mostly from Walter Scott's *Marmion*, just published and not immediately to Jane's liking. Fellow-guests on a number of occasions included the Rev. George Moore, eldest son of the Archbishop of Canterbury, who had married Edward's sister-in-law Harriot Bridges. Jane had always been fond of Harriot and she was anxious to see what the new husband was like. She had said catty things about him to Cassandra (perhaps about his jumped-up origins, for it was common gossip that his grandfather had been a butcher) and she had sworn that she would never like him; but now that she met him she was properly cautious. James's wife took an instant dislike to him: he had a reputation for arrogance and Mary was always ready to think herself slighted. Even Jane was bound to agree that 'his manners were not winning', but she was prepared to give him a chance. Later, at a dinner given by kind old Mrs Knight, she observed that he ordered his wife about and grumbled a good deal, but she conceded that he could tell a good story when disposed to do so. She never felt she had quite weighed him up, although she was sufficiently self-assured in his presence to stop him and engage him in conversation when she met him by accident in a London street. On a later trip into Kent she seized gladly on the opportunity to visit him and Harriot in their rectory at Wrotham.[31]

Happy as the Austens were at Southampton, the arrangement could not last. Frank, inevitably, was posted elsewhere and without him the rent for suitable accommodation was too demanding. It was Edward who finally, if belatedly, came to the rescue. In 1809 he offered his mother and sisters a house on either his Kent or his Hampshire estates. Without hesitation they chose the small house at Chawton which had previously belonged to the Knights' steward. There Jane was to fulfil her ambition to publish novels, refurbishing earlier versions of *Sense and Sensibility*, *Pride and Prejudice* and *Northanger Abbey*, and writing *Mansfield Park*, *Emma* and *Persuasion*. It was to be her home until her untimely death from Addison's Disease in 1817.

Chawton, like Steventon, was a village set in the heart of the Hampshire countryside. Once again a short stroll along a country lane brought Jane to the parish church every Sunday. There was seldom an occasion when the family pew was deserted, for the sisters did not like to be away from home together. The vicar, the Rev. John Rawstorne Papillon, was a distant cousin of the Knights' and Jane was a frequent visitor at the vicarage. She seems to have had no difficulty in keeping up with the latest news about appointments in the church. 'If you have not heard it is very fit you should,' she wrote on one occasion to Cassandra,

> that Mr Harrison has had the living of Fareham given him by the Bishop, and is going to reside there; and now it is said that Mr Peach (beautiful wiseacre) wants to have the curacy of Overton, and, if he *does* leave Wootton, James Digweed wishes to go there.[32]

The incumbent of a parish regarded it as his duty to show hospitality to new clergy coming into the neighbourhood and sooner or later Jane met them at Mr Papillon's dinner-table. She could be as scathing about them as ever: reporting on 'two strange gentlemen, a Mr Twyford curate of G[t] Worldham, who is living in Alton, & his friend Mr Wilkes', she added: 'I don't know that Mr T. is anything except very dark-complexioned, but Mr W. was a useful addition, being an easy, talking, pleasantish young man . . . '[33] She no longer assessed the local clergy as possible dancing partners as she had once done, for she had decided when leaving Southampton that she was too old for dancing; nor did she see them as possible husbands (although Mrs Knight had suggested, perhaps only half jokingly, that she might marry the bachelor vicar of Chawton). She was more interested in them as possible members of the local Book Society, of which she was an assiduous promoter. In this capacity her most useful catch was Mr White, rector of the neighbouring parish of Newton Valence and a nephew of the famous naturalist, the late Gilbert White of Selborne.[34] Her friendliest association, however, was with Mr Benn, the vicar of nearby Farringdon, whose unmarried sister she had taken under her wing.

Steventon was only seventeen miles away. Lack of a carriage made it impossible for the Austen ladies to visit there on a regular basis but one or another of them could go occasionally and stay for a few days either with James and Mary or with friends in the neighbourhood. Jane was always sure of a welcome at Ashe rectory, for although Mr and Mrs Lefroy were no longer there – Mrs Lefroy had been killed by falling from a horse in 1804 and her husband had not long outlived her – their eldest son George had succeeded his father as rector.

Mrs Austen and Jane stayed for a fortnight at Steventon parsonage in 1812, after which Mrs Austen, who retreated into old age much sooner than she need have done, never left Chawton again.[35] James rode over regularly to see his mother and sisters and usually stayed a night or two. He was no longer in very good health and had taken to a diet of bread and water and meat. He had become more introspective of late and was more often to be found writing poetry. Jane thought well of his 'verses' and was sorry when she missed an opportunity to show some of them to Mrs Knight.[36]

James at this time was having trouble with his teenage daughter Anna, who did not get on well with her step-mother. A possible solution seemed to be to send her as often as possible to Chawton, where her grandmother was pleased to have her. Jane loved Anna, but found her a bit of a handful, particularly as she attracted a good deal of attention from young men. Invited by the Whites to attend festivities on Selborne Common for the King's birthday, Anna was reported by Miss Benn to have been 'very much admired by the Gentlemen in general' – including, presumably, the Volunteers, engaged for the occasion.[37] Anna was bosom friends with Harriet Benn, one of the vicar's daughters at Farringdon, and the two of them spent long hours together in intimate conversation in the arbour of the vicarage garden.[38]

When Anna was still only sixteen she fell wildly in love with a man twice her age, the Rev. Michael Terry, one of the sons of the Terry family of Dummer. He was handsome and in line to be presented to the living at Dummer when the present incumbent died; but quite apart from the difference in age he was totally different from Anna in temperament – it seemed unlikely that an attachment between the two of them would last. The combined efforts of the Austen family, including Jane, to keep them apart were of no avail. Mr Terry, poor man, having been shy and retiring all his adult life, was completely captivated by the attentions of the lovely young girl and applied to her father for permission to pay his addresses. James, in spite of his misgivings, could find no reason to refuse and the engagement was announced in 1810. James's worst fears were unfortunately fulfilled, for Anna almost immediately began to have second thoughts: having upset the whole family by insisting on an engagement, she upset them even more by very soon breaking it off.[39] Three years later she fell violently in love again, this time with Ben Lefroy, youngest son of Jane's girlhood friend at Ashe. Ben lived with his brother at Ashe rectory and was near enough to Steventon to visit Anna every day: her stepmother said that she had never seen a couple so foolishly devoted.[40] Unfortunately Ben too was of a serious and unsociable disposition and the engagement was arranged amid general disapproval: Mrs Austen was made quite ill every time she thought about it.[41] Marriage found the pair living at Hendon with Ben's second brother, Edward: Jane seized upon the chance to visit them when she was staying with Henry in London.[42] To everybody's dismay, Ben seemed content for quite some time to live on Anna's small dowry rather than embark on the clerical career for which he seemed destined. He ultimately fulfilled the family's hopes by taking Holy Orders but Jane did not live to see the day.

Jane and Cassandra could and did get away for longish journeys now and again, their absence being made easier by the fact that Martha Lloyd had come to live with them and could be left with Mrs Austen. Cassandra liked to keep up with the Fowles at Kintbury, where Fulwar had succeeded his father as vicar, and Jane with her friend Catherine Bigg from nearby Manydown, who had married an elderly clergyman, the Rev. Herbert Hill, and gone to live at Streatham. The sisters also took it in turn to visit their brother Edward at Godmersham. Jane was increasingly critical of many of Edward's guests, whose social pretensions often seemed to her to be out of all proportion to their intelligence. The clergy were not necessarily an exception: 'I sat by Mr Chisholme [rector of Eastwell]', she wrote after one of the inevitable dinner parties, '& we talked away at a great rate about nothing worth hearing.'[43] However, she very much liked Mr Sherer, the vicar of Godmersham (new since her last visit), and she was really sorry when he had to go away temporarily to look after another of his parishes.[44]

The greatest excitement in Jane's life at this time were her trips to London where her brother Henry, after serving for a number of years in the Oxfordshire militia, had established himself as a banker. Henry knew enough of the business world to be able to place his sister's manuscripts with publishers but he liked to have her on hand occasionally to help matters along. He entertained Jane lavishly and spent a lot of time showing her around art galleries and taking her to theatres, seconded sometimes by their cousins Mary and George Cooke, whose parents had taken lodgings in Bentinck Street. Jane grew increasingly fond of her godfather, the Rev. Samuel Cooke, and visited him and his wife probably more than once at their parsonage in Great Bookham.

Henry was unfortunately one of the many people in Britain whose financial affairs were thrown into chaos by the aftermath of war. In March 1816 his family heard the shattering news that he had become bankrupt. Edward lost heavily by the crash, having stood surety for Henry when he took on the receivership-general of Oxfordshire; other relatives were affected in varying degrees. Henry himself was the first to recover his spirits. He had more than once in his life toyed with the idea of taking Holy Orders: in 1796 he would probably have left the Militia and entered the church if he could have been sure of obtaining a living. (Thomas Knight in his will had named him as second choice for the next presentation to the rectory at Chawton should John Rawstorne Papillon refuse it. Henry had gone to some trouble to investigate the prospect before deciding that it was too uncertain.)[45] Now, at the age of forty-five and after two previous careers, he could not afford to be so nice. So, 'the old learning was to be looked up', as his niece Caroline afterwards put it, and he went to Oxford to see about ordination.[46] He was ordained deacon on 21 December 1816, priested the following February and appointed assistant curate at Chawton. 'Our own new clergyman is expected here very soon, perhaps in time to assist Mr Papillon on Sunday', Jane wrote to her friend Alethea Bigg on 24 January 1817:

> I shall be very glad when the first hearing is over. It will be a nervous hour for our pew, though we hear that he acquits himself with as much ease and collectedness, as if he had been used to it all his life.[47]

Jane had always appreciated Henry's willing nature and lively talents; her pride in his new role was one of the comforts that she enjoyed during the few months of life that remained to her. On 24 May 1817 he and a nephew from Godmersham, William Knight, rode in the rain beside her coach, lent to her by her brother James, on her last journey to Winchester.

Chapter 2

Patronage

The clergy who figured so prominently in Jane Austen's life and novels carved out their careers within a system of patronage which had its roots far back in medieval times and had gathered strength since the Reformation. In the days before education was provided by the state, and before competitive examination and interview became the accepted mode of selection for posts, patronage (the bestowal of favours by persons with the necessary degree of wealth, influence or power) had to be negotiated from start to finish, whatever career the aspirant had in mind. The church was no different in this respect from the armed forces or the civil service, nor did many people think it should be. By the mid nineteenth century, opinion had veered in favour of change in all three cases; only in the twentieth century has the patronage system that flourished in the eighteenth century been condemned as less appropriate for the church than for other institutions.

In Jane Austen's day it was virtually impossible to become ordained in the Church of England without a degree from one or other of the country's only universities, at Oxford and Cambridge. This doubtless precluded many poor boys from thinking of the clerical profession, for in the course of the eighteenth century it had become more difficult for them to obtain places at either university. The free grammar schools, which had provided the minimal amount of classical learning necessary for entry, had fallen into decay. The practice of giving free board and lodging in the colleges to poor scholars in return for service at meals and in chapel also declined as colleges preferred to employ paid staff.[1] Scholarships were available, but only in particular circumstances. The public schools and the better endowed of the grammar schools each had several in their gift and distributed them among their pupils more or less at will: George Austen acquired a scholarship to St John's College,

Oxford, from Tonbridge School, to which his uncle Francis had paid his fees. The university colleges themselves also had scholarships at their disposal, but here preference was given to applicants who were descended either from the founder of the college or from the founder of the scholarship as the case might be. During the middle ages it had been considered appropriate that a man who gave away large sums of money for benevolent purposes should compensate subsequent members of his family for the money they might otherwise have inherited from him, by giving them preferential treatment in the allotment of his charitable funds. Although opposition to the practice of favouring 'Founder's Kin' was beginning to be heard by the end of the eighteenth century, the privilege was not actually abolished until 1854.[2] Jane Austen's two brothers James and Henry acquired scholarships to St John's by claiming kin through their mother with the sixteenth century founder of the college Sir Thomas White; James's son Edward, who could have repeated the claim, preferred in 1817 to take up a scholarship at Exeter College for which he was the only applicant and which he obtained by virtue of his mother's descent from Lord Craven.[3]

At the university, prospective clergy followed the same syllabus as all other undergraduates and consequently found themselves in a position to rub shoulders with future peers, legislators, and landowners. Some were the younger brothers of these more fortunate eldest sons but it is not surprising that many serious-minded young men from humbler backgrounds should have regarded the main advantage of three or four years' residence in a college not as scholastic so much as the chance to make cultivated friends and establish useful contacts. Jane Austen probably had both things in mind when she criticized Mr Collins in *Pride and Prejudice* on the grounds that 'though he belonged to one of the universities, he had merely kept the necessary terms, without forming any useful acquaintance'.[4] Once admitted to a university, obtaining a degree was not difficult: it was afterwards that the problems began. Ordination was not possible before the age of twenty-three; as some students went up to university at a precociously early age (James Austen entered at fourteen) they were left with a good deal of time to fill in. Those who already had a parish lined up (like James Morland and Edmund Bertram, whose fathers were in a position to provide for them) might decide to give themselves a few years' experience 'in the world' before launching themselves into a cure of souls. Others would need to consider that, with the B.A. as their only recommendation, they might find it impossible to make a favourable impression on a patron with a really good living to offer and that they might end their days as mere assistant curates on meagre stipends. Hence, although no further training was officially necessary, many aspiring clergy began upon the search for a university fellowship. Academically these were not difficult to obtain but candidates might have to wait anything from two to six years for one to fall vacant. In Henry Austen's case, the opportunity came just as he was about to escort his attractive cousin Eliza back to her home in France; he had to forgo the pleasure of the trip to take up the proffered place.[5]

Fellowships had the advantage that they could be renewed apparently ad infinitum. Financially they were less advantageous: the average value stood at about £100 a year at the end of the eighteenth century. As this was not a princely sum many Fellows sought to supplement it by taking on certain clerical duties once they were ordained. A common practice was to hire themselves out to take services at £5 a year in the parishes within riding distance of their college. If all these openings were full they could obtain leave of absence and join the countless young clergymen who operated in the same way from home or from lodgings in one of the market towns. According to Arthur Young, the latter abounded with such 'gallopers', who sped around the countryside on Sundays doing duty in as many parishes as they could reach, gabbling through the office 'in a manner perfectly indecent' and striding from the pulpit to the saddle to ride away to the next engagement 'as if pursuing a fox'.[6] It was impossible for them to keep accurate timing; parish clerks rang the bell for the service whenever they saw the clergyman approaching. In bad weather services were simply cancelled.[7]

A Fellowship was no longer tenable once the holder decided to marry. He had then to look either for a curacy or a benefice. Technically he could not be in charge of a parish until he had served for a suitable length of time as an assistant; in practice this rule could be circumvented by the type of person lucky enough to be given a benefice straightaway. Most candidates found that even a curacy was not easy to obtain, for the clerical profession had become very overcrowded by the last decades of the eighteenth century.[8] Curacies were of two kinds. There were those where the incumbent was himself resident in the parish but was either unable or unwilling to do all the work, and those where the incumbent was absent and the curate virtually in charge. Neither type gave security of tenure, though in practice a curate in charge of a parish was seldom dislodged unless the incumbent (perhaps newly appointed) decided to come into residence: Jane Austen, when staying with her brother at Godmersham in 1813, found that the rector was about to move off for three years to his second parish at Westwell, this being the only decent way of evicting a curate whom he had discovered to be unsatisfactory.[9]

Since vicars chose their own curates and paid for them out of their own funds, aspirants often began by making a personal approach to any vicars known to them – fathers and uncles who held benefices were an obvious touch – before advertising in such journals as the *Gentleman's Magazine*. There was a natural tendency to be on the look-out for sick and elderly parsons who might be persuaded that they needed to retire to a heath resort, leaving both house and parish in the care of a younger man.[10] There is something about the sheer length of the speech Henrietta Musgrove makes to Anne Elliot, when the two of them are on holiday at Lyme and Henrietta is trying to prepare the way for her young man, Charles Hayter, to take over the duties of the Rev. Dr Shirley of Uppercross, which suggests that Jane Austen had heard it all many times before:

> I cannot help thinking it a pity that he [Dr Shirley] does not live entirely by the sea. I do think he had better leave Uppercross entirely, and fix at Lyme. – Do not you, Anne? – Do not you agree with me that it is the best thing he could do, both for himself and Mrs Shirley? – She has cousins here, you know, and many acquaintance, which would make it cheerful for her, and I am sure she would be glad to get to a place where she could have medical attendance at hand, in case of his having another seizure. Indeed I think it quite melancholy to have such excellent people as Dr and Mrs Shirley, who have been doing good all their lives, wearing out their last days in a place like Uppercross, where, excepting our family, they seem shut out from all the world. I wish his friends would propose it to him. I really think they ought. And as to procuring a dispensation, there could be no difficulty at his time of life, and with his character. My only doubt is, whether anything could persuade him to leave his parish. He is so very strict and scrupulous in his notions; over scrupulous, I must say. Do not you think, Anne, it is being over-scrupulous? Do you not think it is quite a mistaken point of conscience, when a clergyman sacrifices his health for the sake of duties, which may be just as well performed by another person? – And at Lyme too – only seventeen miles off, – he would be near enough to hear if people thought there was anything to complain of.[11]

If Charles Hayter had obtained the post, a further crisis would have arisen when the Rev. Dr Shirley died, for there was no guarantee that the latter's successor would continue to employ the young man. Hayter would in all probability have been back where he started, looking for another curacy or for a benefice. Some 10 to 15 per cent of ordinands failed to make any sort of headway in the church and, after a few years, either transferred to the teaching profession or disappeared into obscurity.[12]

Wanted—A Curacy in a good sporting country, near a pack of fox-hounds, and in a sociable neighbourhood; it must have a good house and stables, and a few acres of meadow ground would be very agreeable—To prevent trouble, the stipend must not be less than 8ol.—The Advertiser has no objection to undertaking three, four, or five Churches of a Sunday, but will not engage where there is any weekly duty. Whoever has such a one to dispose of, may suit themselves by sending a line, directed A. B. to be left at the *Turf Coffee House*, or the gentleman may be spoken with, any tuesday morning at Tatterfall's Betting Room.　　　　　　C.

A fictitious advertisement published by James Austen in his satirical journal *The Loiterer*, 7 February 1789.
(*British Library*)

Of the clergy who obtained benefices, some had to wait as long as fifteen years before doing so, whereas others walked into one at once.[13] The chances of obtaining a living have been referred to as a gamble, but some participants in the game had the dice loaded in their favour from birth. Of the 11,600 benefices in England and Wales at the end of the eighteenth century, the patronage of about 2,500 belonged to bishops and cathedral chapters: the best chance of a young man getting one of them was to discover that he was related to a bishop or canon. Of Jane Austen's clergy acquaintances, the two with the richest livings were George Moore, son of the Archbishop of Canterbury, who presented him to the parish of Wrotham in Kent, and Richard Buller, son of the Bishop of Exeter, who was presented to the parish of Colyton by the Dean and Chapter of Exeter.

Another sizeable group of livings (some 600) was in the gift of Oxford and Cambridge colleges and of the public schools: these were looked upon as provision for fellows and masters who wished to escape from their celibate profession into matrimony. In the early decades of the eighteenth century, colleges had bought up advowsons at such a rate that they had been forbidden by an Act of 1736 from owning a quantity more than half the number of their fellowships. With the average tenure of a fellowship running at about ten years, college livings became increasingly difficult to obtain.[14] Elections to them were held in college halls. James Woodforde secured the rectory of Weston Longeville at an election in 1784 at New College, Oxford, where he was Fellow and Sub-Warden, recording in his diary:

Nov. 5. The Warden received an account of the death of Dr Ridley, Rector of one of our livings in Norfolk . . .

Dec. 6. Master Senr publickly declared this afternoon in M.C.R. his intention of not taking the living of Weston. I therefore immediately being the next Senior in Orders canvassed the Senior Common Room, and then went with Master into the Junr Common Room and canvassed that. Junr Common Room pretty full . . .

Dec. 15. We had a meeting of the whole House in the Hall at 12 o'clock, to present a Person to the Living of Western Longeville . . . Hooke and myself were the two candidates proposed. Many learned and warm arguments started and disputed, and after 2 hours debate the House divided and it was put to the Vote, when there appeared for me 21 votes, and for Mr Hooke 15 only, on which I was declared and presented with the Presentation of the Rectory. The chief speakers for me were the Warden, Mr Holmes, Mr Webber, Mr Gauntlett, and Dr Wall . . . I treated the Senr Common Room with Wine and Fruit in the

afternoon and in the evening with Arrac Punch and Wine. I treated the Jun[r]
Com: Room with one dozen of Wine afternoon and in the evening with Arrac
Punch and Wine. I gave the Chaplains half a dozen of Wine, the clerks 2 bottles
and the Steward one bottle.[15]

Of Jane Austen's acquaintances, the incumbent at Harpsden, successor
to her maternal grandfather, obtained his living from All Souls College,
Oxford; and her early suitor Samuel Blackall ultimately secured the
living of Cadbury (a prize he had long coveted) from Emmanuel College,
Cambridge; but neither her father nor her brother James found provision in this way. Fellows generally were advised not to wait for a college
living if they could secure one elsewhere.

Another 1,100 or so livings were in the gift of the Crown. In practice,
presentation of these was in the hands of the First Lord of the Treasury
(the Prime Minister), who bestowed the right upon actual or potential
supporters of the government in the House of Commons. None of the
parishes Jane Austen knew came into this category. However, since
members of the House of Commons were nearly all landed gentry,
Crown livings could to all intents and purposes be counted along with
the very large number of parishes – at least 5,500 – where the appointment of the incumbent was in the gift of a private landowner. With this
situation Jane was well acquainted.

As with cathedral livings, the surest way of obtaining a benefice from a
private owner was to be related to him. Gentry had taken it for granted
since the middle ages that they must provide for their families, with the
result that dynasties of clergy had built up all over England. 'I like first
Cousins to be first Cousins, & interested about each other', Jane Austen
once wrote;[16] which was just as well because, thanks to the combined
efforts of Thomas Knight and his kinsman Francis Austen, cousins on
her father's side of the family were to be found in parsonages in many
parts of the southern counties. George Austen succeeded his cousin
Henry first at Shipbourne and then at Steventon; Henry moved on to
West Wickham; another cousin, Thomas Bathurst, one-time curate at
Steventon, was given the rectory of Welwyn in Hertfordshire; another
branch of the family, the Motley-Austens, was established at Chevening
in Kent. Mrs Austen's family was equally well-endowed, thanks to the
Leighs of Stoneleigh and Adlestrop: the Hon. Mary Leigh established
Edward Cooper in the rectory at Hamstall Ridware and gave James
Austen his first benefice at Cubbington, a parish which he kept as a
source of income throughout life although he seldom visited it.[17]

Failing a blood relationship with a patron, a clergyman could sometimes secure preferment through marriage. Thomas Fowle and Noyes

Lloyd secured their fortunes in the church when they married cousins of the 6th Lord Craven, one of the most considerable patrons in the southern counties. Friendships could be equally profitable, whether begun at the university or on the hunting field: it was probably thanks to their common interest in hunting over the countryside south of Basingstoke that James Austen in 1791 was presented to the vicarage of Sherborne St John by William Chute of The Vyne. A few of the clergy were so much a part of the gentry that they owned advowsons themselves and could lawfully appoint themselves to livings – a practice with which Jane Austen saw nothing wrong, since Catherine Morland's father, who had apparently provided for himself in this way, is described at the beginning of *Northanger Abbey* as 'a very respectable man'.[18]

Jane Austen took it for granted that patrons should cater for their relatives and friends. She accepted without question the practice which allowed a patron to install a 'caretaker' priest in a parish until a young man he particularly wished to provide for came of age. She invented a temporary placement of this kind to allow Charles Hayter to marry Henrietta Musgrove towards the end of *Persuasion* – he being extremely lucky in that the prospective beneficiary was very young indeed.[19] There were, however, conventions governing such transactions, the subtleties of which are now difficult to unravel. The agreement had to be drawn up in such a way that there was no hint of simony – James Austen, to his wife's horror, turned down a benefice worth £300 a year because he so much feared 'the ugly word'.[20]

The nepotism and favouritism which later generations found so alien to their notions of disinterestedness and fair play were not, in fact, the worst aspects of the patronage system. If bishops were conscientious in carrying out ordination procedures, the sons, nephews and dependants chosen by private patrons could be assumed to be as well qualified as anyone else. There was always, it must be supposed, the danger that a young man who had no sense of vocation would enter the church simply because a living was reserved for him by his father or uncle: William Jones, a hard-working Hertfordshire parson who had had no such opportunities himself, thought that quite a number of 'unwary youths' fell into this trap, and 'what uphill drudgery and how tedious must the several services appear when not the *heart* but the *lips* only are engaged', he reflected.[21] Jane Austen, however, would probably have denied that the danger was at all great. A little family persuasion did not seem to her at all amiss: when Ben Lefroy was faced in 1813 with the offer of a curacy he did not feel ready to take, she joined with the rest of his friends in pronouncing him 'maddish' to turn it down. Providing the candidate was not wholly averse to taking Orders – and she could not imagine that Ben was – she saw no reason why he should not take advantage of good fortune.[22] Thomas Gisborne, whose work she is known to have read in 1805, argued that:

> to him who sees no reason to think that he shall not promote the glory of God and the good of mankind as much in the church as in any other profession . . . , the prospect of obtaining, by the aid of his friends and relations, a competent provision in the church may lawfully be the motive which determines him to that line in preference to another.[23]

As with all other aspects of the system, the line between right and wrong was subtle and not easily understood by outsiders. To Mary Crawford in *Mansfield Park* it seemed obvious that Edmund Bertram had taken Orders simply because his father had reserved a good living for him, but to Edmund himself the issues were more complex.[24] 'The knowing that there was such a provision for me probably did bias me', he admitted:

> Nor can I think it wrong that it should. There was no natural disinclination to be overcome, and I see no reason why a man should make a worse clergyman for knowing that he will have a competence early in life. I was in safe hands. I hope I should not have been influenced myself in a wrong way, and I am sure my father was too conscientious to have allowed it. I have no doubt that I was biassed, but I think it was blamelessly.

There was of course also the chance that a young man with a genuine vocation would be put off by the difficulty of obtaining a benefice, but Jane Austen does not seem to have been greatly disturbed by the possibility. She manoeuvred even Mary Crawford into the position of admitting that it would be madness for anyone to take Orders without the prospect of a living.[25] What she did deplore was the commercial spirit which had crept into the system of patronage during the eighteenth century. Advowsons were a form of property and, as landowners increasingly regarded their property as a source of speculation, a good deal of trafficking regularly took place. It was a common practice to put advowsons up for sale, or even for auction, permanently or for a long term; the value of the living was advertised in the newspapers along with the life expectancy of the existing incumbent. The going price varied from year to year: in *Sense and Sensibility* John Dashwood estimated it at £1,400 for a living valued at £200 a year.[26] Jane Austen's father had benefited from this practice, his uncle Francis in 1770 having purchased the next presentation to both Deane and Ashe that he might bestow whichever became vacant first upon his nephew. Her friend Mrs Lefroy had also benefited from it, for when, contrary to expectation, the living at Deane fell in first, Francis Austen sold the next presentation at Ashe to another rich uncle, Benjamin Langlois, so that he too could provide for his nephew, the Rev. George Lefroy. Jane Austen nevertheless disapproved of such transactions. In *Mansfield Park* she made the worthy Sir Thomas Bertram suitably chagrined and apologetic when he was obliged by financial difficulties to sell the next presentation at Mansfield. Noticeably, it is the ungentlemanly John Dashwood in *Sense and Sensibility* who regards these practices as the only rational behaviour for men of the world to adopt.[27]

As far as the clergy were concerned, the most burdensome result of patronage was that a great many livings in the Church of England were extremely poor. During a discussion in Parliament in 1802 it was ascertained that about 1,000 of the benefices in England and Wales were worth less than £100 annually, while another 3,000 or so ranged between £100 and £150 – at a time when the latter sum was thought to provide only the barest necessities.[28] It was universally agreed that the state could do nothing to improve the livings, since to do so would be tantamount to subsidizing owners of private property. Yet a poor clergyman was distinctly hampered in his ministry, cut off from educated companionship, deprived of books and devoid of means of giving material assistance to the sick and helpless.[29] Some tried to make ends meet by teaching or by more menial tasks; others – amounting to about a third of all clergy – tried to improve their income by acquiring more than one benefice.[30] If the parishes which formed a plural holding were contiguous, or not too far apart, one clergyman might do duty in both or all; he could then let out the spare living accommodation as Mr Austen did at Deane.

Pluralism was a departure from the old principle of 'a priest in every vill' and Evangelicals within the church raised their voices against it but to no avail. Critics in Parliament in 1802 were silenced when Sir William Scott, an eminent ecclesiastical lawyer, demanded to know how the public could require universal residence of the clergy when 'so large a proportion of the benefices in this kingdom do not pay more than what most of us in this House pay for our upper servants'.[31] It was of course apparent that what some clergy did of necessity others emulated from greed. The word is perhaps too harsh for James Austen but the fact remains that it was not dire poverty that drove him to accept three parishes at a combined income of £1,100 a year.[32] The English clergy was not as pluralistic as some contemporaries thought or most historians have believed: whilst some two thirds remained in possession of a single parish, only some 6 per cent held more than two benefices and of these a mere handful had four or five. Yet they were as pluralistic in rich counties as in poor ones and this brought the whole church into disrepute.[33] The only check on abuses was that if parishes were more than thirty miles apart permission for non-residence had to be sought from the bishop. Since bishops themselves were noted for accumulating benefices *in commendam*, permission was not difficult to obtain.

A corollary to pluralism was that the cultivation of patrons became an ongoing necessity. The Rev. Thomas Fowle, who obtained the living of Kintbury from the Earl of Craven, saddled his son with the name of Fulwar Craven Fowle as a sign of respect. The latter, having duly received the parish of Enborne from the same source, continued to pay court:

> Eliza [Fulwar's wife] has seen Lord Craven at Barton, & probably by this time at Kintbury, where he was expected for one day this week. She found his manners very pleasing indeed. The little flaw of having a Mistress now living with him at Ashdown Park, seems to be the only unpleasing circumstance about him.

Jane reported acidly.[34] In *Pride and Prejudice* Elizabeth Bennet, who seems to have been a trifle naive in such matters, could not understand why her friend Charlotte should have been so ready to accompany Mr Collins on his humiliating visits to Rosings until she recollected that Lady Catherine de Bourgh might have other livings to dispose of.[35] The worldly-wise Mr Bennet was conscious that Darcy's patronage was even more extensive than his aunt's: when the two of them fell out, his ironic advice to Mr Collins was to 'stand by the nephew. He has more to give'.[36]

A conscientious clergyman would try to place curates in his outlying parishes but a poor clergyman would be unable to pay them and a greedy man unwilling to pay them very much. An Act of 1713 gave bishops the right to insist that curates be paid a reasonable stipend, believed by the legislators to be between £20 and £50 a year; a further law of 1796 allowed bishops in some dioceses to insist on £75; yet whilst there was a glut of curates they undercut each other and many continued to receive very low amounts. On the whole, curates in the 1790s were lucky to receive more than £35; Henry Austen's stipend at Chawton in 1818 was still only £54 12s. 0d. He was in considerable financial difficulties for the rest of his life.[37]

Sometimes a rector or vicar would give his curate the Easter offerings but the task of collecting them from house to house was not always a pleasant one and in a small parish they did not amount to very much. 'Surplice fees' (payments for conducting baptisms, marriages and funerals) were also sometimes granted; but again in a small parish these were unlikely to produce munificent returns. Occasionally a stipendiary curate was given a share of the tithes, but seldom if ever was it known for the total income of a curate to exceed a half of that of a vicar or a quarter of that of a rector.[38] Numerous proposals for raising curates' stipends were made in Parliament in the early nineteenth century. Invariably they foundered on the argument that they could not be enforced and that many incumbents could not afford to pay larger sums.[39] According to William Jones, writing in his diary in 1803, 'a journeyman in almost any trade or business, even a brick-layer's labourer or the turner of a razor grinder's wheel' was 'generally better paid than a stipendiary curate'. Young men who had no obvious chance of preferment would do better for themselves and their families 'by making interest for upper-servants in some genteel family', he believed. During the nineteen years he had himself served as a resident curate in the parish of Broxbourne his stipend had never risen above £60. He had been obliged to run a school, which he detested, in order to support his wife and nine children. Even then he was in dire straits:

> The French say – '*Il faut manger!*' We must eat. But we, *literally and frequently*, had not enough of the plainest, commonest provisions. I can truly say that I often pretended to have had enough . . . that there might be more for my small family.[40]

Curates from better-off families than Mr Jones's often called on their parents for continued assistance, but this might merely ease financial burdens at the expense of creating other complications. Henry Rice, newly married to Lucy Lefroy, had to choose in 1801 between seeking a curacy near to his overbearing mother in Kent and accepting Mr Austen's offer of a place at Deane, where his interfering mother-in-law was near at hand ('Mrs L. means to advise them to put their washing out . . .').[41]

The uncertainties of patronage created many personal problems for clergy, of which Jane Austen was only too well aware. For instance, young clergy were almost always advised by their families not to marry until they had a guarantee of being able to support a wife, which might mean waiting for years. Tom Fowle, engaged to Jane's sister Cassandra, took this advice to heart: his family's patron, Lord Craven, had already provided him with a tiny benefice at Allington in Wiltshire and it seemed worthwhile waiting for the better living in Shropshire which Lord Craven meant to bestow on him as soon as it came vacant. Meanwhile, he felt obliged to show respect to his patron by accepting a post as chaplain to the expedition Craven was sending to the West Indies; there the young man died of yellow fever, leaving to Cassandra the £1,000 which was all he possessed in the world.[42] Less biddable couples often decided not to wait, thereby creating problems for all around them. When Mrs Jennings in *Sense and Sensibility* heard that Edward Ferrars and her niece Lucy were proposing to delay their marriage until he was properly settled, she was understandably sceptical:

> Wait for his having a living! – aye, we all know how *that* will end; – they will wait a twelvemonth, and finding no good comes of it, will set down upon a curacy of fifty pounds a-year, with the interest of his two thousand pounds, and what little matter Mr Steele and Mr Pratt [Lucy's father and uncle] can give her. Then they will have a child every year! and Lord help 'em! how poor they will be! – I must see what I can give them towards furnishing their house.[43]

John Lyford, the son of the Austens' family doctor at Basingstoke, had been in a similar situation when he gave up an Oxford Fellowship in April 1799 to marry Miss Lodge, hoping to survive on a £50 curacy: 'Miss Lodge has only £800 of her own', Jane wrote, '& it is not supposed that her Father can give her much, therefore the good offices of the Neighbourhood will be highly acceptable. – John Lyford means to take pupils.' Sadly, they were not needed for long, as poor John Lyford died after a few weeks of matrimony.[44]

If things were difficult for the clergy at the beginning of their career, they were often equally difficult at the end. A curate could not retire unless he had private means, for there were no pensions. A vicar could retire only if he could afford to employ a curate to take charge of the parish. There was also the embarrassment for an elderly clergyman of knowing that someone – often someone he knew – was waiting to step into his shoes. Nobody was likely to be much worried when a thoughtless young man like Tom Bertram went around forecasting cheerfully that the hearty, forty-five-year old incumbent at Mansfield 'would soon pop off', leaving the way clear for Edmund;[45] but what are the elderly Dr Russell of Ashe and Mr Hillman of Deane likely to have thought when they heard in 1770 that their neighbour, George Austen, with a growing family to support, had been promised the benefice of whichever of them 'popped off' first? And what is George Austen, in his turn, likely to have thought when he learnt in 1794 that his son James had been

promised the next presentation at Steventon?[46] Comforting as it may
have been to know that James was provided for, the proximity of a
socially ambitious son and daughter-in-law, cooped up with three children in a very small parsonage house at Deane, may well have pressur-
ized him into retiring in 1801 so that James and his family could at least
move into the larger house at Steventon.

In spite of her acute awareness of such problems, there is no evidence
that Jane Austen wished to see patronage abolished root and branch. No
reasonable person could think in such terms: the system was too much
bound up with tradition, convention and property ownership, for all of
which there was increasing respect in England as a result of the French
Revolution. A few radicals such as Bentham and Cobbett might have
given the impression that this was what they wanted, but their interest in
the cause of true religion was doubtful. Jane Austen would certainly
have agreed with a modern writer, Gordon Rupp, that 'touting and
toadying, the use of money and interest for clerical advancement, find
little support in the New Testament',[47] but she did not think that such
discreditable practices were an inevitable consequence of patronage.
Like many people of her time, she believed that it was possible to operate
a corrupt system incorruptly.

Much could be done by observing the ordinary rules of gentlemanly
conduct. Patrons should regard their powers of patronage in the church
as a trust, not as an asset for investment. On finding themselves with a
vacant benefice and no member of their family available to fill it, they
should take trouble to find a suitable candidate. The proper example
was given by Colonel Brandon in *Sense and Sensibility*. In such circumstances Brandon sought out the young man who had been recommended to him in order to ascertain that he was worthy of preferment.
A patron would be more likely to do this if he knew that he was going to
live in close contact with the incumbent: in Colonel Brandon's case the
parsonage at Delaford was 'within a stone's throw' of the manor house.[48]
Hence Jane Austen's approval of parishes where church, parsonage and
manor house were next door to each other.

There is no suggestion from Jane Austen that she expected patrons to
increase the endowments of their beneficed clergy – hers was not an age
in which patrons showed great munificance towards the church – but she
did expect them to provide a reasonably comfortable parsonage house.
This was important if clergy were to be persuaded to reside in their
parishes and she was clear that they should reside. She had nothing but
scorn for clergy who neglected their parishes simply because they had
the opportunity to live in greater style elsewhere, an opportunity Mary

Crawford hoped Edmund Bertram would follow if she married him. Archdeacon Paley, in a charge to his clergy in 1785, suggested that non-resident clergy could do their duty to their parishioners perfectly well by distributing tracts from the S.P.C.K.[49] Jane was not of this opinion. According to her friend Mrs Barrett, she was attacked by an Irish dignitary for being 'over particular about clergymen residing on their cures', but she stuck to her guns.[50] As Sir Thomas Bertram pointed out in his ponderous way:

> a parish has wants and claims which can be known only by a clergyman constantly resident . . . Human nature needs more lessons than a weekly sermon can convey . . . If [the clergyman] does not live among his parishioners and prove himself by constant attention their well-wisher and friend, he does very little either for their good or his own.[51]

Clearly a clergyman who was a pluralist could not reside in all his parishes. Although none of the clergy in Jane Austen's novels appear to have been pluralists (except, possibly, Edmund Bertram, who may have kept Thornton Lacey when he moved to Mansfield), she was too practical a woman to denounce pluralism if it was the only means of providing clergy with a decent standard of living. The situation has its parallels in the twentieth century, when the Church of England has found it necessary to combine parishes, sometimes as many as four or five in number, under one clergyman, who even in a motorized age can do no more than hold a minimum number of services in each church, sometimes on alternate Sundays. Jane Austen's stand seems to have been that a clergyman who held more than one benefice should do his best to install resident curates in those he did not live in himself, and should make the curacies 'quite as good as he could afford'.[52] This her father had done during the later years of his ministry at Steventon and Deane, thereby providing at Deane a house, a job and an income for his son James. If the same had been done in more of the 40 per cent of parishes which lacked a resident clergyman, the career prospects of young ordinands, as well as the care of souls, might have been considerably improved.[53]

The ongoing relationship between an incumbent and his patron was also something which concerned Jane Austen. There must be none of the sickening obsequiousness that Mr Collins thought it necessary to display towards Lady Catherine de Bourgh. Gratitude and a determination to fulfil the patron's expectations were right and proper, as George Austen demonstrated throughout life; but there must be no fawning, no boot-licking, no obvious servility. There was nothing wrong with Mr Collins' resolve to show unfailing courtesy towards his patroness and her relatives; his only fault was in proclaiming to all the world that he was about to do so.[54] The patron or patroness, for their part, must show a kindly concern for the incumbent's welfare but not interfere with his private concerns. We know from Charlotte Collins that Lady Catherine was 'a very respectable, sensible woman indeed, and a most attentive neighbour', but she carried attention too far when she thought that her position gave her a right to regulate the Collinses' housekeeping as though she were actually paying their bills.[55] Equally, the incumbent and his wife must not sponge on their benefactor, as Lucy Steele clearly intended to do on Colonel Brandon, and as Mrs Norris had done on Sir Thomas Bertram. (Admittedly Mrs Norris was Sir Thomas's sister-in-law, but judging by her behaviour at Sotherton Court she would have done it anyway.)

Patronage has never been abolished in the Church of England: it has simply faded into the background as large landed estates have been broken up and as the gentry, or their descendants, have become less interested in carrying out their obligations. Its disappearance has not been all gain. At its best it implied a caring attitude on the part of local elites which Jane Austen would have been sorry to see lost. Patronage had an important role to play in the proper functioning of the neigh-bourhood, a concept that was central to her social thinking. Its gradual assumption into the hands of the bishops – a category of persons in whom she showed very little interest – was a development she could not possibly have foreseen: bishops in her day were not great administrators and, with the best will in the world, could not have managed to visit regularly the numerous tiny parishes in their vast dioceses.[56]

Chapter 3

The Parson's Education

In the spring of 1783 Mrs Austen heard that her twelve-year-old niece, Jane Cooper, was to be sent to Oxford to be educated and cared for by her father's sister, Mrs Ann Cawley, the widow of a former Master of Brasenose. It seemed a good idea to Mrs Austen tó send the ten-year-old Cassandra with her, and since Jane, though only seven, did not like to be separated from Cassandra, she had to go too. The little girls were not very happy with Mrs Cawley, who was stiff and formal in her manners, and they were no doubt pleased when their brother James, who was then in residence at St John's as a Fellow, arrived at the house to take them out for the day. James, however, was so eager to impress his sisters that he had laid on a formidable programme for their entertainment: according to stories told later by members of the family, he took them sightseeing through more 'dismal chapels, dusty libraries, and greasy halls' than Jane cared to remember.[1]

No more than a few months had elapsed before Mrs Cawley moved house to Southampton, taking the girls with her. This ended the only direct experience Jane Austen is known to have had with life in a university town. Back home at Steventon, and later in life, she met a good many of her brother's university acquaintances and numerous neighbours' sons home for the vacations. Among them she is likely to have heard a few of the silly and disparaging comments which young men sometimes make to impress their peers or to hide their own lack of confidence. A couple of such remarks found their way into her novels and have often been quoted as evidence that Jane Austen shared the poor view of university life which Edward Gibbon put about in his memoirs. In fact they were designed to tell us more about the people making them than about the institutions to which they referred. John

Thorpe in *Northanger Abbey* is typical of the lout who thinks it clever to boast about drink:

> Oxford! there is no drinking at Oxford now, I assure you . . . Nobody drinks there. You would hardly meet with a man who goes beyond his four pints at the utmost. Now, for instance, it was reckoned a remarkable thing at the party in my rooms, that upon an average we cleared about five pints a head. It was looked upon as something out of the common. *Mine* is famous good stuff to be sure. You would not often meet with anything like it in Oxford – and that may account for it. But this will just give you a notion of the general rate of drinking there.[2]

In a different vein Edward Ferrars seeks to evade Mrs Dashwood's enquiries into his lack of a career with a mixture of self-deprecation and nonchalance:

> unfortunately my own nicety, and the nicety of my friends, have made me what I am, an idle, helpless being. We never could agree in our choice of a profession . . . ; – and, at length, as there was no necessity for my having any profession at all, idleness was pronounced on the whole to be the most advantageous and honourable, and a young man of eighteen is not in general so earnestly bent on being busy as to resist the solicitations of his friends to do nothing. I was therefore entered at Oxford, and have been properly idle ever since.[3]

Edward Gibbon, who entered Magdalen College, Oxford, as a gentleman-commoner in 1752, left behind him in his memoirs a lurid account of lazy, pleasure-loving tutors abandoning their pupils to dissipation and idleness.[4] If Jane Austen ever read this account, which became increasingly popular after its publication in 1796, she probably knew better than to place much confidence in it. Gibbon had made poor use of his time at the university and, like Edward Ferrars, was tempted to give the institution a share of the blame for his own failures. That there was a good deal of hard drinking amongst both undergraduates and their seniors Jane Austen was clearly aware: her hero Edmund Bertram, who was unlikely to court dissolute company, remembered having to support young men who leaned heavily on his arm down the length of a street.[5] She also knew that not all students were intellectual giants:

> We had a Miss North & a Mr Gould of our party; – the latter walked home with me after Tea; – he is a very young Man, just entered at Oxford, wears Spectacles, and has heard that *Evelina* was written by Dr Johnson . . .

she wrote witheringly in 1799.[6] But from her father and her eldest brother she knew that there was good scholarship to be had at the universities. The learning that they, and other graduates of her acquaintance, brought with them from the universities profoundly affected her own attitudes to life and revealed itself significantly in her novels.

During Jane Austen's lifetime, and for some decades after, the two British universities of Oxford and Cambridge were assumed to exist chiefly to provide a flow of clergy for the Church of England and to defend its faith against attack. It has been suggested that a somewhat different view of their purpose might have been developing during the seventeenth century, when both universities began to be respected for providing an education which seemed to fit graduates for any choice of career; during the eighteenth century, however, they reverted in popular estimation to their traditional role as seminaries for the clergy. By the end of the century, only 9 or 10 per cent of undergraduates entered for law and medicine; approximately 60 per cent of all graduates, mainly from the Arts faculties, went into the church.[7]

Jane Austen's letter to the Rev. James Stanier Clarke, protesting her inability to write about the life of a metropolitan clergyman, suggests that she believed that the most learned products of the universities went into urban parishes. Her list of the subjects she thought she would need to cover in order to simulate the conversation of such clergymen testifies to the extensive education she thought they had received. At no point either in her letters or in her novels does she suggest that even the rural clergy, with whom she was much better acquainted, were ill-trained. From remarks made by Edmund Bertram in *Mansfield Park*, it appears that she would have liked the clergy to undergo some training in elocution to enable them to perform the liturgy more effectively, but otherwise she seems to have assumed that they were fully equipped academically for their task: her complaint against the likes of Mr Collins and Mr Elton was not that they were undereducated but that they were underbred.[8] Yet she must have known that it was possible for a man to achieve ordination without presenting much evidence of attainment in any branch of knowledge whatever, let alone in the doctrines he was about to impart. At neither Oxford nor Cambridge was much attempt made to test the industry of undergraduates until near the end of their period of study. At the former, where residence was officially four years but often shortened to three, candidates for the B.A. were required at intervals after their second year to take part in three traditional 'disputations'; but although the taking of these tests was strictly enforced little good was achieved by them, since the subjects disputed were banal and predictable and ready-made aids could easily be obtained. The final obstacle was an oral examination based partly on prescribed texts and partly on three classical authors of the undergraduate's own choice. The examination was often perfunctory and failure virtually unknown. At Cambridge the much admired Senate House Examination, introduced towards the end of the eighteenth century and extended in 1808, was much more searching, but success in it was necessary only for an honours degree. The vast majority of candidates remained content with an ordinary degree, for which the requirements were no stiffer than those found at Oxford.[9]

In addition to a degree, a man thinking of ordination needed a testimonial from his college vouching for his fitness. This was seldom refused on academic grounds. Having acquired the necessary document, the candidate had then to find a bishop willing and able to devote time to ordain him. This was often the most difficult part of the whole business – a situation which allowed Lucy Steele to remark, in her vulgar way, of Edmund Ferrars: 'As soon as he can light upon a Bishop, he will be ordained.'[10] The bishop (or his representative) was supposed to satisfy himself that the candidate was competent in Latin, sufficiently versed in Scripture, and acquainted with the liturgy and the Thirty-Nine Articles, but bishops varied as to how they interpreted these instructions.[11] Some assumed that a candidate equipped with a university testimonial required no further scrutiny: Ben Lefroy, ordained by the Bishop of Oxford in 1817, was merely quizzed about his connections with George Austen, whom his lordship remembered. Only a few took their responsibility more seriously. James Woodforde was surprised to find that his examination at the hands of the chaplain to the Bishop of Oxford in 1763 was no trifling matter:

> I was quite half an hour examining. He asked me a good many hard questions. I had not one question that Yes or No would answer . . . Mr Hewish is a very fair Examiner, and will see whether a Man be read or not soon.

Henry Austen, who had taken some trouble to revise his knowledge of the Greek Testament a good twenty years after graduating, was disappointed when the bishop refrained from asking him any questions on it on the assumption that he would not be able to answer them. Most candidates knew that little preparation was necessary: even the conscientious Edmund Bertram, when he was preparing for ordination at the hands of the Bishop of Peterborough, merely said goodbye to his family, mounted his horse and went to stay with a clergyman friend in the cathedral city for a week.[12]

With examination requirements generally so lax, it would have been surprising if there had not been a good number of undergraduates at Oxford and Cambridge prepared to idle away their time. It was mostly the noblemen and gentlemen-commoners who notoriously did so. Ordinary undergraduates aspiring to a profession, and especially those destined for the church, were expected to engage in serious study regardless of the fact that little of its fruits would be needed for examination purposes. To encourage them to work, disputations were held regularly in college halls and ante-chapels, and declamations both oral and written could be presented before a master. While the universities seldom fulfilled their statutory obligations to provide lectures, in the colleges much sound instruction and advice was available. All students upon entry were allocated tutors, many of whom in the colleges regarded themselves as standing *in loco parentis* and gave guidance to their pupils in both reading and behaviour. When Jane Austen's nephew went up to Oxford she waited eagerly to hear which tutor he had been given.[13] James Austen thought so highly of the Rev Dr Marlow, his tutor at St John's, that he maintained respectful contact with him for many years afterwards. Such men could sometimes be called upon voluntarily to help graduates who were preparing for ordination, there being no theological colleges available for the purpose.[14]

The most significant feature of the education received by the clergy at this time was not its desultory or perfunctory nature, which has been very much exaggerated, but the fact that, apart from the hurried perusal of a few theological texts prior to ordination (George Pretyman Tomline's *Elements of Christian Theology* was published especially for the purpose), it was exactly the same as that given to undergraduates with other careers, or with no career at all, in mind. Graduates who received Fellowships were supposed to study for a higher degree in divinity, regarded as the queen of the sciences, but many managed to evade this obligation, either because the fees were too high or because the real attraction of life in a senior common room lay in the pursuit of proctorial and bursarial posts. Neither James Austen nor his father, both of whom spent ten or eleven years at Oxford, appears to have contemplated a doctorate. Although George was a good scholar, he was also known as 'the Handsome Proctor' and was active in university politics.[15]

For the B.A., Oxford University offered undergraduates a course in which two thirds of the time was devoted to the classics and one third to what was called the 'sciences' (logic, rhetoric, Euclid, morals, and politics). Immersion in a series of pagan authors might have been thought an unsatisfactory preparation for the scores of young men destined for the care of souls (the Rev. William Jones thought it encouraged many clergymen to extol 'Heathen virtue' rather than 'Christian morals'),[16] but it was believed to be important that they should receive the same education as other gentlemen, among whom they were going to live. The latter for their part might have been expected to complain at having to submit themselves to the religious instruction dispensed willy-nilly within the colleges, but this was believed to be just as important for future landowners bestowing livings in the church as for future clergy hoping to receive them. At Cambridge classics had been almost entirely abandoned in favour of mathematics, which occupied some three quarters of the syllabus, whilst the remaining quarter was devoted to moral philosophy; but again the course was the same for all. William Cockburn, as Christian Advocate to the University in the early years of the nineteenth century, believed that the growing strength of Methodism was due in large measure to the lack of biblical knowledge and hence of preaching skills on the part of the Anglican clergy. His proposal for remedying the defect was that biblical study should be added to the syllabus generally: 'a certain degree of ecclesiastical knowledge is indisputably valuable to all', he argued.[17] In spite of the increased respect for religion which pervaded England in the decades following the French Revolution, there was still a fear of producing an overdominant clergy; the way forward seemed to be to give not just the clergy but the whole of the educated class a bigger does of religious instruction.[18]

In August 1788 the Countess Eliza de Feuillide (formerly Eliza Hancock), George Austen's niece, visited Oxford with her mother and took the opportunity to call on her cousins James and Henry, both of whom were in residence at St John's. 'We visited several of the Colleges, the Museum, etc.', she reported to her cousin Philadelphia Walter,

> & were very elegantly entertained by our gallant relations at St John's, where I was mightily taken with the Garden & longed to be a *Fellow* that I might walk in it every Day, besides I was delighted with the Black Gown and thought the Square Cap mighty becoming. I do not think you would know Henry with his hair powdered & dressed in a very *tonish* style . . . [19]

The flighty young lady seems not to have noticed the religious atmosphere of the place, although historians have sometimes described it as overpowering. Almost all heads of houses and the majority of dons in the colleges were in Holy Orders or under obligation to proceed to them. Every college had its chapel at whose services attendance was obligatory during term; although the obligation could sometimes be evaded, at others it was strictly enforced by disciplinary action. In addition to college prayers, which even Edmund Bertram remembered as tedious in length,[20] two university sermons were preached every Sunday by senior members in Holy Orders for the edification of their colleagues and juniors. While attendance could not be enforced (the university church of St Mary was not large enough to accommodate the entire body of undergraduates), large congregations were expected in term-time. At Oxford all undergraduates had to subscribe to the Thirty-Nine Articles when they matriculated. At Cambridge there was no such ruling, but in fact most undergraduates were at least nominally Anglican in view of the fact that it was impossible to receive a degree without professing to be '*bona fide* a member of the Church of England by law established'. A movement in the 1770s for the abolition of religious tests for candidates for degrees was believed to be inspired by hostility to the church, and its supporters in Parliament were roundly defeated.[21]

The universities were heavily committed to defending the established faith, on which the whole of government and society was believed to rest. Surprisingly in these circumstances, neither Oxford nor Cambridge authorities believed that their approach to theology need be wholly traditional. Oxford was more conservative than Cambridge but both were open to the winds of change. In earlier times, the Anglican church had placed great importance on the teaching of the early Fathers of the church and on the definitions which had emerged from the Councils of the first four centuries of the Christian era. It now seemed, however, that the complications and technicalities of this approach had favoured dangerous political doctrines such as the Divine Right of Kings, embodied in seventeenth-century England by the Stuarts. With the installation of the Hanoverian dynasty it was deemed wise to put aside all mystifications and base the teaching of the church, like the political establishment which it supported, on an appeal to reason. The result was the growth of 'natural religion', based on the ideas found in Locke's *Essay concerning Human Understanding* (1690) and *The Reasonableness of Christianity* (1695), supported by Newtonian philosophy.[22]

The significance of 'natural religion' for eighteenth-century modes of thought was the emphasis which it placed on science on the one hand and morality on the other. At neither Oxford nor Cambridge were the physical sciences taught directly as part of the undergraduate syllabus: this was hardly thought to matter in the age of Enlightenment, when all knowledge seemed to work together towards a greater understanding of the universe and of the place of human beings in it. Many Anglican scholars seized upon Newton's discoveries as proving beyond doubt that the world was not the unpredictable and threatening environment that it had once seemed to be: on the contrary, it was an orderly system created by a beneficent God who had clearly intended human beings to be happy in it. His ways no longer seemed inscrutable: they could be divined by the use of reason. The story that Newton, merely by watching apples falling from a tree, had been able to discover the divine law which governed the motion of all earthly and celestial bodies seemed to make science everybody's subject, at least in its observational aspects. Amateur botanizing and astronomizing became extremely popular with the literate public. Women, excluded from the universities and hence from study of the classics at the higher levels, took to science as a pursuit in which even men could claim only amateur status: in *Mansfield Park* it is Fanny Price who seeks to draw Edmund Bertram out into the garden so that they can star-gaze together.[23] The idea that the whole of the universe witnessed to God's providence steadily gained ground in the general subjects taught under the heading of 'sciences' at Oxford, whilst at Cambridge, with its greater sympathy for mathematics, the theological aspects of Newtonian science permeated the moral philosophy of the undergraduate syllabus without difficulty.[24]

This was the kind of teaching George Austen took with him from the university to Steventon in the 1760s and imparted to his sons and boarding pupils as well as, presumably, to his congregation. How far Jane Austen joined in the formal lessons in her father's study we do not know, but she seems to have used some of the same school books as the boys, as well as having free use of her father's library. In a letter of 1813 to her brother Frank, on convoy duty in the Baltic, there is a suggestion that they had shared at least the same history lessons:

> It must be real enjoyment to you, since you are *obliged* to leave England, to be where you are, seeing something of a new Country, and one that has been so distinguished as Sweden . . . Gustavus-Vasa, & Charles 12th, and Christina, & Linnaeus – do their Ghosts rise up before you? – I have a great respect for former Sweden. So zealous as it was for Protestantism![25]

Among the individuals she saw fit to recall to Frank's mind, Linnaeus had done much to promote the idea that 'scripture and reason equally assures us that this astonishing machine, the Universe, was produced and created by an infinite architect'. Above all, the numbers of species of plants and animals had seemed to him proof that their creation was the work of a wise and beneficent calculator. Not until the mid nineteenth century did Darwin shatter such comfortable thoughts.

The idea that there was a pre-established order among living creatures accorded well with the idea that harmony had been intended to
reign among human beings also. To Locke it was only reasonable that
men should recognize that everybody had an equal right to subsistence
and an equal right to use their mental faculties in a search for happiness
and well-being. In the general flight from the more mystical aspects of
religion, an overwhelming emphasis on morality ensued. As early as the
seventeenth century, John Tillotson had argued both as a tutor at
Cambridge and as Archbishop of Canterbury that 'the great design of
the Christian religion' was 'to restore and reinforce the practice of the
natural law or, which is all one, of moral duties'. Tillotson's sermons,
proclaiming the eminent reasonableness of God's commandments,
remained extremely popular throughout the eighteenth century as part
of the armoury which parish clergymen took with them into their
pulpits. The message was repeated by other distinguished clerics from
the Cambridge stable: Thomas Herring and Matthew Hulton, both
archbishops in the 1740s and 1750s; and Richard Watson, William Paley
and John Hey in the later part of the century. Of all these divines, the
work of William Paley was particularly successful in permeating the
ranks of the Anglican clergy as they issued from the universities. A
knowledge of his *Principles of Moral and Political Philosophy* (1785), based
on lectures he had given as a tutor at Christ's, was said to be sufficient,
along with two books of Euclid's geometry, to get a man an ordinary B.A.
at Cambridge,[26] whilst a rapid reading of its early chapters was advised
as preparation for ordination among candidates everywhere. If anything further should be desired, the *Anatomy of Religion* published in
1736 by Joseph Butler of Oriel College, Oxford, was considered worth
consulting. Both books scorned patristic learning and advanced an
apologia for religion which Paley frankly stated to be based on utility.

In 1803 William Jones complained in his journal that on the rare
occasions when the majority of parish clergy deigned to preach,

> the name of Christ is scarce ever heard, nor any of the characteristic doctrines
> of His holy religion. The watchword or *catchword* (for I hardly know which to
> call it) is 'Morality'.[27]

This was clearly the emphasis in the clerical milieu familiar to Jane
Austen, for when in *Mansfield Park* Edmund Bertram found himself
having to defend the role of the clergy in the society of the time he did so
in terms which were at least as much utilitarian as spiritual:

> I cannot call that situation nothing which has the charge of all that is of the first

importance to mankind, individually or collectively considered, temporally or
eternally – which has the guardianship of religion and morals, and consequently of the manners which result from their influence.[28]

Yet a reaction to the neglect of revealed religion had already set in.
Admittedly the influence of Evangelical convictions (as distinct from the
earlier Methodist revival) was less keenly felt at Oxford than at Cambridge and it was graduates of the former university that monopolized
the parishes of the southern counties best known to Jane Austen; but her
cousin Edward Cooper was a notable exponent of the new trend and she
was certainly well-acquainted with its standpoint.[29]

At first, Evangelicalism was mainly an individual experience, as in the
case of Wilberforce in his famous encounter with Isaac Milner; but the
latter's election as President of Queens' College in 1788, combined with
the appointment of Charles Simeon as incumbent of Holy Trinity, gave
the movement a firm base within the University of Cambridge. Isaac
Milner decried the way in which many of his fellow-clergy had substi-
tuted 'the miserable fragments of our depraved faculty of reason, in the
room of the influence of God's Holy Spirit'. His brother and fellow
Evangelical Joseph Milner blamed Locke for 'the fashion in introducing
a pompous display of *reasoning* into religion'. These and similar remarks
tended to create the impression that the Evangelicals were adverse to
scholarship, a trait which Jane Austen, with her admiration for her
father and brother, was not likely to have appreciated. Oxford divines
were willing to accept that the lack of respect for revealed religion in
France had been to blame for the onset of revolution, but their remedy
for an excess of reason was not a direct appeal to the Holy Spirit so much
as a more scientific study of the Scriptures through a more thorough
competence in the learned languages. This was more likely to have been
to Jane Austen's taste, for she was delighted when in 1813 she could
report to Cassandra that she had heard their young relative, Henry
Walter, spoken of as 'the best classick in the University'. 'How such a
report would have interested my father!' she added proudly.[30]

In 1870 James Austen's son (James Edward Austen-Leigh) wrote a
memoir of his aunt Jane, in the course of which he referred to having
read that the clergy of the late seventeenth century were greatly inferior
in culture to the laity of that time. 'The charge is no doubt true, if the
rural clergy are to be compared with the higher section of the country
gentlemen who went into parliament and mixed in London society, and
took the lead in their several societies,' he conceded,

but it might be found less true if they were to be compared, as in all fairness they ought to be, with that lower section with whom they usually associated. The smaller landed proprietors, who seldom went farther from home than their county town, from the squire with his thousand acres to the yeoman who cultivated his hereditary property of one or two hundred, then formed a numerous class – each the aristocrat of his own parish; and there was probably a greater difference in manners and refinement between this class and that immediately above them than could now be found between any two persons who rank as gentlemen.[31]

The inference of the passage was that the clergy were if anything more rather than less cultivated than the majority of local gentry – a conclusion to which the writer was drawn by comparing his memories of his grandfather, the Rev George Austen, with the stories he had heard of the contemporary John Harwood of Deane, who liked to begin all his remarks with a round oath and whose ignorance of the world beyond the hunting field was so great that he had to consult the parson to find out whether Paris was in France or France in Paris.

The Rev. George Austen, however, personified a change which had only begun to take place in the character of the clergy in comparatively recent years.[32] In the late seventeenth century many of those occupying the smaller and poorer country parishes had never attended a university and were notoriously unlearned. Those who took degrees were mainly from poor families and, though not uneducated, they could probably with fairness be described as uncultured. At university they had probably worked hard to acquire a little patristic learning, knowing that their status and authority was going to depend on a connection, however humble, with great skills and mysteries.[33] By the mid eighteenth century young men from middle-class families were entering the church in greater numbers. They were both more ambitious than their predecessors and more aware of the learning and culture prevalent among the upper classes. After associating at university with men destined for positions in the highest ranks of government and society, they came in for something of a shock when they arrived at some isolated village to take up their clerical duties. James Woodforde, after visiting most of the farmhouses in a vain search for lodgings, was delighted when the squire agreed at once to accommodate not only him but also his horse – until he discovered that the squire was accustomed to drinking with one of the local farmers from 10 in the morning till 8 at night, and probably looked upon the young curate as a welcome addition to the convivialities.[34]

Under such circumstances, it was hardly surprising if some of the clergy opted for the coarser aspects of country life and took to eating, drinking and hunting with the Squire Westerns of the locality. Such pursuits did not necessarily prevent them from carrying out their parochial duties: Benjamin Newton, rector of Wath, kept greyhounds, hunted the fox, coursed the hare and fished the rivers with the wealthiest of local society, but nevertheless did duty conscientiously in his parish church twice a Sunday. He also read a good deal and proved himself capable of commenting on Gibbon's *Decline and Fall*, quoting Blackstone, and comparing Gisborne with Paley on points of style and content.[35] Dr Grant, whose gourmet habits were such that his wife had to pay the cook extra wages, could nevertheless be described as a good preacher.[36] A reputation for joviality doubtless made these men popular in certain quarters, but the Rev. William Jones was probably right in believing that excessive indulgence in such pleasures as dining and wining with the local gentry gave the clergy as a whole a bad name: Mary Crawford was apparently repeating a common accusation when she said that the clergy had nothing to do but eat.[37] Archdeacon Paley was one of those who recognized the importance of the clergy setting a better example. In a charge to the clergy of the diocese of Carlisle in 1785, he regretted that parsons devoted so much of their time to ignorant pursuits, and urged them to take up intellectual interests such as natural history and astronomy. Paley would have approved of Edmund Bertram's star-gazing, which he described as 'a proper, and perhaps the most proper of all possible recreations for a clergyman'.[38]

Jane Austen's father was one of those clergy who, in the middle of the eighteenth century, resisted any temptations he might have had to join in traditional county pastimes and opted instead for a cultivated way of life. Like others of his kind he became, as his grandson rightly recalled, 'a sort of centre of refinement and politeness'.[39] The blend of unpretentious piety and simple moral truth which the Rev. George Austen conveyed to his children was doubtless appreciated by his acquaintance at large, but just as important in helping to raise the prestige of the clergy was his reputation as a man of taste and learning. His enthusiasm for the classics was long remembered by his family, while his love of a well-turned English sentence was one of the things which according to Henry Austen he handed on to his talented daughter.[40] He bought books on a considerable scale, his library numbering some 500 volumes when he retired.[41] He had a lively interest in current topics of debate, which he fed by subscribing to the *Spectator*, and a delight in plays and novels which Jane Austen transferred to the charming Henry Tilney in *Northanger Abbey*.[42] His gentlemanly manners, his wit and his *savoir faire* made him a welcome neighbour and a more than acceptable guest even among his sophisticated connections in Kent. 'What do you think of my uncle's looks?' enquired his lively niece Eliza, whose cousin Philadelphia Walter had recently been favoured with a visit from the Austen family:

> I was much pleased with them and if possible he appeared more amiable than ever to me. What an excellent & pleasing man he is; I love him most sincerely.[43]

After his death there was found among his possessions that most characteristic sign of the eighteenth-century scholarly gentleman, a small astronomical instrument in a black chagreen case. Jane Austen sent it on to her brother Frank as a keepsake.[44]

Not all of the country gentry liked this scholarly approach on the part of the clergy. In *Persuasion*, Charles Musgrove is said to have regretted the fact that his future brother-in-law, the Rev. Charles Hayter, was not the sort of man to take advantage of the sporting opportunities afforded by a curacy in the heart of some of the best preserves in the country. Jane Austen, however, spoke well of Hayter – a young man who had chosen to raise himself above 'the inferior, retired, unpolished way of living' followed by his own father as squire of Winthrop, to lead instead the life of 'a scholar and a gentleman'. Jane expected her clergymen to be readers: it is a black mark against Mr Collins that he is discovered to be unable to concentrate on the large folios in Mr Bennet's library.[45]

One of the ways in which scholarly clergymen made their influence felt was by taking pupils from among the sons of the local gentry. We do not know what teaching methods the Rev. George Austen used in his little boarding school at Steventon parsonage, but it is reasonable to think that Locke's *Thoughts on Education* had made as much impression upon him as upon other Oxford graduates. 'May I be able to copy the sound, admirable advice he [Locke] gives persons engaged in the tuition of youth!' prayed William Jones after setting up his own school in 1780.[46] Locke's essay was not concerned with scholastic attainment so much as with bringing up children from middle-class and gentry homes to think and behave in a cultivated manner. Ideally he advocated the appointment of private tutors, since schools tended to instill old and lifeless classical scholarship and to expose boys to the corrupting society of bad companions. In practice he would probably have stretched a point for Steventon parsonage, where Mrs Austen presided over health, diet and clothes (all of which he thought important), whilst Mr Austen managed to make lessons sufficiently palatable to enable his pupils – even the less gifted – to remember him with affection. Like Jane Austen in her novels, Locke assigned as much importance to the mother as to the father in the upbringing of children. Between them parents were to inculcate breeding, manners and character into the young, along with a modicum of more of less useful knowledge, such as would benefit either the businessman or the landowner as he went about his daily tasks.

Chapter 4

The Parson's Income

Jane Austen in her novels is notoriously unclear as to the sources from which her characters derive their income. Not only is she understandably vague about 'business' and 'trade', she is scarcely more specific about cases where such alien enterprises are not at issue. Emma Woodhouse is a considerable heiress but we are left guessing as to whence Mr Woodhouse derived his fortune – he owns very little land and there is no mention of 'funds'. It is perhaps not too surprising, therefore, that for her clergy characters she has a mere handful of fleeting references – a phrase here and there – to what she must have known to be their major sources of income: tithe and glebe. In consequence, her novels may inadvertently give the modern reader the impression that the clergy of the Church of England were more dependent on patrons than was in fact the case; for although patrons provided them with their appointments in the first place they did not provide them with their daily bread.

In regard to material assets, the clergy of the Church of England were in a unique position. There was no central organization to which the whole of the church's property belonged. In each parish the rights, lands and buildings – including the church itself – devolved in freehold upon the parish priest. He held them, however, only during his period of office, after which they passed via sequestrators into the hands of his successor. He could not alienate them, and must not wilfully damage them or allow them to depreciate through neglect, but must hand them on in as flourishing a condition as possible. Brought up against this background it is understandable that Jane Austen should have regarded all inherited property as a trust, and that she should have criticized spendthrift owners such as Sir Walter Elliot, and even heedless prospective owners such as Tom Bertram, for improper stewardship.

Tithe, or the right of the clergy to receive a tenth of the annual gross product of all cultivated land in the parish, had been recognized by custom since the ninth century. It had become confused over time, particularly since the Reformation, and was a mixed blessing to the clergy. Curates on a fixed stipend might envy the parsons a right which supposedly cushioned them against inflation; parsons were more likely to complain that it put them on bad terms with the farmers and reduced their popularity in the parish. For reasons which can only be conjectured, this aspect of a parson's situation impinged so little upon Jane Austen's consciousness that it never figures in her letters or novels. She was merely amused when James Stanier Clarke suggested she should show what good could be done by abolishing tithes. The subject is not mentioned in the conversation between Mary Crawford and Edmund Bertram during their visit to Sotherton Court – the passage in the novels which discusses most explicitly and fully the role of the clergy in the society of the time.

There could be no denying that, with the rapid improvements in agriculture during the eighteenth century, parsons stood to gain enormously from a financial point of view by the existence of tithe. To do so, however, they had to assume the role of tax-gatherer and to be forever on the look-out for their rights and dues. A survey carried out for the Younger Pitt in the early 1790s revealed that tithing in kind – a practice which required the parson to visit farms regularly and check on the amount of produce due to him – was still not uncommon in a dozen or so counties, including Hampshire and Kent.[1] Most of the clergy, however, had pulled down their tithe barns (often situated opposite the front door of older parsonages) or converted them to other uses and made agreements with the farmers for receipt of a money payment based on the estimated yield of produce per acre. A parson with an eye to his rights needed to renegotiate these 'compositions', as they were called, as soon as they became unrealistic and to make sure also that they were adjusted to include land newly brought into cultivation. He could do this with each farmer separately, or for the parish as a whole. He could also let out his tithes on lease if this seemed the most satisfactory way of obtaining an income from them: large landowners in particular were often willing to take them on board and recoup the money with interest from their tenant farmers as a proportion of the rent. What with one thing and another, a parson by the beginning of the nineteenth century could easily spend as much time negotiating tithes as a modern clergyman has to devote to money-raising activities in his parish, and without the excuse that his efforts benefited anybody but himself. Mr Collins, with his usual devastating candour, placed it at the head of a clergyman's duties. 'The rector of a parish has much to do', he informed the company at Mr Bingley's ball (most of whom probably knew all about it already). 'In the first place, he must make such an agreement for tythes as may be beneficial to himself and not offensive to his patron.' Only second must he think of writing sermons.[2]

There was often some confusion in the minds of ordinary people as to who actually owned tithes. Mrs Jennings in *Sense and Sensibility* seems to have thought that the tithes at Delaford belonged to Colonel Brandon, the patron of the living, for on hearing that he had offered the benefice to her niece's betrothed 'she was not only ready to worship him as a saint', we are told, 'but was moreover truly anxious that he should be treated as one in all earthly concerns; anxious that his tythes should be raised to the utmost . . . '[3] There was certainly a sense in which an increase in tithes benefited the patron of the living, for it enhanced the value of the benefice which he had the power to sell or bestow; but in a direct way he benefited only if he was the 'impropriator' of the tithes. In almost half the parishes of England the 'great tithes' (levied on cereal crops such as wheat and oats) had been 'impropriated' by a layman, leaving only the 'small tithes' (on produce such as lamb, chickens, fruit and eggs) for the parish priest. In two of James Austen's parishes, Cubbington and Sherborne St John, the great tithes had been impropriated by the respective patrons, the Leighs of Stoneleigh Abbey and the Chutes of The Vyne.[4] Whoever held the great tithes was technically the rector of the parish. He might be himself a clergyman, willing to carry out the spiritual duties of the benefice; if not, he must appoint a vicar or a curate. When Colonel Brandon informs Edward Ferrars that Delaford 'is a rectory', he is making a point of telling him that as incumbent he will receive the whole of the tithes.[5] One can sympathize with Mrs Jennings for not understanding the significance of the remark; but a clergyman would certainly have understood what was at issue, for in impropriated parishes it was common for the lay rector to receive three-quarters of the total yield of the tithe. In some instances – such as in the parishes of the Home Counties, where vegetables were grown on a large scale for the London market – the small tithes could be extremely valuable; but in most parishes the added difficulty of levying them detracted from their already small value. Vicars were known to grumble that they had been given 'not livings but leavings'.[6]

It could be an unpleasant business for a parson to go around his parish insisting on his tithes, yet if he failed to do so he could be accused of running down the benefice not only for himself but for his successors. Some were known to be extremely energetic in the matter and to pursue backsliders in the courts. According to Arthur Young, tithes were levied more assiduously in England than in any country known to him on the Continent.[7] Lay impropriators were more rigorous than clergy in their demands. Often the latter only made a push when they were about to leave a parish. 'My father is doing all in his power to increase his Income by raising his Tythes, &c.', Jane reported when the family was preparing to leave Steventon, '& I do not despair of getting nearly six hundred a year' (a sum he would subsequently expect his son James to collect and send to him in his retirement).[8] There was probably a lot to do to catch up, George Austen having been one of those parsons who preferred teaching boys to taxing farmers.

It is possible that George Austen was all the more interested in his tithes because he was leaving his other source of income – the glebe – for James's benefit as resident curate. He was under no obligation to do so; he could have let it out for his own profit and merely paid his son a £50 stipend as he did the new curate at Deane; but the interest James showed in the horses and livestock at Steventon suggest that he was to be the owner of the farmland attached to the benefice.

The glebe was an area of land donated to the church (often in the distant past) for the benefit of the incumbent. During the eighteenth century the area was frequently extended, for owners of newly-enclosed land in the parish liked to free it from tithe by arranging to hand over a few acres to the church. Assessments in such cases were often generous to the clergy, whose permission as tithe-owners had to be obtained before enclosure could go forward: in areas of rapid enclosure the average extent of glebe doubled and trebled.[9] Bishops encouraged parsons to insist upon an amount of land equal in value to the tithe as it might be expected to have become after enclosure and in many parishes they drove a hard bargain. In addition it was possible from 1776, when the most important of the Gilbert Acts was passed, for parsons themselves to add to the glebe by borrowing money to the extent of three years net income of the living and paying it back at a fixed rate of interest over thirty-one years. The money could be borrowed from anybody willing to lend it and the facility became so popular that a positive wave of endowment resulted, at the clergy's own expense.[10]

With glebe, unlike tithe, there was no built-in necessity to harass anybody else in order to make a living. Parsons were therefore tempted to concentrate on it. The danger was obvious. They could soon be accused of spending too much time on it, like Henry Fielding's Parson Trulliber who was 'a parson on Sundays, but on all other six might properly be called a farmer'. Defenders of the clergy, such as Sir William

Plan (1821) of the glebe land at Steventon, with additional
fields numbered 3-14 which the Rev. George Austen
rented from the Knight family.
(*Jane Austen Memorial Trust, Chawton*)

Scott who spoke on the subject in the House of Commons in 1802, argued that the clergy were obliged by the mere existence of glebe to become farmers and that, provided they did not overdo the business, it had many praiseworthy features:

> In this country the parish priest is, by the very constitution of his office, in some degree an agriculturist; he is *ex officio* a farmer. He is to take care, undoubtedly, that the ecclesiastic shall not merge in the farmer . . . ; but the moderated and subordinate practice of farming supplies many means of cheap subsistence for the clergyman and his family; many means of easy kindness and hospitality to his poorer parishioners; and many motives of pleasing attachment to the place which furnishes the healthy and amusing occupation of his vacant hours.[11]

Which was all very well, but a family can need other things beside food; and if tithes were too burdensome to collect, or insufficient to pay college fees for grown-up sons, who was to tell the clergyman that he ought not to enter the market with his surplus produce? Once he had done so, he would soon find that, with landowners all around him adopting commercial practices and new methods of agriculture, he was bound to do the same if the glebe was to remain viable. The days of the poor clergyman subsisting on the produce of his one cow were over; if the glebe was too small for profitable farming, the best thing to do was either to rent more land to go with it or to let it out to a neighbouring farmer who could make better use of it. This was tacitly recognized when, in 1802, Parliament rescinded laws of Henry VIII's reign which forbade clergy to take leases on the glebe.[12]

George Austen's experience at Steventon was probably typical of that of a clergyman with a modest endowment. He was a scholarly man, not the sort that might have been expected to take to farming; but he was proud of his parish and soon eager to show off his 'lands' to his family and friends.[13] As time went on, with his sons to educate and a houseful of students to feed, he became increasingly aware of the potential of farming both as a source of income and as a supply of food. The original glebe at Steventon was quite small – about three acres; but in addition Thomas Knight allowed his incumbent to take a lease on 200 acres of farmland at nearby Cheesedown, famous for its pigs. Admittedly, George Austen employed a steward, John Bond, to keep the accounts and carry out much of the day-to-day supervision – there are no reports of him attending hogs to fairs as Parson Trulliber was said to do, or getting a bull to his cows like Samuel Johnson's clergyman-friend in Leicestershire;[14] but he kept a keen eye on the market, comparing notes with his landowning son Edward on yields and prices.[15] As he grew older, and his sons were no longer a charge on him, he lost some of his interest in farming. John Bond, on whom he had come to rely a great deal, was complaining of getting older too and had to be released from some of the work. Eventually George Austen turned over a part of the arable land adjacent to the house to extend his garden.[16] James, who was never much interested in farming, and preferred to get the bulk of his income from accumulating parishes, gave up the lease on Cheesedown and used the glebe at Steventon chiefly as grazing for his carriage horses.

On the rare occasions when Jane Austen mentions glebe in her novels, she invariably refers to it as meadow.[17] She was perhaps thinking of her brother's three acres at Steventon, although she must have known that parsons with a larger amount of glebe – like the Rev. John Rawstorne Papillon with his sixty-four acres at Chawton – went in for various kinds of farming, as her father had done when he rented Cheesedown. Her vagueness on the subject betrays a certain lack of interest. In spite of handing on numerous messages from her father to Edward in her letters, she disclaimed all knowledge of his farming activities, including even the number of farm hands he employed – perhaps because her mother and Cassandra were overwhelmingly interested in the subject and there was too much talk about it at home. 'You know my stupidity as to such matters', she reminded Cassandra; and indeed she avoided mentioning them in her novels whenever she could contrive to do so. She allowed Elizabeth Bennet to escape into the house rather than be conducted around Mr Collins's two 'meadows'.[18]

The dependence of the clergy on tithe and glebe had the advantage of integrating them into the agricultural community in which they lived, to an extent that modern clergymen have never yet been integrated into the world of industry and commerce. The clergy of the late eighteenth and early nineteenth century were as sensitive as the local farmers to the vagaries of the weather and the rise and fall of the market. Their incomes varied together. Unfortunately, at a time when rural society was dividing out among landowners, tenant farmers and a labour force working for wages, the clergy came to be identified with the two former groups – with the landlords over tithes and with the farmers over enclosure and wages: George Austen with Thomas Knight, the great landowner, and with Harry Digweed, tenant of Steventon Manor, rather than with the unnamed persons he employed as labourers on the farm. This was thought in some quarters to enhance the status of parsons and hence increase the respect shown to them; in others it was thought to undermine their effectiveness. The exploitative nature of capitalism on the land had, however, not yet been fully felt in Jane Austen's lifetime; it was to be some years yet before Cobbett, always on the look-out for unpopular clergy, reported after one of his rides around Hampshire and adjacent counties: 'I cannot conclude my remarks on this Rural Ride without noticing the new sort of language I hear everywhere made use of with regard to parsons; but which language I do not care to repeat.'[19]

In Jane Austen's day economic conditions were such that any parson who showed a little application could hardly fail to increase his income, provided his benefice was above subsistence level in the first place. George Austen, whose two parishes together were thought to be worth £200 a year in the early 1770s, could get as much as £600 from tithes alone by the end of the century and was disappointed in the £300 cleared by 'the farm' (probably Cheesedown and the glebe together).[20] Improvement of this kind was so common as almost to be taken for granted. Hamstall Ridware was said to be worth £140 a year when Edward Cooper was presented to it in 1799, 'but perhaps it may be improvable', Jane speculated.[21] She was presumably right, since the Coopers raised nine children on it. Colonel Brandon described Delaford as 'certainly capable of improvement', and when Edmund Bertram became incumbent of Thornton Lacey he soon found himself being instructed by his clerical neighbour Dr Grant in 'how to turn a good income into a better', which cannot have been a very difficult task since Dr Grant was known to be the most indolent of men, not overcommitted to the Protestant work ethic.[22] It is true that John Skinner, rector of the parish of Camerton in Somerset during the Napoleonic Wars, failed to achieve the increase in income his uncle confidently expected to take place when he bought the living for him, but Skinner was a particularly difficult man, totally without negotiating skills.[23] Post-war depression destroyed some of the more spectacular gains made during the boom years of 1806–12 but it was not generally catastrophic for the clergy.[24] It would be fair to say that throughout Jane Austen's lifetime poverty, on the whole, was experienced only by those clergy whose benefices did not provide an adequate basis from which to start. While this usually happened in areas where the land was infertile, it could also occur if the glebe was too small or if the parish was encumbered by 'moduses' (agreements for fixed rates of tithe, made prior to 1189 and by the nineteenth century almost worthless). Such benefices could hardly be expected to attract a resident incumbent. From the early years of the eighteenth century there existed a rule by which a benefactor who was prepared to give £200 or more to a parish for the purchase of tithe or glebe could apply to the commissioners of Queen Anne's Bounty for the amount to be doubled; but although 3,306 livings had been augmented in this way by 1815 the need throughout the country was so great that the Bounty could only be made available to benefices under £800 in value. In this category there were so many applicants that decisions sometimes had to be made by lot.[25]

With some parishes so underprovided, it was inevitable that suggestions should be floated in Parliament from time to time about the desirability of evening out the endowments. They were resisted usually on the grounds that parsons had not anticipated any such moves when they accepted preferment.[26] This was true but it was unfair to place all the blame upon the clergy. Private patrons and possibly benefactors would also have objected, along with all who had a concern for property rights. It was easier for radicals to bemoan the fact that a benefice had come to be regarded as a freehold estate instead of a cure of souls than it was for statesmen to decide what could best be done about it. In France clerical property had been confiscated out of hand during the Revolution and the clergy guaranteed a stipend from the state; but Edmund Burke had traced so many subsequent horrors to that one sacrilegious act that few Englishmen would have cared to emulate it.[27]

The livings mentioned in Jane Austen's novels do not fall into the lowest ranges of income. They nevertheless vary considerably, between Edward Ferrars' Delaford on the one hand, said to be worth £200 a year, and Dr Grant's Mansfield, estimated in his predecessor's time to have been worth 'little less than a thousand a year' on the other. James Morland was promised a parish worth £400 a year as soon as he was old enough to take orders, while Edmund Bertram could look forward to £700 at Thornton Lacey.[28] These figures (the only ones mentioned) represent the sort of guesswork that went on whenever a benefice changed hands. Rough calculations could be made on the basis of recent crop prices but accurate assessments were difficult to arrive at. In 1796, assessors trying to work out how much compensation Henry Austen would need to pay John Rawstorne Papillon to induce him to give up his claim to the benefice at Chawton disagreed with each other to the extent of £300–400 in their estimate of the annual value of the living.[29]

It is equally difficult to arrive at a picture of the lifestyle made possible by the various levels of endowment, partly because tastes and temperaments differed. There was good sense in the comment made by Mrs Jennings to Elinor Dashwood when she heard that Colonel Brandon had pronounced Delaford living, at £200, to be insufficient to allow the incumbent to marry: 'The Colonel is a ninny, my dear; because he has two thousand a-year himself, he thinks that nobody else can marry on less.'[30] George Austen, with an income rising from £110 a year provided by his one small parish to perhaps £900 at the end of the century, kept a wife and two daughters in reasonable comfort whilst giving four sons an expensive education and maintaining a fifth – the handicapped George – in the care of a local family. He employed three household servants and, for a brief period, until wartime conditions obliged him to cut down on luxuries, his wife and daughters enjoyed the benefit of a private carriage for local visiting. He was always hospitable to family and friends, many of whom stayed at the parsonage for weeks on end. In the early days he was often hard-pressed for money and is known to have borrowed several sums from his brother-in-law, James Leigh-Perrot; but after 1780 this expedient was no longer necessary. From 1773 he took in three or four boys at a time as pupils, teaching and boarding them at a fee which rose from £35 a year to £65; but he was able to relax from this work in 1796. He never regarded himself as affluent – economy in such matters as dress was always a consideration – but he bought books on a considerable scale and undertook journeys to London, Kent, Bath and Gloucestershire from time to time. A decade after his death James Austen, with the same parish as his basic source of income, with fewer commitments and larger sums of additional money at his disposal, lived in greater style but frequently cried out poverty. In the novels, James Morland's benefice at £400 is expected by his father, who has bestowed it on him, to be quite adequate to enable him to marry the penniless Isabella Thorpe; yet Edmund Bertram, with his £700 at Thornton Lacey, has no sooner married Fanny Price than he is looking for an increase in income.[31]

Further complications arise from the fact that most of Jane Austen's clergy characters enjoy private means. We never see Edward Ferrars trying to keep a wife on £200, because he and Elinor happen to have £3,000 between them, which according to Jane Austen gives them another £150 a year. By the time they actually marry and are found to have 'an income quite sufficient to their wants', Edward's mother has come up with another £10,000. Henry Tilney is clearly well endowed at Woodston, for even General Tilney says that were the parish his son's only resource he would not be ill provided for; but Henry's sartorial elegance and smart curricle were not necessarily paid for out of his benefice since he spent half his time living with his father at Northanger Abbey. Dr Grant, whose luxurious style of living is thought to have been modelled on that of the Rev. George Moore at Wrotham, has obviously married money (though Mrs Norris 'could not find that Mrs Grant ever had more than five thousand pounds'). Even Mr Elton, who always gives the impression of being a self-made man, 'was known to have some independent property' when he arrived at Highbury. The only one of Jane Austen's fictional clergy who is actually stated to be entirely without private fortune is Mr Collins. The value of his living is never mentioned but it is obviously not small: the glebe is extensive and the surrounding countryside productive, which augurs well for the tithes he is so keen on. His living allows him to contemplate marriage with a portionless girl but will not furnish the sort of expense he would be at if he socialized among the gentry of his neighbourhood in Kent.[32]

Jane Austen's father never enjoyed much in the way of private fortune. Jane was fully aware of the liberating effects of even the occasional windfall and conversely of the restricting nature of worry about financial commitments. Out of this immediate experience she made a more general point when she insisted upon private means for most of her clergy characters. In her view, a clergyman should behave like a gentleman, as her father had always done. As the characteristic trait of a gentleman was that he had a mind above money, the simplest way of indicating that her fictional clergy were of this nature was to give them a private income – preferably from land. Jane Austen sometimes made allowances for 'a respectable line of trade' (whatever that may mean);[33] but a tradesman, especially if he was a 'capitalist', was by definition engaged in making money. Significantly, Mr Elton's property is ultimately suspected to have come from trade and Mr Elton, like the propertyless Mr Collins, is no gentleman.[34] The pair of them have mercenary minds. Brought up by a miserly father, Mr Collins cannot get used to comparative prosperity but must be forever talking about it, telling the Bennets that he is above regarding little losses at cards, assessing everything around him in terms of cost and weighing up the advantages and disadvantages of marriage for all the world as if he were in the counting house.[35]

The picture of a privately-endowed clergy is to some extent realistic for, as benefices increased in value, the gentry began thinking it worthwhile to put their sons into them. Parents who did not wish their sons to become idle spendthrifts thereby assured them of a position in landed society without incurring the expense of buying them an estate. Edmund Bertram and Henry Tilney are fictional examples of a trend which was particularly common in rich agricultural counties such as Hampshire and Kent, where Jane Austen's experience lay;[36] among her own acquaintances she could have pointed to Michael Terry of Dummer and Tom Chute of The Vyne. The extent to which the gentry infiltrated the clerical profession should not be exaggerated – the numbers are unlikely to have exceeded 20 per cent of the clergy in the country as a whole;[37] but it was a trend of which Jane Austen seemed to approve since it raised the social status of the clergy. Some members of the gentry class continued to regard a career in the church as inferior to one in the armed forces or the law but, if we are able to believe Jane Austen, it was only certain types of women who did so – Mrs Ferrars and her daughter Fanny; Mary Musgrove; Mary Crawford – selfish, empty-headed or cynical women all. The only male character who scoffs at the role of clergyman is Robert Ferrars, the prize ass of the novels.[38]

Chapter 5

The Parson's Dwelling

Parsons have often been considered luckier than other men in that they could expect to be provided with a house rent-free to live in. Yet up to the middle of the eighteenth century this was for most of them no great blessing, since the majority of parsonage houses were humble, not to say mean, dwellings – hardly better than the cottages of the poor. At the beginning of the century many still had earthen floors and consisted basically of one room, with a couple of sheds built on to serve as kitchen and wash-house and perhaps a garret in the roof space. There were exceptions of course. The parsonage at Colyton, where Jane Austen visited Richard Buller and his wife in 1801, was a large Tudor residence of 1529, bearing the arms of Henry VIII and Catherine of Aragon over the doorway and boasting stained-glass windows like those of the nearby church. Her maternal grandfather's rectory at Harpsden was also a sizeable house, dating from the late seventeenth century. On the whole, however, parsons were expected to make do with the peasant accommodation that had satisfied their celibate predecessors before the Reformation.[1]

The church took no corporate responsibility for providing adequate accommodation for the clergy, this being generally assumed to be the responsibility of patrons. From 1704 the latter could apply to the governors of Queen Anne's Bounty for help with the task. Certain improvements to parsonages became common: floors were boarded over, single rooms were divided to furnish a study and modest extensions were made. The result was often a hotch-potch building such as that which served for a parsonage house at Deane, where no two rooms were on the same level and ceilings were so low that a tall man could not stand up straight under them. The whole was so tiny that Jane Austen once likened it to a carriage with basket and dickey.[2] Even this could be considered princely when compared with the total lack of accommodation which persisted in some 3,000 parishes well on into the nineteenth century.[3]

In 1733 an Act of Mortmain put an end to the availability of the Bounty for the provision of parsonages, but shortly afterwards the clergy themselves began to take a hand. The more ambitious ordinands who appeared in the middle decades of the century were not likely to be content to live in a cottage, especially if they became magistrates with an added dignity to maintain. Since an incumbent could do what he liked with his parsonage house, short of selling it, many of them decided either to 'improve' them or pull them down and build anew. This galvanized a certain number of patrons into activity, among them Thomas Knight. It was at this point that George Austen left Oxford to take up residence in his Hampshire parish. The parsonage house at Steventon was occupied at the time by a bachelor curate who had done duty for a number of years on behalf of the non-resident incumbent; like many houses in such circumstances it was not in a fit state to receive a married parson hoping to bring up a family. It had been described in a diocesan report of 1696 as consisting of 'two bays of building, outletted at the west end and part of the south side over the cellar'. At some time since then it had been given a Georgian front on the north side but the rooms behind had probably not been greatly changed. The Austens therefore moved into temporary residence at Deane parsonage (empty because the Rev. William Hillman chose to live in greater style at Ashe Park), whilst the Rev. Edward Bathurst was transferred elsewhere and the house at Steventon got ready for them.[4] Since neither George Austen nor his bride had much in the way of private fortune, it seems likely that the building operations were paid for by Thomas Knight (although it is worth recording that the latter had done nothing to improve the parsonage at Chawton, which was described by Henry Austen in 1796 as 'exceedingly bad').[5]

Unlike Colonel Brandon, who went down to Delaford to inspect the parsonage when Edward Ferrars and his wife were about to enter it, and Lady Catherine de Bourgh who was in residence at nearby Rosings when Mr Collins was installed at Hunsford, Thomas Knight was not at hand to supervise: the Austen grandchildren who subsequently wrote about the upgrading of the house were probably right to attribute most of the planning to their grandfather. It is not known precisely what he did but, according to Anna Lefroy, 'he added and improved, so that in those times Steventon came to be regarded as a very comfortable family residence'. From drawings made by Anna at a later date we know that the house had a square and regular front with two windows at each side of the doorway on the ground floor, five windows on the floor above and three dormer windows in the roof. Another granddaughter, Catherine Hubbock, tell us that the two windows to the left of the door lighted the best parlour and the two to the right the kitchen. The front door opened straight into a small 'common parlour', above which was the girls' bedroom. According to Catherine there were seven bedrooms in all on the first floor and three in the attic. Some of those on the first floor presumably stretched out over the two projecting bays at the back of the house. At the ground level these provided a series of pantries at one end and at the other a study for Mr Austen, with a bow window facing south.[6]

With seven bedrooms and three garrets the house offered more accommodation than many of the parsonage houses newly built at the time. Typical of these was the parsonage at Haworth, whence the redoubtable Grimshaw sallied forth to drive the drunks out of the pubs on Sundays and where at a later date the Brontë family lived and wrote. Built around 1740, the front door gave on to a dark passage, to one side of which was the living room with a stone-flagged store room behind and to the other the parson's study with the kitchen behind. Straight ahead, the stairs led up to a small room without a fireplace, and four bedrooms. Even more humble were the plans offered in 1752 by William Halfpenny in his *Useful Architecture in Twenty-One New Designs for Country Parsonages, Farm Houses and Inns*, and in 1756 by Isaac Ware in his *Complete Body of Architecture*. Both writers were under the impression that clergy needed rather less space than would have been found in a small farm building.[7]

The house at Steventon was a considerable financial asset to George Austen, in that the three garret rooms allowed him to take in boarding pupils. Half a century later his son Henry, who had started his third career on a £50 curacy, was glad enough to accept a temporary incumbency at Steventon in order to be able to teach a handful of young boys.[8] The building was also considered gracious in its time, with its balanced Georgian front expressing dignity, order and restraint and its fashionable bow window providing both space and light at the back. Yet by the early years of the nineteenth century it was beginning to be regarded as both incommodious and insufficiently imposing. The rooms were no doubt small, as in all eighteenth-century houses (twelve to fifteen feet square being the usual dimensions). On the ground floor, especially, there must have been a higher ratio of persons to rooms than was later considered acceptable, even though Mrs Austen followed the contemporary practice of using what was virtually the entrance hall as a sitting-

An ideal vicarage house, with separate entrance to the study
and Venetian windows giving on to the landscaped garden.
From Ackermann's *Repository of Arts*, January 1817.

room. James Edward Austen-Leigh, brought up at the parsonage just after his aunt Jane left it, remembered the inadequacy of the kitchen quarters and the lack of a servants' hall, much as Catherine Morland remembered the few 'shapeless pantries' and the 'comfortless scullery' in her father's parsonage at Fullerton (at Steventon the three servants occupied the kitchen for most of the day, along with the family.) James Edward also recalled the lack of interior finish – the walls without cornices and the ceilings unplastered, the beams of the bedroom floors projecting into the rooms below in all their naked simplicity. A man like General Tilney, who prided himself on being in the forefront of fashion, would doubtless have voiced in addition his detestation of 'a patched-on bow'. Eliza de Feuillide heard that James Austen when he took over from his father in 1801 had made 'such alterations and embellishments' that it was 'almost a pretty place'; the house was nevertheless pulled down in about 1824.[9]

None of what later came to be regarded as its deficiencies prevented George Austen from leading in it the life of a scholar and a gentleman. It at least provided him with a study which was accessible without having to go through the dining-room, as was the case in so many of the smaller parsonages of the time (Jane Austen knew when John Bond was visiting her father only from hearing his feet along the passage).[10] George Austen was by all accounts as unpretentious as he was refined: he housed his 500 volumes in Hepplewhite bookcases but did not follow the fashion of calling his study the library. There is some indication that his wife and daughters persuaded him to make an effort to bring the family's living arrangements up to date during his last years at Steventon. It was fashionable for ladies to have a 'dressing-room', next to their bedroom, and to use it as a sitting-room both for themselves and (by permission) for other members of the family. In 1798, with the boys gone from home, Jane and Cassandra furnished such a room with their own possessions – an inexpensive carpet, a painted chest of drawers with bookshelves over it, an oval mirror on the wall, a writing-desk for Cassandra's painting equipment, and a piano Jane thought herself reasonably lucky to get eight guineas for when it was sold a few years later.[11] The result could hardly be said to compare with the Coopers' much talked of dressing-room at Harpsden ('How will they convey the furniture of the dressing-room so far in safety?' Jane asked innocently when she heard that Edward was moving to Hamstall Ridware),[12] but the Austen ladies made the most of it. 'We live entirely in the dressing-room now, which I like very much', wrote Jane in December 1798. 'I always feel so much more elegant in it than in the parlour.' Mrs Austen,

PRIDE

AND

PREJUDICE:

A NOVEL.

IN THREE VOLUMES.

BY THE

AUTHOR OF " SENSE AND SENSIBILITY."

VOL. II.

London:

PRINTED FOR T. EGERTON,

MILITARY LIBRARY, WHITEHALL.

1813.

Title page to the first edition of *Pride and Prejudice*.

who was beginning to think herself an invalid, had insisted on having a bedroom with a sitting-room on the same floor even when staying for only one night in an inn at Dartford three months earlier; she was no doubt ready enough to take tea in the new dressing-room each evening before retiring.[13]

In the rest of the house there can have been little space for the profusion of tables, desks and flower stands which Jane noticed scattered about the rooms of the country houses she visited, yet several new pieces of furniture were ordered in 1800. After annoying delays in delivery, Jane reported to Cassandra in November:

> The Tables are come, & give general contentment. I had not expected that they would so perfectly suit the fancy of us all three, or that we should so well agree in the disposition of them; but nothing except their own surface can have been smoother. The two ends put together form our constant Table for everything, & the centre piece stands exceedingly well under the glass; holds a great deal most commodiously without looking awkwardly. They are both covered with green baize & send their best Love. The Pembroke has got its destination by the sideboard, & my mother has great delight in keeping her money & papers locked up – The little Table which used to stand there, has most conveniently taken itself off into the best bedroom, and we are now in want only of the chiffoniere, which is neither finished nor come.

Jane was so proud of the new furniture, especially the tables, that she was bitterly disappointed when the latter fetched only a small amount of money at the sale a year later.[14]

Meanwhile the Rev. George Lefroy had built himself a rather more elegant parsonage when he arrived to take up his duties at Ashe in the 1780s. With a beautifully proportioned front elevation and a handsome segmented fanlight over the door, the rooms were large enough for balls to be given there in the 1790s.[15] Folding doors could be thrown open to combine the dining-room with the drawing-room, whose windows looked over the garden at the side of the house. Since 'a private dance without sitting down to supper' was considered 'an infamous fraud upon the rights of men and women' (as we learn from *Emma*), a refreshment room must also have been provided somewhere – perhaps, as at Many-down, in the conservatory, lighted up for the purpose.[16] The parsonage at Great Bookham, occupied by Jane Austen's godfather Samuel Cooke, would doubtless have lent itself even more easily to such festivities, had Mrs Cooke been of the same mind as 'Madam' Lefroy: a large, three-storeyed, yellow-brick building with wide eaves and an Adam doorway, it could have been outstripped in grandeur only by the rectory at

Wrotham where Jane Austen visited her relative by marriage, Harriot Bridges, in November 1813. Harriot's husband, the Rev. George Moore, had pulled down the old rectory when he arrived in the parish and commissioned Samuel Wyatt to build a replacement in 1801–2. Its classical front and domed bay were almost as impressive a sight as the ruins of the former episcopal palace nearby. Its fame went before it: 'I shall be glad to see Wrotham', Jane confessed.[17]

With John Rawstorne Papillon also pulling down a parsonage house and building a new one at Chawton in 1804, Jane Austen was clearly accustomed to 'improvement', which was the fashionable gentlemanly occupation of the eighteenth and early nineteenth centuries. Like all movements it had its own vocabulary and its own specialized publications, which she drew upon when she described Mrs Dashwood's plans for improving her four-bedroomed cottage at Barton:

> These parlours are both too small for such parties of our friends as I hope to see often collected here; and I have some thought of throwing the passage into one of them with perhaps a part of the other, and so leave the remainder of that other for an entrance; this, with a new drawing-room which may easily be added, and a bed-chamber and garret above, will make it a very snug little cottage. I could wish the stairs were handsome. But one must not expect everything; though I suppose it would be no difficult matter to widen them.[18]

Windows were especially vulnerable to change. Small leaded casements were ripped out during the eighteenth century in favour of the double-sash: an advertisement for the sale of the living of Camerton in 1800 announced proudly that all the upper windows of the rectorial house were sashed.[19] At the same time – although it was to be some years before John Buonarotti Papworth, the fashionable villa architect, declared Gothic to be the most appropriate style for parsonages – Gothicism was creeping into the design of windows. The Rev. James Skinner as the new incumbent of Camerton may have been pleased enough with sashes for the bedrooms but for the ground-floor rooms he decided to install Gothic windows with stone mullions, thereby causing the ceiling to have to be raised and those of the bedrooms to be carried three feet into the roof space.[20] The curious hybrid known as a sashed Gothic window was among the improvements Edward made to the house he provided for his mother and sisters at Chawton. Meanwhile, more stylish houses were having French windows installed. These, like the verandah, the patio and the porch, were part of the current aesthetic movement to bring the outside of the house into closer communion with the inside; yet far from producing an atmosphere of simplicity, they often created a far greater degree of sophistication. When Dr Grant at Mansfield had the windows of his parsonage 'cut down to the ground', and his elegant sister-in-law from London sat in front of them playing her harp, the scene quite captivated the country-bred Edmund Bertram.[21]

As the clergy rose in status, and more and more of the gentry presented their own sons to the livings in their gift, a further phase of improvement began. 'It is a family living, Miss Morland', General Tilney explained concerning Woodston, 'and the property in the place being chiefly my own, you may believe I take care that it shall not be a bad one.' The parsonage in question proved to be a 'new-built, substantial stone house' (stone having acquired a special cachet) with a commodious, well-proportioned dining-room, a gentleman's study for the parson, and a prettily-shaped drawing-room lit by the latest style of French window.[22] It was when Jane Austen's brother inherited the property of Thomas Knight and began to think of clerical careers for his sons that Steventon parsonage was pulled down and replaced by a handsomer house built on higher ground. Many an old parsonage was built on low ground and hence liable to floods: at Deane the whole area of the church and parsonage was impassable in the year that George Austen left it for Steventon. There the garden of the parsonage sloped down towards the house with the result that the ground floor was inundated when heavy snows thawed.[23] The location of the older parsonages was also found unsuitable in other ways. They were very often in the village, close to the church, as were many of the older manor houses. As the gentry moved out to fine new houses a distance away, the parsons liked to follow; so the provision of a parsonage near to the gates of the manor house was often a prerequisite to finding an incumbent of suitable social standing. No doubt Sir Lewis de Bourgh had borne this in mind when building Hunsford parsonage, which Mr Collins described with immense pride as 'separated only by a lane from Rosings Park'.[24] It is not difficult to imagine Mr Collins, like the parson in a Rowlandson print of 1810, going around her ladyship's drawing-room with notebook in hand, taking down the arrangement of the furniture in the hope of emulating it in his 'humble abode'.[25]

The taste for improvement could become quite a mania and prove difficult for others to live with, as Mary Crawford discovered when she was staying with her uncle the admiral.[26] Jane Austen often treated it with detached irony in her novels, yet she by no means disapproved of the general trend. She felt none of the nostalgia John Clare later expressed, in his poem 'The Parish', for the old wattle-and-daub parsonage standing among the 'melancholy row' of peasant cottages, 'needing like repairs'; nor did she regard such living conditions as showing a greater sympathy for the poor. She expected her clergy to improve their dwellings as far as they were able. It was clearly not entirely Mr Elton's fault that his parsonage at Highbury was rather a poor sort of house (we are never told who the patron was); but Mr Elton had private means and, if he had been other than self-centred and shallow, he could have done more than 'smarten it up' in a superficial way.[29] To Jane Austen a well-kept parsonage was a sign of a responsible attitude to religion, property and public duty. 'Neat' and 'tidy-looking' were words which she liked to use in connection with them; in the last years of her life she would dearly have liked to see her niece Anna installed in one.[28] In spite of her amusement at the pettifogging nature of some of Mr Collins's improvements, she would allow Elizabeth Bennet to show nothing but admiration for the general state of his parsonage, which is said to have been modelled on one inhabited by an Austen relative at Chevening in Kent;[29] and she implied that Catherine Morland had grown in maturity when she gave up hankering after 'Gothick' manor houses and began to dream instead of 'the unpretending comfort of a well-connected parsonage'.[30]

Yet Jane Austen was aware that improvement could lead to ostentation and empty show, which she greatly deplored. She made her attitude on this point quite clear in the discussion which took place at Mansfield Park between Henry Crawford and Edmund Bertram when the latter was about to become rector of Thornton Lacey.[31] The parsonage there was already an exceptionally handsome one, described by Crawford as 'a solid walled, roomy, mansion-like looking house, such as one might suppose a respectable old country family had lived in from generation to generation through two centuries at least, and were now spending from two to three thousand a year in'. He nevertheless began devising plans for its improvement, which would include turning the house round at an angle of 45 degrees so that the principal rooms no longer faced north, and making a new garden at what was formerly the back of the house, sloping gently down to the south east. 'By some such improvements', Crawford urged, 'you may give it a higher character. You may raise it into a *place* . . . [The house may] receive such an air as to make its owner be set down as the great land-holder of the parish by every creature travelling the road.' Such transformations were not unknown and Jane Austen was appalled by the false ambitions which lay behind them. Yet she was in favour of the not inconsiderable improvements envisaged by Edmund himself. Surprising as it may seem, this conscientious, sincere and unassuming young man was all for making the parsonage house look like that of a gentleman instead of that of a mere local squire. It was also he who first suggested that, to achieve this aim, the farmyard which obscured the view of the house from the road would have to be removed. Admittedly, he did not go as far as Crawford and agree that the whole of the farmyard area should be 'planted up to shut out the blacksmith's shop', but he would presumably have done something of the kind with the land on either side of his proposed new drive. Edmund, in fact, adopted the attitude we are led to expect from Charles Hayter, another of Jane Austen's favourite characters, when the day should come for him to inherit his father's estate. 'Without beauty and without dignity', Winthrop was 'hemmed in by the barns and buildings of a farmyard'. Charles Hayter, in his determination to be a gentleman, would 'make a different sort of place of it', we are assured.[32]

Enthusiasm for improvement was after all not merely a fashion: it was a key concept of the eighteenth and nineteenth centuries, with twin roots in the agricultural and industrial revolutions on the one hand and the Enlightenment on the other. The word 'improvement', like 'taste' and 'fitness', had a moral as well as an aesthetic meaning. Widespread prosperity, it was believed, would release and encourage the essential reasonableness of mankind: people would become more gracious, more considerate, more dutiful, more humane. Since these were public virtues, there was much to be gained from proclaiming them to the world in outward signs and symbols: 'gracious living' was an art worth pursuing not only for the sake of those in enjoyment of it but for the sake of all who beheld it. A show of wealth alone (for instance by building a house which merely proclaimed its owners to be the biggest landowners in the area) was vulgar; but a show of wealth combined with discrimination and taste was a witness and an education to mankind.

It was all the more deplorable that 'improved' vicarages were by no means universal. When Mrs Austen and her daughters moved into the small house at Chawton which had previously belonged to Edward's steward, James Edward Austen-Leigh believed it to be 'quite as good as the generality of parsonage houses then were, and much the same in style'.[38] It was not a new house – perhaps early Georgian. From the front it appeared to be rectangular but in fact it was L-shaped, with a gravelled yard in the interior angle partly enclosed by outhouses on the two remaining sides. The front door opened on to an entrance hall, capable of being used as an extra little room, with a dining-parlour on the right (where Jane wrote her novels) and a drawing-room on the left. An unidentified set of 'offices' ran along the upright arm of the 'L'. A narrow staircase led to six bedrooms, which along with two garrets accommodated Mrs Austen, Jane and Cassandra (sharing a room), Martha Lloyd, two maidservants and a man, leaving the 'best' bedroom (like the state bedroom in grander houses) free for guests, and one of the garret rooms free for an accompanying servant.[34] Nephews and nieces who visited it in their youth remembered it as spacious, but this was probably because of the unusual number of outhouses in which they delighted to play as children.[35] In the house itself the rooms were small, with the low, crooked ceilings that Mr Palmer commented on so rudely when he visited Barton Cottage (a house not unlike the typical parsonage in lay-out).

In spite of being so grateful for the house at Chawton that she did not like to criticize it in any way, Jane Austen did once admit that the walls were sometimes damp: the proximity of a large pond, which overflowed in wet weather, cannot have helped.[37] James Edward said that there was room to receive other members of the family as visitors, but when Jane's brothers arrived, with their wives, servants and children, the house became impossibly crowded and somebody – either Jane of Cassandra or Martha – had to move out.[38] Deane parsonage was even more cramped: when Martha Lloyd and Jane Austen stayed there in 1799, in order to be able to travel with James and Mary in their carriage to the Kempshott ball, Mary's baby and his nurse had to sleep on the floor whilst the two young ladies occupied the same room and slept in a 'shut-up' bed – a mattress with front legs that could be folded back, and the whole tipped up on hinges to be stowed away into a cupboard which simulated a wardrobe.[39] Difficulties were likely to be caused in parsonages anywhere when elderly relatives had to be accommodated: Kintbury parsonage was crammed when Fulwar Fowle, who had moved in as the new incumbent, continued to house his parents and in addition took in two spinster relatives along with the mother of one of them, who had nowhere else to go.[40]

Henry Crawford, inspecting the village of Thornton Lacey round about 1812, was surprised to find that the parsonage there was not 'a scrambling collection of low single rooms, with as many roofs as windows', nor was it 'cramped into the vulgar compactness of a square farmhouse', these being apparently the norm.[41] In spite of the widespread craze for building, there was clearly still a large number of patrons who were loth to spend money on parsonages when they had no sons to install in them. Worse, parsonages were often allowed to become extremely dilapidated; many were virtually falling down. In 1818 the parsonage houses in 2,183 parishes were declared by their incumbents to be 'unfit' for them to live in. Some were too big, others not considered grand enough, but a great many were genuinely unsuitable for habitation.[42] Jane Austen's county of Hampshire had its share of such houses, a state of affairs which Cobbett in a typically irate passage blamed on both patrons and parsons: 'Of all the mean, all the cowardly reptiles that ever crawled on the face of the earth, the English landowners are the most cowardly', he wrote after riding around Hampshire in 1826. '[They] see their own parsons pocket the tithes and glebe rents and suffer the parsonage house to fall down'.[43]

There undoubtedly existed, in most parts of the country, landowners who had impropriated the tithes of their parishes and preferred to employ a £50 curate, living in a dilapidated cottage, rather than install a vicar in a decent vicarage; and there were also parsons who allowed parsonages houses to fall into disrepair as an excuse for non-residence. However, the reasons for the widespread decay were more complicated than Cobbett allowed. Pluralism could not easily be eradicated whilst there were large numbers of extremely poor parishes. The problem of what to do with the extra parsonages was compounded if the latter had been 'improved' beyond the capacity of a clergyman without independent means to support them (as Mrs Leigh-Perrot suspected had happened at Ashe when in 1820 she thought of buying the living for her great-nephew).[44] In many parishes the non-resident incumbent allowed the redundant parsonage house to remain empty rather than go to the trouble of letting it out. If a curate was employed, he was sometimes given the option of living in the parsonage house rent free or at a nominal charge; but if the house was too large he might prefer to spend a part of his small stipend on renting more comfortable lodgings. Mary Russell Mitford in *Our Village*, an essay based on an amalgam of the villages she knew in Hampshire and Berkshire, described as a familiar feature of such places the respectable-looking house with 'fine flowered window-blinds' and a brass knocker on the door which signalled the curate's lodgings -- 'apartments his landlady would call them; he lives with his own family four miles off, but once or twice a week he comes to his neat little parlour to write sermons, to marry, or to bury, as the case may be'.[45]

A curate living in a parsonage house at least helped to keep the fabric warm and hence relatively free from damp; but curates seldom had enough money to carry out even the most essential repairs necessary to maintain the property. The Church of England in Jane Austen's time accepted no responsibility for repairs: each clergyman was supposed to keep his own house in order and if he failed to do so his successor could claim compensation for 'dilapidations', either from his predecessor or, if the latter had died, from his executors.[46] This often led to bitter dissension among clergy and clergy widows: 'Dr Grant and Mrs Norris were seldom good friends', we are told in *Mansfield Park*, 'their acquaintance had begun in dilapidations'.[47] Nobody had ever worked out whether an incumbent's obligation to carry out repairs extended to clergy houses in which he did not himself reside: George Austen seems to have accepted responsibility for repairing the little house at Deane to the tune of £100 when his son James, who had lived there as his curate, left it in 1801; but he was probably an exception.[48] As houses became more and more ruinous they were less and less likely to attract a resident incumbent; pluralism was thus both a cause and an effect of the widespread decay. A rise in status among the clergy also caused its own problems: the well-off Rev. William Hillman preferred to pay rent in order to live in style at Ashe Park rather than inhabit the tiny rectory at Deane, much as Tom Chute preferred to stay on at The Vyne and gallop off to his parish on a Sunday rather than go and live there.[49]

A curate who was allowed to live in a redundant parsonage house sometimes regarded himself as getting a better financial deal than one who had to pay board and lodgings elsewhere in that, provided he had enough capital to purchase tools and plants, he could grow produce in the garden. James Woodforde found this a great boon when he was curate of Babcary, even though he resided there only a few days at a time: 'Very busy all day planting my peas and beans', he noted in his diary.[50] These, along with cabbages, were the most common of the vegetables grown at the time: the Austens at Steventon were unusual in thinking potatoes worthwhile (Mrs Austen was still planting and digging up her own potatoes when she was in her seventies at Chawton).[51]

In *Persuasion*, Jane Austen was at pains to point out that the rectory at Uppercross in which the saintly Dr Shirley had lived out his long ministry was easily distinguishable from the nearby labourers' cottages.[52] The 'compact, tight parsonage, enclosed in its own neat garden, with a vine and a pear-tree trained round its casements' was clearly in a different category from the dwellings of the poor, which, according to Jane Austen's remarks in *Emma*, were usually surrounded by a mere mud plot, unattractive and unkempt.[53] In making this distinction she may inadvertently have given the impression that the typical parsonage garden of the time resembled what is now regarded as the traditional cottage garden. The latter, whose small plot of ground was crammed with a mixture of flowers and vegetables, shaded by ancient fruit trees combining usefulness with charm, was an invention of the garden designers of the late eighteenth century. Jane Austen was well acquainted with their writings on the subject. Sir Uvedale Price, reacting against the monotony of the square grass plots which accompanied the houses of most model villages, suggested in 1794 in *An Essay on the Picturesque* that philanthropic landowners seeking to enhance their own credit would do better to house their labourers in cottages with gardens that were less uniform. He suggested as an ideal 'frame' for a cottage a large tree, 'embracing it with its branches'. Honeysuckles, vines or jasmines could clamber over the porch, and fruit trees accompany the flowers and vegetables. The whole could suitably be surrounded – not, as one might expect from Price, by wild and luxuriant bushes but by a neatly clipped hedge, since 'neatness and regularity are so connected with the habitation of man that they must always please on a small scale and where the connection is immediate'.[54] This essay had a profound influence on cottage gardens, some of the best of which were to be found in Hampshire;[55] yet it was misleading of Jane Austen to give the impression that parsonage gardens were also of this type. The clergy of the Church of England had long been impressed by the so-called Natural Style in gardens, developed in the early decades of the eighteenth century by Pope and Kent and sold to owners of the great estates of England in a somewhat extreme form by Lancelot 'Capability' Brown. It was these gardens, not Uvedale Price's ideal cottage surroundings, which they tried, within their limited means, to copy.

The cult of the Natural Garden, which was one of England's major contributions to the Enlightenment, owed much to pagan beliefs in the essential goodness and virtue of mankind, but the clergy of the Church of England were ready, characteristically, to adapt it to their own purposes. In fact they were to the forefront in developing and promoting it: at least sixteen clergymen are known to have written important books on the subject.[56] The Garden of Eden, they were convinced, had been a tranquil and harmonious place, spoilt only by the insidious promptings of man's pride and disobedience. If the formal garden of the seventeenth century, with its geometrical flower-beds, topiary hedges and rectangular ponds suggestive of man's tyranny, were replaced by a scene which was more natural but had not yet run wild, would it not tranquillize the mind of the beholder and give him or her an encouraging glimpse of the paradise that could be regained through Christ's redemption? The writers of the books on Picturesque travel that were so popular at the time were fond of describing nature as a painter;

why not, therefore, make the garden into a portrait of Eden before the Fall?

Not many clergy were ever in a position to practise these ideas on a grand scale. An exception was Mrs Austen's cousin, the Rev. Thomas Leigh. His rectory was something of a family living, for it had been occupied at one time by Mrs Austen's uncle, the famous Theophilus Leigh of Balliol, and the parsonage house stood in close proximity to the ancestral home of the Leighs at Adlestrop. At the turn of the eighteenth and nineteenth centuries the formal garden which Sir William Leigh had made famous at Adlestrop Park in Stuart times, along with the less distinguished garden belonging to the parsonage, was transformed by Humphry Repton at the instigation of the Rev. Thomas Leigh. Jane Austen, who had visited Adlestrop with her sister shortly before the changes took place, and who was on the scene again with her mother shortly afterwards, derived from them much of the hostile comment she made on Repton in *Mansfield Park*.[57]

Jane's attitude to landscape gardening was always engagingly ambivalent. Her reading of Cowper, which included his famous poem *The Task*, had taught her that mankind should show humility to nature and not treat the countryside with the ruthlessness of a Capability Brown. As Cowper wrote:

> Improvement, the idol of the age,
> Is fed up with many a victim. Lo! he comes –
> The omnipotent magician, Brown, appears . . .
> He speaks. The lake in front becomes a lawn,
> Woods vanish, hills subside, and vallies rise,
> And streams, as if created for his use,
> Pursue the track of his directing wand . . .

As a lover of nature Jane Austen might have been expected to prefer Brown's 'natural' if idealized landscape to the highly formalized gardens he destroyed; but not so, for although she presented the formal garden in a far from attractive light in her description of Sotherton Court, she had learnt also from Cowper that Brown had no respect for the social amenities provided by such gardens. Terraces, arbours and shrubberies had been destroyed by him, and the unmown grass of the park swept up to the windows of the house, which in the English climate hardly seemed reasonable. On both counts she ought to have appreciated Repton. The latter constantly urged upon his clients the need to pay attention to 'the character and situation of the place to be improved' and, as one who saw house and garden as an entity, he was eager to restore the half-way stages which in the past had enabled the timid to enjoy the outdoor scene without venturing into the wild. Unfortunately Repton, whose career began at a time when the most spectacular clients for landscape gardening had been creamed off by Brown, found himself dealing for the most part with owners whose chief objective was to make their estates more impressive: hence his emphasis on providing a grand 'approach' to the house, if necessary by destroying labourers' cottages en route, and an expansive 'prospect' from the windows, even if it involved chopping down avenues which obstructed the view.[58] At a time when Jane and her mother and sister were hard pressed to maintain a decent standard of living, she understandably did not take kindly to Repton's showy 'improvements' at Adlestrop. These included 'removing' a pool whose limpid surface distracted attention from the rest of the garden, and diverting the spring which fed it so that it cascaded over artificial rocks down the hill in front of the house. The further plans which the Rev. Thomas Leigh aimed to carry out in conjunction with Repton for the 'improvement' of Stoneleigh Abbey as soon as he came into possession of the estate doubtless seemed to Jane the height of ostentation, envisaging as they did the creation of a huge colonnade between house and garden, an alteration in the course of the river to bring it nearer to the south wing of the house, the removal of a small island and the building of a new bridge to improve the approach.[59]

In *Pride and Prejudice*, which was completed in its earliest form some years before Jane's visit to Adlestrop, she described as one of the delights of Pemberley the very sort of garden which Repton constantly advocated – a garden which gave the satisfying impression of being natural but which was in fact carefully arranged for the comfort of visitors and residents.[60] Mr Darcy's house, though approached through impressive woods offering wild paths for the intrepid to explore, gave more immediately on to a smooth lawn, shaded by beautiful oaks and chestnuts and bounded by a stream with paths alongside which could be trodden with impunity by the least adventurous of walkers. The stream, 'of some natural importance', had been 'swelled into a greater, but without any artificial appearance. It banks were neither formal nor falsely adorned'. Elizabeth Bennet, we are told, 'had never seen a place for which nature has done so much'. Pemberley's grounds were nevertheless the result of a judicious mixture of nature and art and as such exemplified, to one reader at least, the entire character of Jane Austen's approach to life. After some persuasion Charlotte Brontë had opened at last the pages of *Pride and Prejudice*:

> And what did I find? . . . a carefully planned, highly cultivated garden, with neat borders and delicate flowers; but no glance of bright, vivid physiognomy, no open country, no fresh air, no blue hill, no bonny beck.[61]

Though most parsons had to make do with a fairly modest area of garden, they did their best to introduce as many features of this domesticated Natural Style as they could encompass. The kitchen garden, as being purely utilitarian, was usually separated from the rest of the grounds and hidden either by a wall, as was traditional on large English estates, or by a fence or hedge.[62] The remainder of the garden was then given over to a judicious mixture of lawn, shrubs, gravel paths, turf and trees. A French visitor to England in 1784 was particularly surprised at the passion for lawns, which could often be seen attached to the new suburban 'villas' that were growing up near to towns and cities as well as to parsonages:

> Such gentlemen as are not rich enough to have parks have what is called a lawn, a small stretch of land round the house with a number of narrow paths, beautiful turf, and a little clump of trees, the whole being kept with extreme tidiness. They design these little pleasure grounds themselves. It is all they need to give them a sense of proprietorship and to provide them with a walk for half an hour before dinner.[63]

Even Ashe rectory, facing as it did immediately on to the road like a Georgian town house, managed to have a lawn at the side, screened by a tall yew hedge, behind which Mrs Lefroy's guests could stroll on summer evenings.[64]

Eighteenth-century gardens were for both walking and sitting in, the sitting being done at intervals along the way, when meditation or conversation were called for. Few parsons could have had a garden as large as Mr Collins's, capable of being set out in walks and cross walks (a circumstance which strengthens the view that Jane Austen copied it from a particular vicarage garden known to her at Chevening in an affluent region of Kent);[65] but even in the smallest garden it was considered essential to provide somewhere for the occupants of the house – especially the ladies – to stroll. At the Austens' house in Southampton the problem had been partly solved by utilising the old city wall, which bounded the garden on one side and was accessible to ladies by means of a flight of steps; but a more usual device, employed in gardens both great and small, was to plant a shrubbery.

First mentioned in a garden dictionary in 1739, the shrubbery had quickly shown its advantages over the former wilderness. Unlike the latter, which required forest trees and took up considerable space, a shrubbery could be planted near to the house: ladies could easily escape into it to find either the solitude or the intimate companionship for which they were all supposed to crave. They needed, it was thought, both quietness and shade: direct sunshine was considered harmful and tanned complexions were not yet fashionable. Capability Brown's gardens, devoid of shrubberies, caused an outcry largely because, with their trees not yet grown, they supplied too little shade: Cowper actually compared Brown's gardens to the scorched plains of India, complaining that Englishmen had to carry umbrellas to keep off the sun when walking across them. 'Our fathers knew the value of a screen', he moaned,

> . . . and in their shaded walks enjoyed at noon
> The gloom and coolness of declining day.
> We bear our shades about us; self-deprived
> Of other screen the thin umbrella spread,
> And range an Indian waste without a tree.[66]

The parsonage garden at Steventon, though lacking a lawn, was remembered by Anna Lefroy as having a shrubbery at the back of the house when her grandparents and aunts lived there in the 1770s.[67] Later in the century a shrubbery was often the first consideration of anyone designing a garden: Edward and Elinor Ferrars, newly married, hurried off to their parsonage 'to project shrubberies'.[68] Dr Grant, whatever his faults may have been, allowed his wife to plant a shrubbery (the thoughtless Mrs Norris still had only a 'hot park' attached to the little house she occupied in her widowhood).[69] In the Grants' shrubbery Fanny Price and Mary Crawford 'sauntered about together for many a half-hour', the latter marvelling, in her snobbish town-bred way, that 'a country parson should ever aspire to a shrubbery or anything of that kind', the former praising the quiet simplicity of the place and rhapsodizing on the astonishing variety of nature exemplified by the evergreen:

> The evergreen! How beautiful, how welcome, how wonderful the evergreen!
> . . . In some countries we know that the tree that sheds its leaf is the variety, but
> that does not make it less amazing that the same soil and the same sun should
> nurture plants differing in the first rule and law of their existence.

The craze for evergreens was comparatively new. The laurel was admired for its prolixity, the privet for its compactness – a feature especially useful in the designing of arbours (Mary Russell Mitford described an arbour which was 'a complete sentry-box of privet' in her tiny garden at Three Mile Cross).[70] The privet, indeed, came to be regarded as so typically English that when a memorial garden was planted around the spot where Sir John Moore was buried at Corunna it was surrounded by a privet hedge, parched and windswept on the headland. Flowering shrubs were also popular. The Rev. William Gilpin deplored the habit of planting them in shrubberies because they smacked of artificiality but, although Jane Austen admired Gilpin's travel books, this was a view she could not accept. Peonies and honey-suckle and even roses she thought looked well in a shrubbery – few small gardens had room for a separate rose garden, which in any case was often tiresomely hot, as Fanny Price discovered. Hearing that the roses in the shrubbery at Southampton were 'of an indifferent sort', Jane planned to get a few of the better kind, and also a syringa – 'I could not do without a syringa for the sake of Cowper's line', she told Cassandra. She was thinking of the poet's walk on a bleak winter's morning and of his longing for springtime with its 'syringa, ivory pure'. The same line (from Cowper's poem, *The Task*) put her in mind of a laburnum 'rich in streaming gold', and she talked of getting one of those too. Current bushes and raspberry canes were also likely to find a place in the shrubbery, the whole assortment frequently merging into a small orchard. The garden which Edward provided for his mother and sisters at Chawton exemplified the type: 'Trees were planted each side to form a shrubbery walk . . . which gave a sufficient space for ladies' exercise', Jane's nephew recalled. 'There was a pleasant, irregular mixture of hedgerow, and gravel walk, and orchard, and long grass for mowing.'[71]

The mention of a gravel walk is of some significance. Gravel paths, in preference to paved walks or paths of beaten earth, had been introduced on large country estates early in the eighteenth century and had gradu-ally made their way into smaller gardens, where their drawbacks did not become apparent until the invention of the lawn-mower in the nine-teenth century. Stephen Switzer, one of the pioneers of the Natural Style, forecast in 1715 that English gardens would eventually surpass all others because of the superiority of English gravel.[72] The advantage of gravel was that it allowed ladies to walk along natural-looking winding paths through orchards and shrubberies without getting their feet wet: Sir Thomas Bertram, mindful of Fanny Price's health, advised her to walk only 'on the gravel' (quite rightly, it seems, since Marianne Dash-wood nearly got her death of cold from walking heedlessly in the long grass.)[73] Mrs Austen was a great believer in gravel and was delighted when their neighbour at Chawton, Mr Prowting, opened a gravel pit at the entrance to his house: 'Tolerable gravel', Jane pronounced it.[74] Gravel was useful, too, for the semi-circular carriage drive, or 'sweep', which was considered the proper type of entrance to a gentleman's residence. Steventon parsonage was given a sweep as soon as the Austens moved into it. Of the clergymen in Jane Austen's novels, only Mr Elton and Mr Collins lacked a sweep: the former because his vicarage was 'an old and not very good house, almost as close to the road as could be', and the latter because his front garden had to be small enough for him to see Lady Catherine driving down the lane in one of her many vehicles. Both these clergymen were of doubtful pedigree.[75]

Whilst lawns, shrubberies and pleasant walks exemplified the graciousness of nature, trees were more expressive of the age-old grandeur of God in His universe. Silviculture, though still valued for its economic potential, was discussed in aesthetic terms for the first time during the eighteenth century, attention being paid to varieties of colour and height.[76] Trees in a landscape could enhance the prospect or accentuate the fall of the ground; when well-grown they could become the glory of the entire garden, as were the cedars at Thomas Leigh's Adlestrop. In large quantity they could give the sombre effect which was the nearest a garden could get to the sublimity so dear to latter-day exponents of the Picturesque. They were appreciated also for their shade: 'We walk a great deal, for the woods are impenetrable to the sun even in the middle of an August day', wrote Mrs Austen to her daughter-in-law during her sojourn at Stoneleigh Abbey.[77] Her own garden at Steventon contained a significant number of trees in proportion to its size, as we know from Jane's lamentations after a great storm in November 1800: 'I was sitting alone in the dining room, when an odd kind of crash startled me', she wrote to Cassandra.

> In a moment afterwards it was repeated; I then went to the window, which I reached just in time to see the last of our two highly valued Elms descend into the Sweep!!!!! The other, which had fallen I suppose in the first crash, & which was the nearest to the pond, taking a more easterly direction sunk among our screen of chestnuts and firs, knocking down one spruce fir, beating off the head of another, & stripping the two corner chestnuts of several branches, in its fall. This is not all. One large Elm out of two on the left hand side as you enter what I call the Elm walk, was likewise blown down . . .

This was at the front of the house; at the back, Anna Lefroy remembered the stupendous height of the silver fir that grew at the end of the terrace.[78]

Far from thinking the garden sufficiently supplied with trees, however, George Austen a few months before the storm occurred had contemplated incorporating a portion of the glebe meadow into the vicarage garden and planting it out in the approved fashion. James Woodforde had carried out a similar scheme at Weston Longeville in the 1780s and many clergy did the same as soon as they felt they could afford to give up a piece of pastureland for the purpose.[79] This seems to have been the clerical equivalent of the fashion for 'emparking' displayed by great landowners in the eighteenth century. Jane reported good progress with the plans at Steventon in a letter to Cassandra in October 1880. 'The Bank along the *Elm Walk* is sloped down for the reception of Thorns and Lilacs: & it is settled that the other side of the path is to continue turf'd & be planted with Beech, Ash, & Larch', she wrote. A month later dissension had set in and Jane, whose opinion seems not to have been valued in these matters, wrote rather less enthusiastically:

> A new plan has been suggested concerning the plantation of the new enclosure on the right side of the Elm Walk – the doubt is whether it would be better to make a little orchard of it, by planting apples, pears, & cherries, or whether it should be larch, Mountain-ash & acacia. What is your opinion? I say nothing, & am ready to agree with anybody.

Fruit trees, though not accepted as woodland, were after all more practical from a housekeeping point of view. At Chawton, where Jane was in charge of the wine for the household, she kept an anxious eye on the state of the fruit crop in the garden: 'There are more gooseberries and fewer currants than I thought at first. We must buy currants for our Wine . . .', she wrote on one occasion.[80] Many types of fruit were grown at the time. In addition to apples, pears, plums, gooseberries and cherries, numerous berries and currants were popular, and peaches, apricots and grapes were commonly found out of doors in the southern counties. Many different varieties were available and their relative merits were of wide interest: even Dr Grant, whose concern in gardening was confined to eating the produce, could enter into dispute with Mrs Norris over a Moor Park apricot.[81] Nor were orchards wholly despised from an aesthetic point of view, since they could be said to combine practicality with beauty, which was one of the ideals of the time. The Wordsworths spent many an evening sitting in the orchard they had planted at Dove Cottage.[82]

If the improvements at Steventon were unfinished when James Austen took over a year later, he is likely to have found them an embarrass-

Steventon Rectory (Hants.), where Jane Austen lived between 1775 and 1801; a drawing by Jane Austen's niece Anna, who was brought up there after her aunt had left. The house was pulled down about 1824.

The thirteenth-century church of St Nicholas, Steventon, where Jane Austen's father officiated as rector between 1764 and 1801, when his son James took over as curate. The spire of the church was added in Victorian times.
(The Parochial Church Council of St Nicholas' Church, Steventon)

3 Jane Austen. The only portrait known to be authentic, done about 1810 in pencil and watercolour by her sis[
Cassandra. Younger members of the family afterwards thought it made Jane look less sweet-tempered than t[
remembered her and it was altered for inclusion in James Edward Austen-Leigh's *Memoir* in 1869.
(*National Portrait Gallery*)

4 The Rev. George Austen, Jane Austen's father. A
miniature painted in 1801, the year of his retirement.
(*Jane Austen Memorial Trust, Chawton*)

The Rev. James Austen, Jane Austen's eldest brother.
A miniature of about 1790, when he was twenty-five
ears old and serving as a curate at Overton.
Jane Austen Memorial Trust, Chawton)

6 The Rev. Henry Austen, Jane Austen's fourth
brother. A miniature of about 1820, when he was
approaching fifty and serving as temporary rector at
Steventon. (*Jane Austen Memorial Trust, Chawton*)

7 Adlestrop Park (Gloucs.), which Jane Austen visited in 1806 when she was staying with her mother's cousin, th
Rev. Thomas Leigh, at the nearby rectory. Built by Sanderson Miller in the mid eighteenth century, it was owned b
Mrs Austen's half cousin, James Henry Leigh. The gardens were landscaped by Humphry Repton. Engraving fro
J.P. Neale, *Views of the Seats of Noblemen and Gentlemen* (1823).   (*Manchester Central Library*)

8 Stoneleigh Abbey (Warwicks.), visited by Jane Austen and her mother in 1806, when it was inherited by th
latter's cousin, the Rev. Thomas Leigh, rector of Adlestrop. The neo-classical west wing, whose forty-five windov
and twenty-six bedchambers were counted with astonishment by Mrs Austen, was added to the medieval and Tud
portions of the house between 1714 and 1726.

Godmersham House (Kent) in the late eighteenth century. Jane Austen frequently visited the house after it was inherited in 1798 by her third brother, Edward, who was adopted by his father's cousin, Thomas Knight. From Edward Hasted, *The History and Topographical Survey of the County of Kent* (1778-99).

0 Chawton House and Church (Hants.), English school, *c.* 1740. Jane Austen was a regular visitor at the 'Great House', owned by her brother Edward, during the last eight years of her life when she lived at the 'Small House' on hawton High Street. She was a regular worshipper at St. Nicholas' Church. The nave and the wooden-sided belfry f the church were destroyed by fire in 1871. (*Knight Family*).

11 Bath. An aquatint published by Archibald Robertson in 1792, showing Lansdown Crescent still incomplete. Strangely, it also shows to the right the neo-Gothic chapel of All Saints, a proprietory chapel designed to accommodate the new residents but not completed until 1794, and on the extreme right the forthcoming Christ Church, Montpellier Row, built between 1795 and 1798. Both churches, like the crescent, were the work of John Palmer. (*Bath City Library*)

12 Southampton, showing a section of the medieval city wall and in the distance the twin spires of Holy Rood (left) and St Michael's. The house to the right of the latter is similar to the one in which Jane Austen lived between 1806 and 1809, with a garden leading down to the wall, which at that time fronted directly on to the sea. From R. Mudie, *Hampshire* (1838). (*Manchester Central Library*)

3 Alton (Hants.), with the Norman tower of St Lawrence's Church on the right. In 1811 Jane Austen walked the one and a quarter miles from Chawton to Alton with her niece Anna and the latter's friend Harriet Benn, who were seeking mourning clothes in preparation for the king's death. From R. Mudie, *Hampshire* (1838). (*Manchester Central Library*)

4 St Paul's, Covent Garden, described by its architect, Inigo Jones, as 'the handsomest Barn in England'. Jane Austen knew the church from staying with her brother Henry in nearby Henrietta Street. Engraving by Thomas H. Shepherd.

15 Thomas Secker (1693-1768), Archbishop of Canterbury, after Sir Joshua Reynolds. Jane Austen was familiar with Secker's *Lectures on the Catechism*, which was a widely used manual in her time. (*National Portrait Gallery*)

16 William Cowper (1731-1800), by George Romney, 1792. Jane Austen wrote to her sister Cassandra, 18 December 1798, 'My father reads Cowper to us in the evening, to which I listen when I can.' (*National Portrait Gallery*)

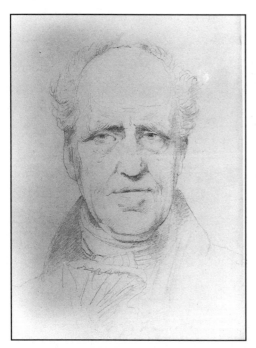

17 The Rev. George Crabbe (1754-1832), by Henry William Pickersgill. Jane Austen so much admired his poetry that she professed to wish she had been his wife. (*National Portrait Gallery*)

18 Hannah More (1745-1833), by Henry William Pickersgill, *c.* 1820. Jane Austen refused to be persuaded by Cassandra into reading Hannah More's novel *Coelebs in Search of a Wife*, saying that she did not like Evangelicals. (*National Portrait Gallery*)

ment, for his wife Mary, who was economical in her ideas and not the sort of woman to be carried away by visions of beauty, looked on the whole subject of gardening as disagreeable. Yet even he took on some sort of a project in 1808, having decided that he could lessen the expense by avoiding outside labour and getting his own men to do the necessary trenching, by degrees.[83] Henry Tilney, whose father had provided him with an excellent kitchen garden at Woodston before he was old enough even to enter the living, and who was in any case not in a position to have to consider expense, had no need to be behindhand in the gardening stakes: when Catherine Morland visited him at his parsonage for the first time she found him 'bringing his genius to bear upon a meadow'. Only two sides of it were as yet planted but Catherine, suitably impressed, was prepared to think it 'prettier than any pleasure ground she had ever been in before, though there was not a shrub in it higher than the green bench in the corner'.[84]

It is unlikely that every clergyman who added a few acres of pasture-land to his garden was deliberately pursuing some inspired vision of the divine plan. Some merely followed the latest fashion – any fashion that took their fancy, including the craze for oriental art that passed in waves over the English elite in the late eighteenth and early nineteenth centuries. William Cowper wished they would devote their money to worthier objects:

I could not help wishing that the honest vicar, instead of indulging his genius for improvements, by enclosing his gooseberry bushes within a Chinese rail, and converting half an acre of glebeland into a bowling green, would have applied part of his income to the more laudable purpose of sheltering his parishioners from the weather during their attendance at divine service. It is no uncommon thing to see the parsonage house well thatched and in exceeding good repair, while the church perhaps has scarce any other roof than the ivy that grows over it.[85]

John Clare saw the desire for lawns and parks as mere status-seeking. Many parsons certainly spent more on improvements than they could rightly afford. The Rev. John Rawstorne Papillon, for instance, after rebuilding his rectory in 1804, wrote to his father in 1805:

When you come to Chawton in the Spring and Summer, as I hope you will, you will find a considerable alteration in the grounds about the house, but I much doubt whether they will meet with your approbation, for I am sensible I have been at too much expense in my plantations, etc., and eight acres of the field at the back of the house, which I attempted to lay down in grass, I have been in a manner obliged to plough up . . .[87]

His enthusiasm for improvement was the more noteworthy in that he was a middle-aged bachelor. Some gentlemen took a personal interest in gardening – Jane Austen described her godfather, the Rev. Samuel Cooke, as positively 'fidgety' on the subject;[88] but it was often a wife who made all the difference as to whether a parsonage and its grounds were improved or not. Before discussing her role it is important to consider the vicinity in which she operated and in which her husband pursued his vocation.

Chapter 6

The Country Parish

James Austen, returning to his studies at Oxford after a few days absence in June 1789, professed to have noticed an astonishing change in the appearance of many of his acquaintance. As he wrote in *The Loiterer*:

> So numerous, indeed, were the black coats, and so dismal the looks of the wearers, that I was almost led to imagine that there must be general mourning.

Closer observation revealed that the sombre gentlemen who thus oppressed his vision were not mourners but newly-ordained clergy, whereupon the satirist proceeded to bemoan the fate of the many graduates – some thirty in June and a similar number in December – who were obliged each year to leave the university and take up clerical duties in country parishes. Only financial necessity could make them do it, he decided.

> Young men in the bloom of life, and in the Heyday of their blood, cut off from all that renders life agreeable, removed from the Scene of their triumphs and the witness of their Glory, and condemned to pass many years in solitary obscurity and insipid quiet. To be obliged to wear black to those who have been usually dressed in brown or blue; to be under the necessity of going twice a week to Church, to those, who for some time, have never gone at all, are very severe mortifications; but by no means the only ones to which this change in their situations will expose them. For in spite of all the fine things which Poets, both ancient and modern, have said on the charms of Solitude, and the happiness of a Country Life, an impartial examination of the matter will convince us, that a dirty Village is not half so good a place to lounge in as the High Street, and that boarding at a Farmhouse is by no means so pleasant as dining at the Cross, the Star or the Angel.[1]

With all its exaggerations, this article touched a genuine chord which might have appealed not only to young curates, whom James Austen had chiefly in mind, but to numerous parsons the length and breadth of England. Not for nothing was the adjective 'obscure' indelibly attached to the term 'country parson': however brilliant the latter may have been, the epithet was transferred to him from his surroundings.

When George Austen left Oxford for Steventon in 1764, the population of the entire parish numbered no more than thirty families. The village itself consisted basically of a single row of cottages scattered intermittently for about half a mile along a lane, each with its vegetable garden surrounded by trees. Behind the lane at one end stood the church and the manor house, with a few more cottages nearby, and at the other end the parsonage, connected with the church by a tree-lined path along a grassy bank. Near the vicarage was a pond, and a maypole with a weathervane that creaked dismally in the wind. A couple of outlying farms and a few isolated homesteads completed the picture of the parish. There was no shop, no inn and no lawyer, teacher, doctor or apothecary. The Austens had to travel seven miles to Basingstoke for their family doctor, Mr Lyford, and Jane and Cassandra had to seize the opportunity on their way home from rare visits to friends to stop off at Andover or Basingstoke and buy such things as drawing-paper and ink. Jane made the most of occasional visits from travelling salesmen to buy stockings and lace.[2]

A drawing made by George Austen's granddaughter Anna of some of the cottages in the village indicates that they were tolerably spacious and well-built – half-timbered, with roofs of slate and stone.[3] Chimneys at both ends suggest that there was more than one living-room and, although the cottages appear to have been basically one-storeyed, dormer windows imply that attic bedrooms had been built into the roof space. Anna's half-brother Edward nevertheless made it quite clear, in his memoir of 1870, that during his grandfather's time at Steventon the occupants of the cottages were nothing if not poor.[4] The men worked on the land, the women eked out a living by spinning flax or wool. Mr Austen had a friendly relationship with his steward, John Bond, whom it is suggested was the model for Mr Knightley's William Larkins,[5] and the Austen children were fond of John and Elizabeth Littleworth who had acted as foster-parents to them in their infancy (Mrs Austen having followed the practice of putting her babies out to be minded until they could walk and talk); but the only other companionship the Austen family could have hoped to find in the parish would have come from the Digweeds, tenants of Steventon Manor. Hugh Digweed, followed in

1798 by his sons Harry and William, rented almost all the land in the parish of Steventon (and neighbouring Farringdon) from Thomas Knight. Their house, hidden in trees immediately behind the church, was a pretty flint and stone building of the reign of Henry VIII, standing in a park of some 170 acres. The Digweeds were much respected in the area as gentleman farmers of long standing (Jane thought that Harry Digweed would be the best employer to take on John Bond when her father retired),[6] but apart from the third son, James, who went to university and subsequently took Holy Orders, they had no pretensions to culture. George Austen's chief connection with them was as joint-owner of the hunting rights of the manor. He himself had no great interest in sport but his sons Henry and Frank, who were roughly the same age as Harry and William Digweed, were enthusiasts and the two pairs of young men often went out shooting together. In the winter the two families frequently met to play cards, a noisy time being had by all.[7]

The only relationship Jane and Cassandra had with the rest of the inhabitants of the village was based on patronage. Women from the cottages came from time to time to work at the parsonage; others were claimants for charity. We hear in 1798 of Dame Staples who came to help with the household chores, and of John Steevens' wife who replaced Dame Bushell as washerwoman. Mary Steevens and Dame Staples figure again at Christmas as recipients of pairs of stockings from Jane's charitable purchases; Mary Hutchins and Dame Kew also received stockings, whilst Betty Dawkins got a shawl and Dame Staples' little daughter Hannah a shift. Earlier in the year Dame Tilbury's daughter had lain in and become a possible candidate for baby clothes. It is true that we also hear of one Betty Londe to whom Jane Austen seemed to feel under a particular obligation, for she wrote to Cassandra in 1798 in terms much like those which Emma Woodhouse used with reference to Miss Bates:

> I called yesterday on Betty Londe, who enquired particularly after you, and said she seemed to miss you very much, because you used to call in upon her very often. This was an oblique reproach at me, which I am sorry to have merited, and from which I will profit.

It seems unlikely, however, that Betty Londe belonged to the same socially respectable class as Miss Bates, or Jane would have referred to her more formally.[8]

The adjacent parishes of Ashe and Deane were even less populous than Steventon.[9] Each had its manor house, but Ashe had only fourteen families of farm labourers when George Lefroy arrived as rector in

1783. Deane included the little hamlet of Oakley, which had a shop where Jane bought the obligatory worsted stockings for the poor and near to which the Wither Bramstons had recently built a large house; even so, the population of the parish numbered no more than twenty-four families when James Austen took up residence as curate in 1792. Dummer, a little further up the hill, had some forty families in the parish as a whole but nobody could say that the village itself was a hive of activity: the cawing of the rooks in the tall trees was often the only sound to be heard. George Whitefield, who served as curate there in 1736, confessed in a letter that he 'mourned like a dove for his Oxford friends'.[10] The isolation of the villages was clear from the state of the roads and lanes which ran through and between them, for all were unpaved and undrained; in wet weather Steventon and Deane were quagmires and the lane between them almost impassable. A heavy farm cart was often the only vehicle that could successfully, if with great difficulty, negotiate the ruts.

William Cobbett, after a strenuous ride over the flinty downs of Hampshire in 1822, wrote appreciatively of the little settlements which had afforded him refreshment:

> The homesteads in the sheltered bottoms, with fine lofty trees about the houses and yards, form a beautiful contrast with the large open fields. The little villages, running straggling along the dells (always with lofty trees and rookeries) are very interesting objects, even in winter.[11]

This was all very well for the passer-by. In *Sense and Sensibility* Edward Ferrars, who as an ordinand knew that he could expect to spend his life in a country parish, commented more prosaically upon the surroundings of a Devonshire village: 'These bottoms must be very dirty in winter.'[12] Writers on the picturesque had for decades been waxing lyrical about the peace and charm of England's villages, fastening usually, as did Uvedale Price, upon features which could be thoroughly tiresome to live with – thatched roofs which harboured damp or streams which were only too liable to flood neighbouring houses and yards when snow melted. William Gilpin, who had little praise for the countryside between Winchester and Basingstoke, nevertheless greatly admired Hurstbourne Tarrant, whose thatched cottages were bunched about a fast-flowing stream crossed by ancient stepping-stones; yet James Austen's friend Peter Debary, who was brought up there in his father's parsonage, decided in 1801 that he had had enough of the country and turned down an offer of a curacy at Deane on the grounds that he would prefer to be nearer London.[13] When Isabella Thorpe, eager to attach her clerical admirer James Morland, protested that 'a cottage in some retired village would be extasy', it turned out that what she really had in mind were 'some charming little villas about Richmond'.[14]

To a young clergyman (and even to one not so young) it was not so much the damp and chill that was likely to depress the spirits as the lack of congenial companionship. The bachelor James Woodforde complained of loneliness every time he was without guests staying at his Norfolk parsonage; and even Gilbert White, for all his communion with birds and animals, felt keenly at Selborne the lack of friends capable of sharing his interests. James Austen, though he appeared to settle down to the business of accumulating parishes, sometimes displayed a restlessness which might have owed something to intellectual frustration: the villagers of Steventon became, if anything, even poorer in his day, as their homespun yarn became less marketable.

By the time Jane Austen published her novels, she had had experience of living in a village rather larger than Steventon. The parish of Chawton had a population of 347 at the census of 1811, rising to 417 during the next ten years.[15] The village itself had about forty houses, and building was going on during Jane's lifetime: one of her last outings was to see some new development taking place 'up Mounters Lane'.[16] The village was more advantageously situated than Steventon, being less than a mile along a main road from the market-town of Alton with its bank, apothecary, lawyer and full range of shops. One of the main trunk roads from London divided just outside the Austens' house, the left fork running to Fareham and Gosport and the right to Winchester and Southampton. Greater accessibility had brought to the village a few residents whose social status was distinctly above that of the agricultural labourers and domestic servants who occupied the majority of the cottages: William Prowting, magistrate and Deputy Lieutenant of the county; his daughter Ann-Mary and her husband Captain Clement R.N.; Mr and Miss Hinton, son and daughter of the former rector of Chawton; Miss Benn, sister of the rector of Farringdon; and other ladylike spinsters of respectable pedigree. The Prowtings, Clements and Hintons occupied sizeable houses, with names such as Chawton Lodge and The Dower House.

Much has been made of the bustling quality of life at Chawton and of the valuable effect this was likely to have had on Jane Austen's fiction. Certainly the sight of mail coaches and post-chaises dashing along the road gave the illusion of contact with the busy world. In July 1816 Jane was able to write to her nephew Edward, home from school at Winchester: 'We saw a countless number of Postchaises full of Boys pass by yesterday morn[g] – full of future Heroes, Legislators, Fools and Villains.'[17] But the contrast with Steventon should not be exaggerated. The traffic which hurtled through the village had little effect upon its life: a contemporary sketch of the main thoroughfare showed the familiar unsurfaced carriageway with the buildings intermittently placed alongside.[18] To the east and south, deep countryside enveloped the little villages of East and West Worldham, Upper and Lower Farringdon, Newton Valence, Hartley Mauditt and Empshott, whose parishes in the year that Jane Austen died had no more than 312 inhabitants (the two Worldhams), 387 (the two Farringdons), 221 (Newton Valence), 57 (Hartley Mauditt), and 97 (Empshott).[19]

That there was some very poor property in Chawton we know from the fate of Miss Benn, evicted from her cottage by 'old Philmore', its tight-fisted owner, who wanted it for his son. It was a miserable enough habitation, shaken by every wind that blew; but nothing better seemed to be available. Many of the houses were damp, if only because a sizeable pond at the junction of the two main roads provided the usual hazards. 'We have had sad weather lately', Jane wrote on 13 March 1816. 'Our Pond is brimful & our roads are dirty & our walls are damp, & we sit wishing every bad day may be the last.'[20] At nearby Selborne water rushing down the hillside had turned the paths into deep ravines. Fortunately there were no mud huts in the village – a fact which Gilbert White had thought was a matter for some pride when he wrote his *Natural History* in 1789.[21]

The majority of the parishes which Jane Austen invented for her novels can be placed somewhere on the scale between Steventon and Chawton. Mr Collins's Hunsford is an enigma, due to the fact that Elizabeth Bennet never visited the village when staying at the parsonage; for the others, a few shreds of information provide a world of knowledge. The sleepiest place is Thornton Lacey, 'a retired little village between gently rising hills' – so retired, in fact, that Henry Crawford counted himself lucky to have stumbled upon it. There was a farm and a blacksmith's forge but no manor house – the parsonage was the only building that looked like a gentleman's residence.[22] Fullerton had at least a squire, and a village lively enough to have a few couples walking through it on a Sunday; but the sight of a post-chaise arriving at the parsonage was rare enough to arouse great curiosity.[23] Uppercross we are told was 'a moderate-sized village', but the manor house and parsonage, and lately the farmhouse renovated and modernized by the squire's son, were 'the only houses superior in appearance to those of the yeomen and labourers'; the squire's daughter felt sorry for the parson and his wife because they had only her family for company.[24] Delaford was regarded by Mrs Jennings as a better place to live in than Barton since it had a butcher's shop, as also had Mansfield; but it was Henry Tilney's Woodston, 'a large and populous village, in a situation not unpleasant', that sounds most like Chawton, in that it had a number of little chandlers' shops and several neat houses above the rank of cottages.[25] The value Jane Austen placed upon the benefices attached to some of these places – £200 at Delaford, £700 at Thornton Lacey – was not intended to give any indication of their size and character, for she was well aware that endowments bore no relation to the amount of pastoral work required. Dummer was as valuable a benefice as Overton, with only a quarter of the inhabitants.

Highbury, which forms the setting for *Emma*, was clearly a larger village than Chawton, which could never have been described, even by its proudest inhabitants, as 'almost amounting to a town'.[26] The main street of Highbury was broad, if irregular, and there was an inn which kept a couple of post horses for hire. There was a large drapery store, a butcher's, a baker's and an optician's; and at the end of the street Mrs Goddard kept a ladies' seminary employing three teachers. There was a lawyer, an apothecary and several businessmen, active or retired. Some of the people mentioned were doing well for themselves – Mr Perry, the doctor, was thinking of setting up his carriage, while Mr Cole, one of the businessmen, had built an extension to his house and had begun to give dinner-parties. Yet the scene was still not a very lively one, as Emma, from a vantage-point at the window of the draper's shop, was bound to admit:

> Much could not be hoped from the traffic of even the busiest part of Highbury; – Mr Perry walking hastily by, Mr William Cox letting himself in at the office door, Mr Cole's carriage horses returning from exercise, or a stray letter-boy on an obstinate mule, were the liveliest objects she could presume to expect; and when her eyes fell only on the butcher with his tray, a tidy old woman travelling homewards with her full basket, two curs quarelling over a dirty bone, and a string of dawdling children round the baker's little bow window, eyeing the gingerbread, she knew she had no reason to complain.

She knew very well, too, that once out of the main street of Highbury a muddy lane ran past the vicarage into fields covered with pools and pollards, whilst on the other side of the village the parish of Donwell was almost entirely rural.[27] Of the many models from Jane Austen's experience which have been suggested for Highbury, the likeliest is Great

Bookham where her godfather Samuel Cooke was vicar. With 500 or so inhabitants, Great Bookham was regarded as quite a town; yet at a distance of a mere mile or so Fanny Burney had been able to live in seclusion with her French *émigré* husband in the 1790s, confessing when she moved away from the area that the only people she regretted leaving were the parson and his excellent wife.[24]

In setting her novels in country parishes, Jane Austen was locating them in what was in fact the heartland of the established church. A clergy list published in 1817 revealed that the vast majority of England's 10,500 parishes had fewer than 500 inhabitants each; nearly 3,000 had fewer than 200 each, and 960 tabled less than 100. The parochial system, which covered the whole of the country with a network of parishes, had developed during the middle ages when England was almost exclusively rural and the population thinly and fairly evenly spread. Numbers had expanded enormously since then, but in a few limited areas only; as far as the majority of people were concerned country life went on as usual. In 1801 four-fifths of England's 9,000,000 people still lived in hamlets and villages, whilst many of the urban fifth lived in towns no bigger than Great Bookham. Only London was a city of great size. As late as 1821, several years after Jane Austen's death, more than three-fifths of the total population still inhabited the countryside, although the sea-ports and the growing industrial cities of the north and midlands were by then growing at such a rate that Liverpool, Manchester and Birmingham numbered 400,000 inhabitants between them.[29]

In the countryside the Church of England could still depend upon a magnanimous patron here and there to build a new church and apply for an Act of Parliament to adjust nearby boundaries and provide a parish for it. In the cities this was less likely to happen, although a 'proprietary chapel', funded by pew-rents, might be built as a speculation by or for an enterprising clergyman. In any case, the need for provision in the rapidly developing urban areas was too great to be left to individual initiative. With Convocation in abeyance from the beginning of the eighteenth century to the middle of the nineteenth, the Church of England had no central organization of its own to decide upon a programme of fund-raising for the building of churches and the endowment of benefices. In 1711 Parliament intervened and passed an act to facilitate the building of fifty new churches in London and its suburbs, the money to be raised from a duty on coals. Nothing was done for other cities until the year of Jane Austen's death, and then it was too little and too late.

Few people in Jane Austen's day could have foreseen that the imbalance of population in favour of the cities would increase so enormously that the country-based church would begin to look like a whale stranded upon the shore. Her generation lived through twenty-five years of war, during which time England's agriculture was vital to her economy and her survival. It was difficult for people to think that it would ever be otherwise: in 1815 Parliament was in no doubt about the desirability of protecting England's agriculture against influxes of cheap foreign corn, which it was felt could never be wholly reliable. Jane Austen herself was not a prophet, whose job it was to observe the direction of straws in the wind, but an entertainer and moralist commenting on behaviour in her time. The likes of Mr Collins, Mr Elton and Dr Grant in their country parishes would be well-known to her readers, whereas a London-based parson such as Mr Clarke wanted her to write about might not.

Jane Austen loved the countryside and, in spite of its restrictions and discomforts, was only truly happy when living in a village. Since it was more common for people to live in the country than in the town, she took it for granted that the clergy either enjoyed it or put up with it. She expected them to do their duty to God and their parishioners and to seek any support they needed in a satisfactory relationship with family and neighbours. That there was sufficient scope for them in a country parish she was in no doubt whatever.

Readers of Jane Austen's novels can be excused for wondering what duties her clergymen in their country parishes were supposed to perform, since they seem to have endless amounts of time and leisure to devote to their private concerns. Mr Elton was always glad of an invitation to fill the long dull evenings by playing backgammon with Mr Woodhouse: the only engagement he missed when he suddenly took himself off to London to get Harriet's picture framed was a meeting of the whist club at the *Crown*.[30] Henry Tilney could spend half of each week away from his parish and even when he was there he had time for his dogs and his horses.[31] Mr Collins was visited by his relatives during what must have been Lent ('Easter was approaching') yet there is no sign that he was inundated with devotional exercises at what is now the busiest season of a clergyman's year: on the contrary, he was able to spend each morning for a week driving Sir William Lucas around the countryside in his gig.[32] Despite this, there is no suggestion that any one of these clerical gentlemen shirked his duty. They may have had their personal defects – Elton and Collins especially; but the former is pronounced by no less a judge than Mr Knightley to be 'a very respectable vicar of Highbury',[33] and Mr Collins is presented to the reader as the type of man who carried out his obligations to the letter. Jane Austen, in fact, combined a high regard for the role of the clergy with a total acceptance of their leisured existence: to her, they were more important for what they were than for what they did.

The formal duties of a parish priest in the late eighteenth and early nineteenth centuries were indeed very much lighter than those expected of a modern clergyman; so light that they allowed for a practice known as 'nominal residence', whereby a clergyman who had no other parish to his name could nevertheless spend most of his time elsewhere. Sir Thomas Bertram admitted that this would be an option open to his son Edmund at Thornton Lacey, eight miles from his beloved ancestral home at Mansfield, were he content to carry out minimal duties only:

> Edmund might, in the common phrase, do the duty of Thornton, that is, he might read prayers and preach, without giving up Mansfield Park; he might ride over, every Sunday, to a house nominally inhabited, and go through divine service; he might be the clergyman of Thornton Lacey every seventh day, for three or four hours, if that would content him.[34]

This was perhaps a mild exaggeration – like Henry Tilney, Edmund may have found that he needed also to be in his parish on a Monday 'to attend the parish meeting' – but the general impression was accurate enough.[35]

The requirements, even on a Sunday, had become fewer in the course of the eighteenth century than they had been at the beginning. It had been the practice earlier in the century to 'read prayers' (in other words, perform the liturgy prescribed by the Book of Common Prayer) twice a day on Sundays. The times were normally 10 a.m., when Mattins, the Litany, and Ante-Communion were offered, and 3 p.m. for Evening Prayer. A sermon was preached at one of the services, perhaps at both. The morning service could take anything up to three hours. The short interval which elapsed before the evening service would then be completely filled with the churching of women after childbirth and the catechising of children and apprentices in preparation for Confirmation: the clergyman could easily be in church all day, eating his lunch in the vestry. As the century wore on, however, pluralism made 'double duty' impracticable in many places, so either morning or evening service was dropped. A practice adopted out of necessity soon came to be regarded as normal and many parishes with a full-time resident clergyman nevertheless fell into the way of having only one service: by the end of the eighteenth century double services survived in less than half the parish churches of England.[36] Jane Austen was accustomed to two services at Chawton but was not at all dismayed if one or the other was cancelled: 'No morning service today, wherefore I am writing between 12 & 1 o'clock', she wrote blithely to Cassandra one Sunday in 1816.[37]

Jane Austen disapproved of 'nominal residence', as Sir Thomas Bertram's rebuke to Henry Crawford makes clear; but this does not mean that she expected the clergy to perform a round of formal duties such as have descended upon them since her day. The most conscientious clergyman was not expected, for instance, to celebrate Holy Communion more than once a month in a country parish. The sacramental element in Christianity was not greatly stressed by the theologians of the time; the taking of *the* Sacrament, as the Eucharist was called, was regarded as an act of special piety or intent which could only reasonably be entered into some few times a year – perhaps only the three times specified as a minimum by the Prayer Book. Jane Austen regarded it as a sign of real devotion in her two nephews at Godmersham that they stayed in church after the morning service to take the Sacrament.[38] The celebration was invariably tacked on to the end of either the morning or the evening service and the clergyman was under obligation to give notice of it a week beforehand.

No clergyman felt obliged to say the Office daily in his parish church. Midweek services were not entirely unknown (a fictitious clergyman advertising in *The Loiterer* for a curacy thought it necessary to specify that he would 'not engage where there was any weekly duty') but they were rare. The advertisement for the living of Camerton in 1800 stated 'the duty is very easy, viz., only once and occasional burials, etc'.[39] Parson Woodforde restored the service on Good Friday which his predecessor at Weston had abandoned, and held services on 5 November (thanksgiving for deliverance from Popish treason) and 30 January (in memory of Charles I's martyrdom);[40] but otherwise midweek duties in church, like those at Camerton, were confined to the occasional wedding and funeral. Even these might take place on a Sunday.[41]

Births were events which called for immediate attention on the part of a conscientious parish priest. In the days when a great many children died in infancy, it was necessary for the clergyman to reach the bedside as soon as possible after the birth and christen the child privately: if the baby was believed to be dying, the priest might be fetched at any time of night or day. If the baby survived, the private 'naming' was expected to be followed some few weeks later by a public baptism at which the godparents were present: in the case of Jane Austen, born in December during one of the coldest winters on record, April came before she was taken out of the house for public baptism. Meanwhile, the mother was 'churched', at a short service whose words were devoted to giving thanks to God for the baby's safe deliverance but which was popularly believed to absolve the woman from the sin of conception. Village people often took a churching more seriously than a baptism and were prepared to pay a fee: Parson Woodforde in the 1780s was charging a shilling if he thought the woman could afford it, sixpence if she was poor. Even these duties could hardly be said to have demanded much time if the adult population of the parish was tiny.

Sick visiting might reasonably be expected to have been more demanding, for there was a good deal of ill-health in the villages; but here too the formal expectations were slender. Sick Communion, for instance, was distributed only once a year, usually at Shrovetide. It was then considered so unusually great a burden that Henry Austen was known to make a special journey into Kent to help the vicar of Godmersham with the task.[42]

So small a complement of active duties left plenty of time for writing sermons. No clergyman, however, was expected to produce an original composition every Sunday. Henry Crawford, assessing Edmund Bertram's commitments at Thornton Lacey, judged that 'a sermon at Christmas and Easter' would be 'the sum total of the sacrifice'.[43] This was an underestimate but not a ludicrous one. Mr Collins, who liked to boast about his obligation to write sermons, in fact produced only two in the period between his ordination at Easter and his visit to Longbourn in November of the same year. In the parlance of the day, he referred to them as 'discourses', and was probably thinking of having them published.[44]

Congregations in Jane Austen's day had a great liking for sermons. Even in a country parish (if we are to believe Edmund Bertram) there were people capable of judging the quality of the delivery if not the content of the message.[45] Texts were noticed, especially by young ladies, who stitched them into samplers: the dewy-eyed Miss Nash kept a note of every text Mr Elton had ever preached on since his arrival at Highbury.[46] It was nevertheless considered perfectly proper for a parish priest on most occasions to take his sermons from books published for the purpose. There were a great many of these on the market: Jane Austen's cousin Edward Cooper published a number of volumes, the third of which was intended expressly for 'country congregations' (Jane did not think much of them, but they sold well into the nineteenth century).[47] A great many parsons throughout the land served their parishioners with a staple diet taken from the sermons of famous preachers such as Tillotson, Thomas Sherlock and Samuel Clarke. Some simply read out extracts from the printed texts; others, more conscientious, would adapt them to suit particular circumstances – which is probably what James Austen was doing when he was said to be labouring over his sermons. A personal or informal approach was distrusted as a sign of the dreaded 'enthusiasm' connected with the Methodists: on a notable occasion when premature darkness prevented William Jones from seeing his notes and obliged him to extemporize, he felt he had to explain the circumstances to his journal.[48] Jane Austen herself never asked for originality in a sermon. She had no time at all for the verbal pyrotechnics with which some City preachers sought to impress their fleeting congregations (though whether she had actually heard any of the latter, or had merely read about them in Hugh Blair's *Lectures on Rhetoric and Belles Lettres*, a much reprinted work cited by Mary Crawford in *Mansfield Park*, is open to some doubt). She liked to hear the same old truths firmly and sincerely delivered, which is probably precisely what she got from her godfather Samuel Cooke, whom Fanny Burney described as 'a goodish though by no means marvellously *rapid* preacher'. It was somewhat against her own inclinations that she admired Mr Sherer's preaching when she first heard it at Godmersham: he was 'a little too eager sometimes in his delivery', she thought, but she forgave him the eagerness because it came from the heart.[49]

When the services, the visiting and the preaching were despatched, there remained the possibility of 'the parish meeting', which sometimes detained Henry Tilney at Woodston on a Monday and conditioned whether James Austen visited his mother at Southampton on that day or not.[50] This was the meeting of the vestry, which as far as church affairs were concerned took place once a year, within a month of Easter, to elect the people's warden, and on as many other occasions thereafter as were necessary. In most country parishes vestries were still 'open' bodies, which all residents in the parish who owned land there were entitled to attend. The rector (or vicar if the parish was impropriate) took the chair, although in his absence it was possible to elect a deputy. The vestry was responsible by canon law for keeping the church (other than the chancel, which was the responsibility of the rector) in good repair; for ensuring that there was enough space and seating for all the parishioners; and for providing such items as were essential for worship – altar, pulpit, desk, font, communion vessels, a Bible and a Prayer Book. If the churchwardens, who were responsible to the archdeacon at his annual visitation, judged that any repairs, alterations or refurnishings were necessary, they laid estimates before the vestry, which could argue and protest but not refuse if it meant impairing the proper use of the building. Having agreed, perhaps to modified plans, the vestry was obliged, if no private benefactions were forthcoming, to allow the churchwardens to levy a rate which fell on all parishioners according to property.

The overwhelming majority of churches in the English countryside were centuries old and repairs could be a major problem. Not all old churches were stout buildings: the church of St Nicholas at Chawton (destroyed by fire, except for the chancel, in 1871) was said to be a poor structure. If a major project was undertaken (as at Newton Valence, where the tower was almost entirely rebuilt in 1813), vestry meetings were likely for a time to be frequent and lengthy. The bishop sometimes set up a commission of enquiry and sent down agents to take evidence. Henry Tilney may have had serious business in mind when he warned Catherine Morland that having been summoned to Woodston for the parish meeting he would 'probably be obliged to stay two or three days'.[51]

Such commitments were not, perhaps, as regular as they should have been. Although more was done to keep churches in good repair than was once thought, vestries in the eighteenth and early nineteenth centuries probably deserved their reputation for slackness in the matter. William Jones complained in 1803 that his church 'had not been repaired, not even whitewashed, for 50 or 60 years, not within the memory of the oldest man in the parish'.[52] In country parishes, too, there was little likelihood that extensions would be needed to accommodate the worshippers or that there would be continual problems over the allocation of pews. If quarrels occurred, they were more likely to be over whether or not to install (or retain) a gallery at the back of the church for the use of singers; it was some such dispute which led James Woodforde to conclude, during one of his curacies: 'Great and many are the divisions in Castle Cary, some almost irreconcilable.' It was perhaps fortunate that organs, which later became a major item of expenditure in churches, were few and far between, and that anti-popish sentiment ensured that there would be few demands for accessories. Nor was there a great deal of architectural reconstruction unless it was paid for by private benefaction, as when the church at Deane was entirely rebuilt by the Wither Bramstons in 1818. Contemporaries did not have the admiration for their medieval churches that Victorian experts were to feel, but few vestries were desirous of pulling them down and building anew.

Mary Crawford had not been living with her sister and brother-in-law at Mansfield parsonage for very long when she came to the conclusion that the clergy had nothing to do. Her experience of Dr Grant, whom she described as 'an indolent, selfish *bon vivant*', confirmed opinions she had heard in London, where clergymen were seldom seen except as preachers on Sundays, that the clergy were of no importance to the life of the community. Compared with a lawyer, a soldier or a sailor, she said, a clergyman was nothing.[54]

In trying to set her right, Edmund Bertram not only defended the role of the clergy as a whole but put forward stunning claims for the particular importance of the country parson.[55] He was able to begin his argument with the assumption that the latter operated on the more fruitful soil, for it was widely believed that country-dwellers were more morally inclined than people who lived in towns. The idea was indeed so common that politicians, including the Younger Pitt, had come to believe that they could make Parliament less corrupt simply by increasing the proportion of county members. William Cowper, whose poetry Jane Austen so much admired, had for decades presented the countryside as a place where men and women could most easily see God's handiwork. In volume after volume of gentle verse, he had instilled in his readers the idea that certain virtues, such as integrity, simplicity, humility and quiet domesticity, were typically rural. Town dwellers readily accepted the myth, for the thought of an ideal milieu from which they had sprung sustained them in the hurly-burly of life; whilst farmers, who should have been the first to question Cowper's contrast between urban settings created by man and the rural landscape untouched by human hand, made no complaints against an attitude which placed them in such a favourable light. London was happily regarded by all as a very special den of iniquity ('Here I am once more in this scene of dissipation and vice', wrote Jane Austen, aged twenty, from a hotel in Cork Street);[56] and since Mary Crawford herself had referred to the capital as a place where 'everything is to be got with money',[57] Edmund was on strong ground in dismissing large centres of population from any argument about the influence of the clergy. 'We do not look in great cities for our best morality', he said.

> It is not there, that respectable people of any denomination can do most good; and it certainly is not there, that the influence of the clergy can be most felt . . . The clergy are lost there in the crowds of their parishioners. They are known to the largest part only as preachers.

A good sermon was not to be despised in the country any more than in the town, he continued, but:

it is not in fine preaching only that a good clergyman will be useful in his parish
and his neighbourhood, where the parish and neighbourhood are of a size
capable of knowing his private character, and observing his general conduct,
which in London can rarely be the case.

A clergyman, Edmund pointed out, 'has the charge of all that is of the
first importance to mankind, individually or collectively considered,
temporally and eternally . . . ; the guardianship of religion and morals,
and consequently of the manners which result from their influence'.
'And with regard to their influencing public manners,' he persisted,

> Miss Crawford must not misunderstand me, or suppose I mean to call them the
> arbiters of good breeding, the regulators of refinement and courtesy, the
> masters of the ceremonies of life. The *manners* I speak of might rather be called
> *conduct*, perhaps, the result of good principles; the effect, in short, of those
> doctrines which it is their duty to teach and recommend; and it will, I believe, be
> everywhere found, that as the clergy are, or are not what they ought to be, so
> are the rest of the nation.

'As the clergy are or are not what they ought to be.' Unfortunately, Jane
Austen's novels are tantalisingly sketchy on the subject of what the clergy
ought to be. Of good Dr Shirley of Uppercross we know only that he has
been 'for more than forty years zealously discharging all the duties of his
office', and of Edward Ferrars that he readily discharges his duties 'in
every particular'.[58] Edmund Bertram is lectured by his father on the
importance of a pastoral presence, but we never see him at work in his
parish. Henry Tilney is presented to us rather as though he were on
probation only, so we must suspend judgement: he spends only half his
time in his parish and his parsonage house is only half completed. In real
life, Jane Austen lavished more praise on her brother Henry's performance as a clergyman than she ever bestowed on James's but he had not
yet been installed in a parsonage of his own when she died.

Of her fictional clergymen, Elton, Grant and Collins clearly fall short
of the ideal, though all have their merits. Mr Elton is frequently
consulted by magistrates and churchwardens; needy persons can appeal
to him at any time; he visits the sick; Mr Woodhouse likes him and Miss
Bates praises his kindness to her deaf old mother; his conduct in church
is admired by the whole parish. But he seems all the time to be trying
simply to create an impression. He can behave rationally with men but
his conceit when it comes to women brings out a deplorable streak of
vulgarity in his nature.[59] Dr Grant writes excellent sermons and shows
commendable hospitality, but the gentlemanliness Mary Crawford gives

him credit for is only skin deep. He signally fails in his home life to set the Christian example which his orphaned sister-in-law, brought up by a godless uncle, so very much needs.[60] Mr Collins's greatest virtue – his pride in his position – is unfortunately, like all his virtues, carried too far. He is meddlesome and interfering and imagines that he has a right to give advice, in circumstances of which he knows nothing, to persons he has scarcely met. Jane Austen cannot have expected her clergy to remain aloof – at Chawton she came greatly to admire the poetry of George Crabbe, whose penetrating study of the vicar in *The Borough* highlights that very fault;[61] but she could not stand interfering parsons, especially when they presumed to prescribe proper conduct for young ladies. Mr Collins sinks himself at the outset of his visit to Longbourn when he cannot think of anything to read out loud to the Bennet sisters other than Fordyce's *Sermons*. Later, his attempt to prevent Elizabeth from marrying Mr Darcy is reminiscent of the bad advice given by the Rev. Dr Marchmont in another literary work Jane Austen greatly admired – Fanny Burney's *Camilla*.[62]

It has always been difficult, even with the best intentions in the world, to describe in detail the role of a clergyman outside the range of his formal duties. Jane Austen did not make the task any easier by giving it to Edmund Bertram, who was only moderately articulate. Edmund did, however, give one important clue as to the sphere in which the clergyman was expected to work. The reference to 'parish and neighbourhood' implies something larger than the confines of the tiny village in which he might find himself residing.

EMMA:

A NOVEL.

IN THREE VOLUMES.

———◆———

BY THE
AUTHOR OF "PRIDE AND PREJUDICE,"
&c. &c.

———◆———

VOL. I.

═══════

LONDON:
PRINTED FOR JOHN MURRAY.
———
1816.

Title page to the first edition of *Emma*.

Chapter 7

The Clergy and the Neighbourhood

'Have you an agreeable neighbourhood here?' enquired Edward Ferrars of the Dashwoods on his first visit to Barton. Similarly Frank Churchill, meeting Emma Woodhouse for the first time, broached a topic which Jane Austen described as usual among new acquaintances: 'Had they a large neighbourhood? – Highbury, perhaps, afforded society enough? – There were several pretty houses in and about it.'[1]

The term 'neighbourhood' has had a variety of meanings over the centuries but – applied to person rather than to an area of land – it has usually implied a community of interest. Jane Austen habitually used it with reference to groups of families sufficiently equal in social standing and living near enough to each other to meet regularly for mutual entertainment and companionship – in other words, the social elite of each of the small residential areas which constituted rural England. She was herself intimately acquainted with two neighbourhoods, rather different from each other, at Steventon and Chawton. Steventon being a small village, with only the Austens and the Digweeds ranking above the status of labourer, the neighbourhood embraced the small landowning gentry of the surrounding parishes: James Holder who had made a small fortune in the West Indies and had come home in middle age to rent Ashe Park; John Harwood, whose family had owned Deane House since the early years of the eighteenth century; Thomas Terry of Dummer; Wither Bramston of Oakley; and at a somewhat greater distance, and hence more loosely connected, the Withers and Bigg-Withers of Manydown and the Chutes of The Vyne. Chawton, being a larger village, virtually constituted a neighbourhood in itself – as Caroline Austen put it, 'There were several families in the village' – but others from Farringdon, Selborne, Newton Valence and even Alton were not excluded. The Chawton neighbourhood differed from that of Steventon in that its members were not all actively engaged in farming: they included for instance, Benjamin Clement, who was a retired naval officer but nevertheless *persona grata* at social gatherings along with landed gentlemen such as John Middleton, tenant of the manor house for a number of years when the Austens first moved into the village. In her novels Jane Austen presents us with neighbourhoods of both types, those of Barton in *Sense and Sensibility*, Mansfield in *Mansfield Park* and Uppercross in *Persuasion* resembling Steventon; and those of Longbourn in *Pride and Prejudice* (close enough to the little town of Meryton to attract retired businessmen such as Sir William Lucas) and Highbury in *Emma* more closely resembling Chawton.

Not that they were exactly alike. A community which is to have any kind of validity must have its own distinctive character. In Jane Austen's England, difficulties of travel gave each neighbourhood a claustrophobic nature which meant that each was likely to develop in subtly different ways. Anne Elliot, having moved only a few miles from Kellynch to Uppercross, felt herself to be something of an outsider in the intimate circle surrounding the hospitable Musgroves: unable immediately to join in the gossip, 'she acknowledged it to be very fitting that every little social commonwealth should dictate its own matters of discourse; and hoped, ere long, to become a not unworthy member of the one she was now transplanted into'.[2] A teasing rivalry could sometimes exist between neighbourhoods, as some prided themselves on their musicality ('Was it a musical society?' Frank Churchill enquired of Emma Woodhouse concerning Highbury), others on their literary interests. Jane Austen insisted that the Book Society to which she belonged at Chawton was much superior to the one formed at Steventon. 'The Miss Sibleys want to establish a Book Society in their side of the country, like ours', she wrote gleefully to Cassandra on 24 January 1813:

> What can be a stronger proof of that superiority in ours over the Manydown & Steventon society, which I have always foreseen & felt? No emulation of the kind was ever inspired by *their* proceedings.[3]

Differences of wealth were sometimes keenly felt: Jane Austen's niece Fanny Knight, who enjoyed visiting Chawton when her aunts were alive, came to think afterwards that the society they had enjoyed there was not as distinguished as that which surrounded her father at Godmersham, while Jane herself always felt that more fashionable clothes, which she could ill afford, were needed whenever she went to stay with her brother in Kent.[4]

Variations in the character of different neighbourhoods were high-lighted against a common background of social convention. The gener-ally accepted routine provided opportunities for almost daily meetings among members of the elite. The men would meet early in the morning for hunting or fishing, returning home to breakfast at about 10 a.m. – a substantial meal to which visitors might be invited. The rest of the time before dinner was then free for making 'morning calls'. These were regulated by a formidable etiquette, it being considered ineligible for ladies to call on gentlemen until the gentlemen had called on each other, and so on; but a newcomer to the neighbourhood could expect to have been absorbed into the routine after a few days' residence. A call of fifteen minutes' duration was considered the minimum for politeness. The time could be extended by the hostess offering refreshments in the way of sandwiches, cold meats, fruit or cake; and this in turn might lead to an invitation to join in a walk, to visit a mutual friend, or to accomplish a charitable errand. Dinner was served at about 4 o'clock (or as late as 6.30 if fashionable town manners were adopted) and was the occasion for more formal hospitality. In addition to the guests invited for the meal, others could be asked to arrive after the dessert and to join in playing cards, listening to music, or forming a set for an impromptu dance. Tea was served at the end of the evening and the guests departed to their homes, to meet perhaps in different combinations the next day. Sunday brought attendance at church, often with walks afterwards. Other opportunities for meeting included book societies and whist clubs (the latter usually for gentlemen only). The usual round of social events might be punctuated in the summer by excursions to local beauty spots and in the winter by balls held in the nearest assembly rooms or in one of the larger private houses.

The conventions governing admittance to the society of any particular neighbourhood cannot now be easily defined, although they were apparently easily recognized by all concerned at the time. At Chawton the Austen sisters were soon receiving visits from the Middletons at the Great House, although it is unlikely that the previous occupants of their 'Small House' as it was sometimes called (Mr Seward, bailiff of the Chawton estate, and his wife) had been on such neighbourly terms; similarly at Barton the Dashwoods were at once entertained by the squire and his lady at Barton Park, although they merely rented a cottage.[5] Differences of status within each neighbourhood seem also to have been clear at the time, though they are equally difficult to rational-ize. The owner of a considerable area of land, even if he were fairly actively engaged in farming like Mr Knightley, would usually be given precedence, though a Mr Woodhouse, who owned no land to speak of, might be given equal respect as a gentleman of independent means long resident in the neighbourhood.

Contrary to what is often said of the society of the time, businessmen were not excluded – provided that they did not devote the whole of their time and energy to their business pursuits. The Gardiners who, though they lived near to their business in Cheapside, were seen to have an interest in travel, sport and matters picturesque, were graciously received by Mr Darcy when they paused on their holiday tour of Derbyshire to look around his house and grounds of Pemberley.[6] At Highbury the saving grace of Mr Weston was that his business in London had always brought him 'just employment enough'. He had managed to keep a foothold in the country and, as soon as he had made enough money, he purchased a small property and virtually retired altogether: when we meet him in *Emma*, in early middle age, his business affairs take him to London no more than once a year.[7] Mr Cole, too, was accepted into neighbourhood circles at Highbury to the extent that he withdrew from his business in town: full entry could only be expected when he had had no concern with it for several years beyond drawing the profits.[8] Land ownership might bestow a special cachet, but the *sine qua non* was not land but leisure. Sir William Lucas, once he was 'unshackled by business', could 'occupy himself solely in being civil to all the world' and was considered an asset to Meryton society. On the other hand, Robert Martin, a young yeoman farmer who grazed cattle on a picturesque site near Donwell Abbey and whose house was by all accounts fully equal in size and elegance to Mr Weston's Randalls, was dismissed by Emma Woodhouse from any possibility of regular social intercourse on the grounds that his farming activities, which were rapidly expanding, would soon be occupying the whole of his day, and that by the time he was middle aged he would be thinking of nothing but profit and loss. Emma's judgement in this matter was endorsed by that of Mr Knightley, who thought well of Robert Martin and would have altered his social standing if he could but felt obliged to confess that he could not.[9]

Each neighbourhood in fact constituted a microcosm of the governing classes of England: a society founded on land ownership and reinvigorated by trade, whilst despising the principles on which the latter was based. It honoured above all a leisurely way of life which allowed its members to enjoy regular social intercourse and to engage in public service without thought of financial gain. In every sphere of government, local and national, personal contacts were valued more highly than political doctrine, while voluntary service was believed to guarantee higher standards of integrity than paid officials could ever achieve.

The similarity between the local and national situation was emphasized by the fact that members of neighbourhood elites mingled with those operating at a higher level on a number of occasions – at hunts and race meetings; at Quarter Sessions and Assizes; on parliamentary hustings; and, in the case of more affluent members of society, in London, Bath or Brighton for the season. Great landowners and members of the aristocracy were expected to put in an appearance at local assemblies in their vicinity, even if they arrived late and departed early like the Osbornes of Osborne Castle in Jane Austen's unfinished novel *The Watsons*.[10] They were also expected to give annual balls to which society from a wide area of the county was invited. 'Did you think of our Ball on thursday evening?' enquired Jane of Cassandra after receiving an invitation from Lord Portsmouth to attend at Hurstbourne,

> & did you suppose me at it? You might very safely, for there I was – On wednesday morning it was settled that Mrs Harwood, Mary [James's wife] & I should go together, and shortly afterwards a very civil note of invitation for me came from Mrs Bramston, who wrote I believe as soon as she knew of the Ball. I might likewise have gone with Mrs Lefroy, & therefore with three methods of going, I must have been more at the Ball than anyone else.

'It was a pleasant Ball', she continued, '& still more good than pleasant, for there were nearly 60 people, & sometimes we had 17 couple – The Portsmouths, Dorchesters, Boltons, Portals & Clerks were there, & all the meaner etcetera, etceteras.' Lord Portsmouth, who as a boy had been a pupil of George Austen's at the parsonage, spoke a word or two to Jane and desired to be remembered to Cassandra.[11]

Hob-nobbing with the aristocracy did not mean that the gentry were necessarily either respectful or approving of those 'above' them. On the contrary, a critical attitude towards persons whose influence was often unmatched by ability was almost *de rigueur*. Jane Austen's letters show that she made no exception to this rule. They abound with ill-natured references to Hampshire personalities such as the eccentric Lord Bolton, whose wife needed a wig and whose eldest son 'danced too ill to be endured'. Cruel vignettes depict Edward's visitors at Godmersham (such as Lady Hatton's daughter Elizabeth, who 'says as little as ever, but holds up her head & smiles & is to be at the Races'; and Lady Hatton herself with her younger daughter Annamaria, who called one morning – 'but I do not think I can say anything more about them. They came & they sat

& they went'). It should be no cause for surprise that at a superficial level Lady Catherine de Bourgh, with her arrogance, impertinence, snobbishness and domineering manner, is made into a caricature of the aristocracy as 'the meaner etcetera, etceteras' saw them.[12]

Like officers of the Army and Navy, the clergy of the Church of England were considered eligible for neighbourhood society by virtue of their profession. This was more than could be said for members of other professions, some of whom might achieve modest gentility but who on the whole were considered either impossibly menial or too presumptuous. Teachers, for instance: Miss Taylor, governess to Miss Emma Woodhouse and constantly given countenance by the latter, was considered highly respectable and ultimately a suitable wife for Mr Weston, but there seemed to be no doubt that Jane Fairfax would be condemned to servility if she took a teaching post in some unknown household.[13] Mrs Goddard, mistress of a boarding-school with forty pupils and several assistant teachers, might be considered fit, along with Miss Bates, to bear the timid Mr Woodhouse company of an evening when he would otherwise have been left alone but, unlike Miss Bates, who was the daughter of a former vicar of Highbury, she was not invited to supper parties with the rest of the neighbourhood. Lawyers were in an equally uncertain position. The Ferrars family allowed the law to be 'genteel enough', but the Bingley sisters despised the Bennet girls for having an uncle who was an attorney.[14] Mr John Knightley, a lawyer in London, was respected as 'a tall, gentleman-like, and very clever man; rising in his profession', but he would in any case have been welcome in Highbury as the younger brother of the local squire; Miss Hawkins' uncle, who was rumoured by the lady's well-wishers to be 'in the law line' at Bristol, was dismissed by Emma Woodhouse on the grounds that he was very likely to be 'the drudge of some attorney, and too stupid to rise'. Emma likewise considered Mr Cox's assistant to be 'a very pert young lawyer'. Mr Cox himself, Highbury's solicitor, was invited along with the male part of his family to sit down to dinner with Mr Knightley and Miss Emma Woodhouse at the Coles', but 'the less worthy' female members were relegated to arrive after the meal. The apothecary and his wife were not invited at all. Mr Perry was said to be about to set up his carriage, a real sign of affluence; but he presumably belonged nevertheless to the shadier section of the whist club formed among 'the gentlemen and half-gentlemen of the place'. When Jane Austen read the early chapters of a novel her niece Anna was writing she scratched out a passage in which a Mr Griffin was introduced to 'Lord P. and his brother', explaining to Anna: 'A Country Surgeon (don't tell Mr C. Lyford) would not be introduced to Men of their rank.'[15]

The precise degree to which the clergy were admitted to neighbourhood society naturally differed from place to place. Personality on both sides was bound to make a difference. The irascible John Skinner, shortly after his induction at Camerton, discovered that the squire, whose house and grounds adjoined the churchyard, had encroached upon the latter with the connivance of the churchwardens. After that, he was unlikely to get on well with the offending gentleman: on the contrary, his incumbency became a continual battle between the two of them, with Skinner increasingly isolated.[16] Mr Collins and his wife Charlotte suffered comparative isolation in their vicarage at Hunsford for the rather different reason that Lady Catherine de Bourgh was only interested in inviting them to dinner when there was nobody better around; and although she told them in her pompous way that she had 'not the smallest objection to their joining in the society of the neighbourhood', they found that the standard of entertaining in their affluent part of Kent was above their touch.[17] Financial circumstances were forced to count to some extent: a poor parson like William Jones of Broxbourne, who could not even afford a full clerical outfit in which to appear in the pulpit, would probably not have had the clothes in which to socialize among the gentry.[18] Having started life as a poor boy in Abergavenny he was, in any case, less likely to feel at home in well-off circles than clergy like Edmund Bertram and Henry Tilney, who were gentlemen born.

When all such qualifications have been made, it seems true to say that the clergy were welcome, at one level or another, in most neighbourhood circles if only to swell the ranks. So few persons of gentility were available, even in the most populous neighbourhoods, that social events were often difficult to arrange. The evenings on which gatherings could be held were restricted by the vagaries of the weather and the phases of the moon: carriages could not manoeuvre in the unsurfaced lanes if there was too much mud or snow – responsible coachmen would refuse to drive along the unlit country roads on dark nights. In consequence, even an energetic organizer like Sir John Middleton of Barton Park, who readily galloped about the countryside for the whole of a morning in his efforts to drum up a party, sometimes had to admit defeat because families were too heavily engaged when the moon was full.[19] Balls tended to fall flat for lack of numbers, as Jane noted again and again during her younger days at Steventon:

17 January 1798: 'The ball on Thursday was a very small one indeed . . . There were but seven couples, and only twenty-seven people in the room . . . '

24 December 1798: 'Our ball was very thin . . . There were thirty-one people . . . '

21 January 1791: 'Our ball on Thursday was a very poor one, only eight couple and but twenty-three people in the room . . . '

Hostesses arranging dinner parties relied on the same people again and again: 'One always knows beforehand what the dinner will be, and who will be there', Mary Musgrove complained on receiving yet another invitation from the Pooles – a sentiment which echoed Jane Austen's experiences at Steventon and again at Chawton.[20] Jane's overbearing aunt Leigh-Perrot, who chose to live at Hare Hatch particularly for the socializing opportunities presented by a new and affluent neighbourhood close to the Bath road, prided herself on dining with thirty families (Mrs Bennet in *Pride and Prejudice* boasted of twenty-four), but in most neighbourhoods the same few families followed each other around from party to party.[21]

The sheer boredom of life in a country house should not be underestimated. 'I should hardly like to live with her ladies and gentlemen in their elegant but confined houses', was Charlotte Brontë's reaction to Jane Austen's novels.[22] However energetically the social round was pursued, it was unlikely to prove wholly satisfying, especially to the younger members of the community. As the Rev. Thomas Gisborne pointed out in 1797:

> the paternal mansion, insulated in its park, or admitting of no contiguous habitation except the neighbouring hamlet, seldom furnishes the opportunity of access to a perpetual circle of amusement. Visitors cannot always be found in the drawing-room, the card-table cannot always be fitted up, the country town affords a ball but once a month.[23]

It was not only young ladies but young gentlemen, supported by their parents or living off rents and investments, who found themselves with very little to do. There was hunting and shooting in the season, but what then? 'The Comfort of the Billiard Table here is very great', Jane Austen wrote from Godmersham in 1813. 'It draws all the Gentlemen to it whenever they are within.' Mr Hurst, in *Pride and Prejudice*, spent all his time playing cards.[24]

Much has been made of the liberating nature of the new fashion in entertainment whereby, instead of sitting in high-backed chairs placed squarely against the parlour walls as old Mr and Mrs Musgrove had been wont to do, family and guests retired to the drawing-room or the library where a grand piano, flower stands, bookshelves and a profusion of small tables allowed everybody to choose their own diversion; but its origin lay partly in the fact that, with the increase in leisure that came in with the agricultural revolution, there was less to talk about. Conversation tended to be desultory and commonplace; it could only be sustained as an accompaniment to other pursuits – as at a typical party at Ashe Park reported by Jane Austen to Cassandra on 20 November 1800:

> Mrs Bramston talked a good deal of nonsense, which Mr Bramston & Mr Clerk seemed almost equally to enjoy. There was a whist & a casino table, & six outsiders. – Rice & Lucy made love, Mat. Robinson fell asleep, James & Mrs Augusta alternately read Dr Jenner's pamphlet on the cow pox, & I bestowed my company by turns on all. On enquiring of Mrs Clerk, I find that Mrs Heathcote made a great blunder in her news of the Crooks & Morleys; it is young Mr Crooke who is to marry the second Miss Morley – & it is the Miss Morleys instead of the second Miss Crooke, who were the beauties of the Music meeting . . . [25]

References to poor conversation abound in Jane Austen's novels, from *Sense and Sensibility* in which we are told that Mrs Ferrars was 'not a woman of many words; for, unlike people in general, she proportioned them to the number of her ideas', to *Persuasion*, in which the men at Uppercross are described as interested only in guarding and destroying their own game and the women in household gossip. Even the Coles' dinner party, which Emma Woodhouse had feared would be wild and unseemly, furnished only 'the usual rate of conversation; a few clever things said, a few downright silly, but by much the larger proportion neither the one nor the other – nothing worse than everyday remarks, dull repetitions, old news, and heavy jokes'.[26]

Under these circumstances, any likely addition to a neighbourhood set was seized upon avidly. Mr Knightley may have had doubts about Frank Churchill from the point of view of moral integrity but, as Emma Woodhouse pointed out: 'We do not often look upon fine young men, well-bred and agreeable. We must not be nice, and ask for all the virtues into the bargain.'[27] At Chawton even the obscure Mr Sweney, who appeared but once at a dinner party and obligingly played card games, all of which were new to him, was sadly missed when it was found that he had had to return to London before he could attend another party two days later. Young men were perhaps at a special premium but even elderly married relatives, visiting for a short time, were looked forward to with interest and subjected to an unremitting round of morning calls and dinner engagements. There was nothing unusual in Mr Gardiner's finding when he visited his sister Mrs Bennet for a week that he never once sat down for an evening with the family.[28]

Clergymen, however modest their social capabilities, were likely to be welcome if they were at all willing to 'join in'. Mr Collins found ready listeners to his stories of opulence and grandeur and fully repaid Mrs Philips for plying him with coffee and muffins by agreeing to make up a table at whist. A young man of the charm and address of the Rev. James Edward Austen understandably delighted Mrs Chute: 'He is a very agreeable companion,' she reported, 'cheerful, lively, animated, ready to converse, willing to read out loud, never in the way . . . '[29]

In the 1780s and 1790s, when dancing at public assemblies was popular in small country towns, clergymen both young and not so young, married and unmarried, were in demand as dancing partners. A few of the extreme Evangelicals might frown upon such frivolous activity, especially as it could conceivably be thought to have sexual connotations, but this attitude was not yet common. Clergymen arriving at a local dance hall, where ladies were frequently obliged to sit against the wall for lack of partners, were not expected to stand and watch. When the Rev. John Calland, rector of Bentworth, stood with his hat in his hand at a Manydown ball, waiting 'to be talked to and abused for not dancing', Jane Austen and her friend Catherine Bigg 'teased him into it at last' – Jane reporting delightedly to Cassandra that he became thereafter 'altogether rather the genius and flirt of the evening.'[30] Later, when assemblies were rivalled in popularity by dances given at private houses for invited guests, even a sanctimonious clergyman like Mr Collins could find excuses for participating, on the grounds that a ball given by a person of known character for respectable people could not have any 'evil tendency'.[31] On one such occasion Jane Austen's 'set', which she carefully enumerated for Cassandra's benefit, included no fewer than five clergymen. A few days later, when Richard Buller and Edward Cooper, the latter with his wife and two children, were staying at the rectory, both gentlemen, joined by John Lyford, accompanied her in her father's carriage to a ball at Ashe. On the way, they called at Deane parsonage to pick up James, whose dancing had so much improved in recent months that Jane decided a ball would be 'nothing without *him*.[32]

Meanwhile card-playing, which had been one of the accomplishments recommended to young clergymen by *The Loiterer* as likely to make them acceptable to their local squire, remained popular throughout the period. James Austen, along with other clergymen in the neighbour-hood, did his full share of it at Steventon, where it was the staple entertainment at the Digweeds' and at the bachelor Mr Holder's: 'Our visit at Ashe Park last Wednesday went off in a come-cá way; we met Mr Lefroy & Tom Chute, played at cards & came home again', Jane wrote to Cassandra on 3 January 1801. Two weeks later, along with James and the Rev. Fulwar Fowle, she dined at Deane with Mr Harwood and his clergyman son John and played at vingt-et-un; four days after that, Austens and Fowles were again at Ashe Park where according to Jane they met nobody but themselves, 'played at *vingt-un* again and were very cross' (Fulwar Fowle being a bad loser).[33]

The clergy could not all be expected to be good conversationalists. There can have been few as accomplished as Henry Tilney, whose skills were clearly something quite new to Catherine Morland, brought up though she had been in a country parsonage. In fact it was a clergyman, the Rev. Matthew Robinson, whose post-prandial nap at Ashe Park Jane Austen revealed to posterity in her letter to Cassandra on 20 November 1800. Still, there was a chance that a clergyman would have something worthwhile to say on subjects outside the range of gossip: books, for instance. The clergy who belonged to Jane Austen's Book Society at Chawton seem to have been the only members capable of making intelligent comments on what they read. The Clements received their one book a fortnight more as a duty than a pleasure, while Mrs Digweed often let hers lie around unread. The latter's reaction when asked if she had enjoyed a volume of parodies on the major poets startled even Jane:

'Oh yes, very much – very droll indeed. The opening up of the house and the striking up of the fiddles.' What she meant, poor woman, who shall say? I sought no further.[34]

Jane Austen's father was probably highly unusual in taking a delight in Gothick novels (a characteristic Jane handed on to Henry Tilney), but the clergy as a whole were noted for their interest in the Picturesque, which formed the background to the novels. Edward Ferrars, despite his protestations of ignorance on the subject, was fully conversant with its themes and terminology. William Gilpin, whose travels in search of the Picturesque were at the root of Henry Tilney's comments on the scenery at Bath, was himself a clergyman.[35] Among poets, too, the clergy could draw upon writers dear to their own hearts: William Cowper's poetry, which George Austen was in the habit of reading aloud to his family on dark evenings, was said to have found its way into every vicarage in England.[36] Reading aloud by one person to the rest of the company was a valuable accomplishment at a time when candles gave out only a small circle of light. Clergymen were expected to be adept at it.

In *Sense and Sensibility* Jane Austen complained that women's talk was habitually more boring than men's. Gentlemen, she thought, could always add a little variety to the constant repetition of local gossip by talking about 'politics, inclosing land, and breaking horses'.[37] All these were topics with which the clergy were likely to be conversant. Land enclosure would obviously attract their attention, for although some three-quarters of the clergy came from professional, trading and small farming circles they acquired an interest in landed property as soon as they acquired a benefice.[38] Even the non-beneficed clergy were connected with agriculture by the fact that the financial structure of the church rested upon tithes. Increasing the productivity of the land, through enclosure and other 'improvements', was a subject which concerned them all.

In the matter of politics, their interest (in both senses of the word) also ran parallel to that of the miscellaneous land-owning class of the rural counties of England. Both clergy and gentry were predominantly Tory, a factor which accounts for many of the hostile caricatures of the period. Their Toryism was more a matter of sentiment than of party doctrine and could embrace some quite contradictory elements (as it did in the case of Jane Austen herself). A romantic attachment to the Stuarts, whose coats of arms had been dutifully erected on the walls of many country churches in the seventeenth century and had remained there in spite of the change of dynasty, was combined with a fierce loyalty to George III and the Protestant Succession; loyalty to the King was combined with a healthy suspicion of courtiers and administration; and an attitude of staunch independence was combined with a suspicion of campaigns to free Parliament from the influence of the Crown lest such campaigns should increase the power of magnates and politicians. The Whigs, in spite of the aristocratic element in their ranks (and perhaps even because of it) were believed to favour disruption in church and state; and although the poorer clergy may be thought to have stood to benefit by a possible change of system, few seem to have been inclined to take the risk.

In the Austens' own county of Hampshire, one of the fiercest electoral contests of the period took place in 1790, when William John Chute of the Vyne and Sir William Heathcote of Hursley Park near Winchester (whose son later married Jane Austen's friend Elizabeth Bigg of Manydown) successfully defeated two opposing candidates who were campaigning for Catholic Relief and Reform of Parliament.[39] Election campaigns were traditionally addressed to 'the clergy and gentlemen of the county', for the incumbents of livings had the right to vote among the 40 shilling freeholders by virtue of their benefice. George Austen cannot have been overlooked in a contest which was reckoned to have cost no less than £40,000 on each side and whose intensity was such that Chute's elder brother died of a fever said to have been brought on by his exertions in canvassing.[40] The cry 'Heathcote and Chute for ever' was still a catchphrase in the Austen household in 1800, when Jane used it with reference to an encounter she and her mother had had with Mrs Heathcote and Mrs Chute at Deane House. 'They had meant to come on to Steventon afterwards,' she added, 'but we knew a trick worth two of that.'[41] Jane tended to steer clear of politicians, usually suspecting Chute of some self-interested motive whenever he made a civil gesture. Her brother James, however, not only cultivated him assiduously for his patronage in the church but took every advantage of his privileges as a Member of Parliament, in which capacity he served almost continuously until after James's death in 1819. Both James and his wife were constantly asking him to frank their correspondence and would sometimes delay answering letters until he arrived home from Westminster. Even Jane and Cassandra sought franks whenever a suitable opportunity arose.[42]

Breaking horses was a subject which might be discussed in several contexts. Landowners and clergy used horses extensively, both for farm work and transport. Animals that were to be versatile needed to be trained to move from the plough to the carriage, and to bear both gentlemen and ladies. It could be a matter of life and death to understand the character and capabilities of the horse, as Mrs Lefroy's tragic death in 1804 by being thrown from a skittish animal made only too clear. An aspect of horsemanship more likely to be discussed at dinner tables, however, was concerned with performance on the hunting field. From the mid eighteenth century, when the fox was added to the deer as a suitable quarry for the chase, many country squires kept packs of hounds with which they hunted indiscriminately over the countryside. Thomas Terry of Dummer, who had hunted red deer in the thick woodlands around Kempshott House when the Prince of Wales was in residence there in the late 1780s, took to fox-hunting in the mid 1790s, and his son Stephen (a year older than Jane Austen and her dancing partner at local balls) became a notable addict.[43] William Chute founded the famous Vine Hunt at about the same time, writing to his brother Tom (later the Rev. Thomas Chute), then in residence at Oxford, for his advice on the purchase of suitable hounds.[44] John Harwood of Deane, on whom it has been suggested that Fielding modelled his Squire Western, was another keen huntsman – all these within a few miles of each other. Any gentleman who could keep the pace was usually welcome to join the hunt and, although mere farmers might be excluded on social grounds, parsons were invariably in this context counted as gentlemen. Wilberforce flattered himself in 1813 that 'the race of buck parsons is nearly extinct',[45] but Jane Austen could count more than one enthusiastic rider to hounds among her clerical acquaintance, including her brother James and his friend the Rev. Fulwar Fowle. James had acquired a taste for the sport at Oxford and, in *The Loiterer*, had advised any young clergyman about to take up duties in a country parish to cultivate not only riding but 'an extensive and accurate knowledge of all sporting matters'. This, he wrote, would not only ensure that a knife and fork was always laid for him at the squire's table, but might produce useful contacts: 'For nothing is more certain than a good shot has often brought down a comfortable Vicarage, and many a bold rider lept into a snug Rectory.[46]

Unlike the fox and other vermin such as rabbits and hares, game birds were considered valuable and could only be shot by permission from the gentleman who held the lordship of the manor. The Rev. George Austen was privileged, by courtesy of Thomas Knight, to share the lordship of Steventon manor with Hugh Digweed, tenant of the manor house; and their sons enjoyed much sport together in the season. Edward Austen, when he became a landowner with extensive woodland, always had plenty of visitors – including from time to time his two clergyman brothers – keen on shooting. The Rev. Gilbert White, in spite of his love of birds, took the sport for granted. Presents of game birds were commonly sent to friends upon the slightest excuse, as Jane Austen discovered when she was looking after her brother Henry during a bout of illness;[47] but killing birds, and even fishing the rivers (for which permission was also required), could hardly be said to have been necessary to maintain the nation's food supply. The sport was all. Jane, without being excessively rigid in her views, disliked too much emphasis on it: she very much hoped that her youngest brother Charles would get good enough weather to enjoy a few days shooting at Godmersham during a well-earned leave from the Navy, but she deplored the continual interest shown in blood sports by her nephews there.[48]

During the French Wars, and particularly during the invasion scares of 1798-1801 and 1804-5, parsons were required to cooperate with gentry in preparations for defence.[49] Lists drawn up by harassed schoolmasters and constables of the men that would be willing to serve in the militia, or in driving waggons and conducting teams of cattle to the army camps, were checked by the clergy at meetings of the vestry and reported to the government with varying degrees of efficiency. Country parsons on the whole met with a less enthusiastic response to their recruiting efforts than their brethren in urban areas: the Rev. George Austen's total of thirty-five men out of the 150 inhabitants which the census for 1801 had revealed for Steventon was unusual for rural Hampshire.[50] Some bishops advised their clergy against playing a more active role in the war, but in other dioceses parsons were free to compete with local squires for the command of the Volunteers. The spirited Fulwar Fowle was put in charge of a rifle company, winning from George III a much-prized compliment as 'the best preacher, the best officer, and the best rider to hounds in all my loyal county of Berkshire'.[51] At Steventon the captaincy of the militia fell to the lackadaisical Mr Holder of Ashe Park, to the annoyance of the Rev. George Lefroy's eager son, serving as his ensign.[52]

In normal circumstances, however, cooperation between clergy and gentry was more likely to be seen in the context of the one important social duty which had long been thought to devolve upon them both: that of dispensing charity. In medieval times the lord of the manor had been expected to ensure that his peasants did not starve. The tradition continued to the extent that a landowner of the stature of Jane Austen's brother Edward was regarded as having a responsibility towards the less fortunate residents on his estates: 'Edward's poor' was a phrase which appears several times in Jane's correspondence. Edward's thirteen-year-old daughter, faced with writing a letter to Aunt Cassandra, chose to tell her about 'our poor' – about 'old Mary Crowcher' who got '*maderer* and *maderer*' and 'poor Will Amos' who went to live in a barn at Builting.[53] A landowner was expected to supply gifts of food, clothing, and perhaps money, to those in need, at regular intervals, usually at Christmas, and at times of bad harvest and bad weather, sickness, bereavement and unemployment. Jane and Cassandra at Chawton frequently acted as agents for the absent Edward in these matters. 'We are just beginning to be engaged in another Christmas Duty, & next to eating Turkies a very pleasant one, laying out Edward's money for the Poor . . .', Jane wrote to Martha Lloyd on 29 November 1812.[54]

Meanwhile the clergy, like the monks of old, were called upon to minister to the poor in a multitude of ways. They usually kept a medicine box from which to dispense homely remedies. They gave advice on domestic economy and helped to place young people in jobs.[55] Unlike the gentry, many of them kept their doors continually open to the poor and were particularly noted for giving them dinners at harvest time and Christmas.[56] They took collections of money for the poor at church doors after Communion services and distributed little sums to queues of people waiting outside; at times of particular hardship, they organized collections around the parish and distributed food and clothing both from their own stocks and from gifts supplied by others. The clergy shared with the gentry a right of entry to the houses of the poor. Although not all were assiduous in visiting, the practice was common enough for Emma Woodhouse to believe that Mr Elton had been on an errand of mercy to a labourer's cottage as soon as she saw him in the vicinity.[57] Mr Collins's zeal in this respect erred as usual on the side of interference: he reported to Lady Catherine 'the minutest concerns' of everybody in the parish, so that 'whenever any of the cottagers were disposed to be quarrelsome, discontented, or too poor' she could sally forth into the village 'to settle their differences, silence their complaints, and scold them into harmony and plenty'.[58]

In addition to charitable efforts on the part of individuals, poor relief was administered through the machinery of local government. Here too the clergy could cooperate to some purpose with the gentry of the neighbourhood, for the parish was not only a pastoral division of the Church of England but an administrative unit of the county. The parish vestry, at its annual meeting, elected not only the churchwarden but two overseers of the poor whose duty it was to collect and dispense the Poor Rate levied upon all landowners in the parish. In accordance with the Poor Law Act of 1601, each parish was responsible for its own paupers, a duty which could be variously interpreted but at least meant that no one should be allowed to starve.

The overseers of the poor were responsible to the magistrates, who met together both locally in Petty Sessions and more grandly in the Quarter Sessions of the county bench. The magistrates were in origin a judicial body, and still met in judgement in criminal cases ranging from infringement of the Game Laws to petty theft; but they had also acquired over the centuries a large number of administrative duties. At Quarter Sessions they both approved the Poor Rate and set a County Rate. This also was levied upon the landowners of the parishes and used for the provision of a wide range of services including the regulation of roads, bridges and markets, the maintenance of law and order, the supervision of gaols and asylums, and the recruitment of militia. In law a magistrate had to be a member of the Church of England and the owner of freehold land to the annual value of more than £100 a year. In

practice the vast majority were country squires, but an increasing minority – amounting to perhaps a quarter of the entire bench – were
beneficed clergymen.[59]

The duties of a magistrate demanded a great deal of time and effort
for no material reward. It was no exaggeration on the part of Emma
Woodhouse to describe Mr Knightley, chief magistrate at Highbury, as
having 'all the parish to manage'.[60] On the other hand, because the
duties were so multifarious and important, the office bestowed great
distinction upon the holder, and for this reason was in great demand in
the rural areas of England (less so in towns, where the duties could be
both unpleasant and more difficult to carry out). In country districts the
nouveaux riches were particularly anxious to gain admittance. No vast
amount of land was needed to produce an income of £100 a year: a
retired businessman might easily score up the required sum from a
small-holding and, having done so, a position on the Bench would clinch
his arrival at gentility. At Highbury Mr Knightley's associates were Mr
Weston and Mr Cole. The Rev. Mr Elton was not, apparently, a member
of the Commission, but we have no reason to doubt Mrs Elton's veracity
when she boasted that 'the magistrates and overseers, and churchwardens were always wanting his opinion'. He was highly thought of for
his attentions to the needy: John Abdy's son could draw him away from a
tea-party to solicit his aid in getting parish relief for his poor old father,
bedridden with rheumatics. The regular meeting which he attended at
the *Crown* could well have been the Petty Sessions, often held in the local
inn, where his advice might have been needed on any number of issues
from a dispute over a right of way to a serious problem arising from
vagrancy or low wages.[61]

Appointment to the magistracy was by the Crown on the advice of the
Lord Lieutenant. This meant that an aspirant must keep on good terms
with the local gentry and thereby ensure that his name was mentioned at
the race meetings and other gatherings where such matters were often
settled. Many a clergyman might have envied George Austen his connection with Lovelace Bigg Wither of Manydown, Deputy Lieutenant for
Hampshire in the 1790s, though there is no evidence that the former
took advantage of it. The knowledge that Bigg Wither, due to illness,
would be absent from a ball in 1799 kept half the gentry of the
neighbourhood away also.[62]

Socializing in the neighbourhood had its price, of course. Clergy who
were fully integrated might be expected to take their turn at hosting
parties as well as attending them. These could be of various kinds. James
Woodforde wrote of bachelor parties at which fellow curates and other

young blades played fives against the churchyard wall.[63] For more decorous events a hostess was needed. A sister or a niece might be imported for the purpose but to play an effective role in all neighbourhood concerns a wife was indispensable in the long term. Before considering the deeper purposes which good fellowship in the neighbourhood might conceivably have fulfilled, it is necessary to pay attention to that important personage in the history of the Church of England, the parson's wife.

Chapter 8

The Parson's Wife

'Why had this sensible man left a career at Oxford to find himself in a poor Hampshire village?' asks one of Jane Austen's recent biographers, when recording the arrival of the Rev. George Austen to take up his duties at Steventon.[1] The answer must surely be that he had wanted to marry. He had been made rector of Steventon in December 1761 but had shown no signs of wishing to leave Oxford until three years later when he married Cassandra Leigh. He might then have counted himself lucky that he had a parish, however poor it may have been, to which he could take his bride. Not all his associates were as lucky. Tom Warton summed up the feelings of many an Oxford don when he rhymed in 1750:

> These fellowships are pretty things,
> We live indeed like petty kings:
> But who can bear to waste his whole age
> Amid the dulness of a college,
> Debarr'd the common joys of life,
> And that prime bliss – a loving wife!
> O! what's a table richly spread,
> Without a woman at its head!
> Would some snug benefice but fall,
> Ye feasts, ye dinners, farewell all!
> To offices I'd beg adieu,
> Of Dean, Vice-praef, – of Bursar too;
> Come joys, that rural, quiet yields,
> Come tythes, and house, and fruitful fields![2]

The news of a clergyman bringing a wife into the neighbourhood always caused a stir: it was taken for granted that she must be absorbed into the tiny social elite of the place. Everybody must call on her: the 'visits in form', as Jane Austen called them in *Emma*, must be paid as soon as possible.[3] Mrs Austen made a great point of instructing her grand-daughter Anna on this piece of etiquette so that she could get it right in a novel she was engaged in writing.[4] After the morning calls must come the formal invitations. A Mr Elton in his bachelor state could be asked to spend an evening playing backgammon with Mr Woodhouse; a Mr Elton married must for the first time in his ministry be asked to dinner at Hartfield. Emma, who would have preferred to avoid him, knew that she had no option: she 'must not do less than others'.[5]

A clergyman arriving in a neighbourhood *without* a wife was equally likely to cause a stir, at least among the female members of the neigh-bourhood, who were bound to look upon him as a possible marriage partner for one or other of the single ladies among them. According to the opening words of *Pride and Prejudice*:

> It is a truth universally acknowledged that a single man in possession of a good fortune must be in want of a wife. However little known the feelings or views of such a man may be on first entering a neighbourhood, this truth is so well fixed in the minds of the surrounding families, that he is considered as the rightful property of some one or other.

Few clergymen were possessed of a fortune to equal that of Mr Bingley, the gentleman of leisure whose arrival at Netherfield occasioned this comment; but apart from the poorest among them, who scarcely ranked above the emerging class of shopkeepers and clerks, they were not unworthy of consideration from a worldly point of view. A living of £300-400 a year, with a decent parsonage house offering free accommo-dation, placed a clergyman on a level with the lesser gentry and made him far from despicable in the marriage stakes. Whatever his antece-dents, his position as a freeholder and his connection with a landed patron qualified him as a gentleman. Mr Collins had some reason to be surprised at the portionless Elizabeth Bennet refusing him and he was probably right when he claimed that there was many a young woman in his parish in Kent who would have jumped at the offer. His connection with Lady Catherine de Bourgh alone was sufficient to make Sir William Lucas regard him as a fine catch for his daughter Charlotte, just as Mr Elton's connection with Mr Knightley of Donwell Abbey dazzled Augusta Hawkins, whose sole claim to gentility until then had been her sister's marriage to the owner of Maple Grove.

In the tight little neighbourhoods of rural England marriage opportunities for women were few and far between. Mothers began on the task of getting their daughters married as soon as they left the schoolroom: it was considered a measure of the way they had brought them up and of their own effectiveness as hostesses that they should succeed in their efforts as soon as possible. 'Lady Lucas will have a daughter married before I have', was Mrs Bennet's bitter reflection on the news that Mr Collins had transferred his attentions from her Elizabeth to Lady Lucas's Charlotte.[6] Successful mothers sometimes became addicted to the marriage game, which provided an outlet for their managerial talents and an interest outside the narrowly domestic:

> Mrs Jennings was a widow, with an ample jointure. She had only two daughters, both of whom she had lived to see respectably married, and she had now therefore nothing to do but to marry all the rest of the world.[7]

Parsons' wives, in a position to introduce their husbands' college friends to the neighbourhood, were at an advantage in the business. Mrs Lefroy at Ashe clearly had a hand in promoting the interest shown by the Rev. Samuel Blackall (one of her husband's guests at the parsonage) in her young neighbour Jane Austen, for when he ultimately cried off she was too sheepish to say much about the matter to Jane herself. 'Perhaps she thinks she has said too much already', wrote Jane to Cassandra.[8]

A clergyman arriving in a neighbourhood often aroused more varied expectations in the marriage market than if he had been a gentleman of the landowning class like Willoughby or Frank Churchill. He might be less demanding as to dowry and social standing. The time had gone by when Fielding and Richardson could give their fictional clergy a happy ending to their adventures in marriage with the lady's maid, but it was still worthwhile for the teachers and parlour boarders at Mrs Goddard's school to peep through the curtains at Mr Elton walking arm-in-arm with Mr Cole.[9] Mr Elton's subsequent history in fact illustrates admirably the fluidity of a clergyman's social position with regard to marriage. He himself thought that he might aspire to the hand of Miss Woodhouse, heiress of Hartfield; Emma thought he could suitably marry Harriet Smith, a modestly educated girl of unknown parentage; he ended up by marrying the youngest daughter of a Bristol merchant with an independent fortune of 'so many thousands as would always be called ten'.[10] It was always possible that a clergyman would have a mind above money, as did Mr Collins, who made it shatteringly clear to Elizabeth Bennet that he was prepared to do the handsome thing by the lady of his choice:

> To fortune I am perfectly indifferent, and shall make no demand of that nature

on your father, since I am well aware that it could not be complied with; and that one thousand pounds in the 4 per cents. which will not be yours till after your mother's decease, is all that you may ever be entitled to. On that head, therefore, I shall be uniformly silent; and you may assure yourself that no ungenerous reproach shall ever pass my lips when we are married.[11]

Another interesting possibility was that a clergyman – if he had waited until he acquired a living before seeking a wife – might be middle-aged, and ready, therefore, to take a woman who was not in the first bloom of youth. For a brief period around 1815, naval commanders returning home from the wars with prize money were in the same position; but clergymen were more common. Ladies who, in spite of visits to London and seasons in Bath (where Catherine Morland had been taken to find a husband), had been passed over in previous years might stand a second chance. Catherine Bigg of Manydown, who had shared with Jane Austen the humiliation of sitting partnerless at balls, was prepared at the age of thirty-five to marry a clergyman considerably older than herself. Mrs Knight did not despair of Jane, who remained single after several years actual *residence* in Bath, finding a husband at last in the middle-aged bachelor vicar of Chawton when she arrived there at the age of thirty-four. Jane, fortunately, liked old Mrs Knight and was in a mood to reply gaily when Cassandra handed on this piece of information:

I am very much obliged to Mrs Knight for such a proof of the interest she takes in me – and she may depend upon it, that I *will* marry Mr Papillon, whatever may be his reluctance, or my own.[12]

Clergymen's daughters were often thought to make particularly good wives for other clergymen and hence to have a sort of lien upon any that became available. It was for this reason that Mary Crawford tortured herself when Edmund Bertram went to stay with a clergyman's family at Peterborough. What if one of the Miss Owens married Edmund?

I dare say they are trying for it. And they are quite in the right, for it would be a very pretty establishment for them. I do not at all wonder or blame them . . . Their father is a clergyman and their brother is a clergyman, and they are all clergymen together. He is their lawful property, he fairly belongs to them.[13]

Jane Austen was not above sharing such assumptions. She persisted in believing that Martha Lloyd was destined to come back from visits to Ibthorpe engaged to the awful Peter Debary;[14] and she did not see why her cousin Mary Cooke should feel curtailed in her marriage prospects just because she had to stay at home with her ailing mother:

> I am very sorry for Mary; but I have some comfort in there being two Curates now lodging in Bookham besides their own Mr Warneford from Dorking, so that I think she must fall in love with one or the other.[15]

Surprisingly enough, the evidence provided by Jane Austen's novels and letters suggests that the purely religious aspects of the prospective husband's occupation were of little concern to women thinking of marrying a clergyman. Of all the female characters in the novels who become attracted to clergymen, only Mary Crawford shows any sign of being at all exercized by the gentleman's religious convictions. Catherine Morland is scarcely interested one way or the other when she learns that the young man who fascinated her when she met him at the Lower Rooms is a clergyman (a fact Mr Allen ascertained only in order to assure himself of Henry Tilney's suitability from a worldly point of view as an acquaintance for his young ward). As for Elinor Dashwood, she is merely pleased that the lackadaisical Edward Ferrars should be pursuing his personal inclination at last, rather than remaining idle to please his mother. Fanny Price defends Edmund's choice of profession against its critics, but one suspects she would have done the same for any other choice he had made. Equally there is no evidence that any of the parsons' wives Jane Austen knew in real life was particularly devout. A woman who married a clergyman, provided he did not belong to the minority of Evangelicals, could be sure that she would not be expected to show more than an ordinary commitment to religious duty: this meant that she could weigh the practical advantages and disadvantages of the match as she would have done those of any other.

The attractions might be regarded as considerable. Once the husband was beneficed, his wife obtained an independent establishment which included a house and garden and probably a farm. She could now entertain her relatives and friends: many a parson's wife became noted for her hospitality (Jane Austen considered it a black mark against Mrs Norris that her bedrooms at the parsonage were seldom filled).[16] Marriage with a clergyman also gave a woman the opportunity to carry out social work, perhaps in conjunction with the lady of the manor, to whatever extent she chose. Parsons' wives were expected at the very least to distribute their husband's charity. In addition, the poor and needy might call at the parsonage house for anything from advice to money. According to Mrs Norris, it was 'unknown how much was consumed in our kitchen by odd comers and goers'.[17] Like Mrs Cooke of Bookham, Mrs Norris was one of many parsons' wives noted for handing out herbal remedies. Some adopted a less homely line and were to the forefront in promoting public health measures. The progress of inoculation against smallpox owed as much to the country clergy and their wives as to the medical profession: Mrs Lefroy is reported to have inoculated the children in her husband's parishes with her own hand.[18] This talented lady also demonstrated the possibilities that were open to a parson's wife as a society hostess in a country neighbourhood. She gave balls of a more sophisticated kind than the dances Mrs Austen arranged for her younger children in the kitchen at Steventon. At Mrs Lefroy's parties, young and old could meet to dine and chat and enjoy themselves; strangers could be made to feel at home; the lordly Chutes, the influential Bigg Withers and the down-to-earth Digweeds could meet on easy terms. Unlike Mrs Elton, who offended the society of Highbury when she arrived from Bristol with her talk of rout parties and iced drinks,[19] Mrs Lefroy knew how to enliven the neighbourhood without suggesting that she despised its unfashionable ways. It was possibly Mrs Lefroy Jane Austen had in mind when she caused Mary Crawford to meditate on the social possibilities of marriage with Edmund Bertram, imagining herself 'commanding the first society in the neighbourhood; looked up to, perhaps, as leading it even more than those of larger fortune'.[20]

To Jane Austen, none of these advantages was worthwhile if the marriage was devoid of affection and mutual respect. She could understand and even sympathize with Charlotte Lucas who at the age of twenty-seven, with little in the way of beauty or fortune, had agreed to marry the odious Mr Collins 'solely from the pure and disinterested idea of an establishment'. She could explain Charlotte's position with real feeling for the plight of women:

> Without thinking highly either of men or of matrimony, marriage had always been her object; it was the only honourable provision for well-educated young women of small fortune, and however uncertain of giving happiness, must be their pleasantest preservative from want.

She appreciated that Charlotte's marriage would facilitate the entry of her younger sisters into the marriage market and free her brothers from the anxiety of having to look after an old maid. Yet she could not approve of the step. Her opinion was the same as Elizabeth Bennet's — that a marriage based purely on such calculations was a betrayal of personality, a sacrifice of 'every better feeling to worldly advantage'.[21]

In real life Jane knew of many clergy marriages that were based on true affection but there were others in which she suspected that worldly pressures had played a major role. 'Tomorrow we must think of poor Catherine', she wrote on the eve of her friend's marriage to the Rev. Herbert Hill (a man of whom she appeared to know no harm except that he was 'quiet' and that he supplied his household with 'very bad baker's bread').[22] She could hardly ever believe that Harriot Bridges, the lively and much-loved youngest daughter of Sir Brook Bridges, could be happy with the formidable Rev. George Moore. 'I had a most affectionate welcome from Harriot & was happy to see her looking almost as well as ever', she wrote on 20 June 1808, having met Harriot for the first time since her marriage. 'I really hope Harriot is altogether very happy – but she cannot feel quite so much at ease with her Husband, as the wives she has been used to', she wrote again, on 26 June. Five years later she was still writing: 'There is nothing to object to in his manners to her, and I do believe that he makes her – or she makes herself – very happy.' Elizabeth Bennet had similarly wondered at Charlotte Lucas's contentment with Mr Collins.[23]

Admittedly there were drawbacks to marriage with a clergyman, even when affection was present. A factor of some importance at the time was that a parson's wife might have to leave the neighbourhood in which she had been brought up, and in which her entire network of relatives lived, in order to accompany her husband to a distant parish – often referred to as being in another 'country' even when it was only a few miles away. The thought of having to leave Goodnestone for Wrotham worried Harriot Bridges more than any other consequence of marrying Mr Moore. Harriot was fortunate in that her connections were wealthy and frequent visiting was no great problem; Jane Austen refused to pity her simply because she could not be in two places at once.[24] Charlotte Lucas's case was different. Neither she nor her parents could afford to be frequently travelling the fifty miles that separated them, as Elizabeth Bennet did not hesitate to point out to Mr Darcy.[25]

To make matters worse, the distant parish might well be buried in the depths of the country. To a woman bred in a town, or accustomed to seasons in London, confinement to a country parsonage all the year round could be tedious beyond endurance. Parson Woodforde was frequently upset because his niece Nancy, who lived with him as his companion and housekeeper, complained of the 'dismal situation' of his Norfolk parsonage, 'nothing to be seen, and little or no visiting, or being visited, etc.'[26] The Rev. William Jones was surprised to find that his wife and daughters actually liked taking boarders and had no wish to give up the practice when his financial circumstances improved: 'It keeps their life from stagnating', he wrote.[27] Mrs Grant was worried from the start lest her town-bred sister should be bored at Mansfield parsonage in the winter; and Mary was indeed bored whenever the rain confined her to the house.[28] Even Mrs Austen, who loved the country when she was young, succumbed to nervous illnesses once her children were grown up and decided that she must remove to Bath. Jane Austen seems, in fact, to have known a large number of hypochondriacal parsons' wives, whose condition was possibly exacerbated by their feeling of isolation. There was her godfather's wife, Mrs Cooke, who had to have her daughter with her all the time. The vicar of Godmersham, Mr Whitfield, was kept in a constant state of worry by a sickly wife. Harriot Bridges' brother Edward, vicar of Lenham, suffered even more from a wife who dragged him off to Ramsgate for the whole of the summer, causing him to have to commute to his parish at weekends: 'She is a poor Honey,' Jane wrote, 'the sort of woman who gives me the idea of being determined never to be well – & who likes her spasms & nervousness & the consequence they give her, better than anything else.'[29]

A far-seeing woman would also have to bear in mind that on the death of a clergyman husband (an event likely to occur sooner rather than later if he were elderly to start with) she would lose not only her breadwinner but the roof over her head. Among the social classes that Jane Austen dealt with, this double fate was shared only by widows such as Mrs Dashwood, whose manor house was inherited by a son unable or unwilling to accommodate his mother. The church made no provision, financial or otherwise, for clergy widows. The patron of a benefice expected the incumbent to live up to his income; unless a wife had private means salted away she could well be in some financial distress after her husband's death. Mrs Austen's income, even when topped up by subsidies from her four sons, amounted to no more than £460 a year – a small sum when Mrs Dashwood and her daughters considered themselves hard pressed to manage with £500. The Austens in Bath soon found themselves moving from pleasant apartments in Green Park Buildings to cheap lodgings in Tib Street, which Mrs Austen regarded as disreputable. Even so her troubles were not as great as those of many clergy widows, for she had given up the vicarage at Steventon of her own accord a few years earlier. It was Jane who had felt the hurt of seeing James eager to get them out of their old home, and of having to sell her books and her piano in order to move into lodgings. She would fully have understood the distress of the vicar's wife in the parish next to William Jones's, whose husband died in harness leaving her with three unmarried daughters and little money. 'How must their hearts droop at exchanging their present large, convenient, beautiful house for a cottage', Jones wrote. 'A rectory, or a vicarage house, is certainly but a caravanseray; for it frequently exchanges its inhabitants.'[30] In these circumstances the husband's patron was seldom willing to help. When the Rev. Noyes Lloyd died in 1789 his patron, the Earl of Craven, was steadily drinking himself to death. It was thanks to George Austen that Mrs Lloyd and her two unmarried daughters were provided with a temporary home at the parsonage at Deane.[31]

The most impoverished characters Jane Austen introduces into her novels are Mrs Bates, the widow of a former vicar of Highbury, and her unmarried daughter. The whole of Highbury society conspires to enable them to keep up appearances, living as they do in a 'very moderate sized apartment' up a dark, narrow stairway in someone else's house.[34] Mr Knightley, chiding Emma Woodhouse for a breach of civility towards Miss Bates, describes her in his straightforward way as poor. 'She has sunk from the comforts she was born to; and if she live to old age, must probably sink more.'[32] If Jane Austen had needed a single model for such a person, she might have found one in Miss Benn, sister to the rector of Farringdon, who lived in Chawton. The neighbourhood rallied around her as that of Highbury rallied around the Bateses. Jane reported in 1813 to Cassandra, who was staying at Steventon:

> As I know Mary is interested in her not being neglected by her neighbours, pray tell her that Miss B. dined last Wednesday at Mr Papillon's – on Thursday with Capt and Mrs Clement – Friday here. Saturday with Mrs Digweed, & Sunday with the Papillons again.[34]

Jane suspected that something of the same kind was beginning to happen to her and her mother when they were alone together in Bath:

> Our tea and sugar will last a great while. I think we are just the kind of people & party to be treated about among our relations; we cannot be supposed to be very rich.[35]

Thanks to the provision by Edward of a rent-free house at Chawton, they were at least in no danger of being driven into the kind of hovel that Miss Benn lived in.[36]

If these were some of the considerations on the woman's side, what of the man's? What might a clergyman be looking for in a wife? Of the seven representatives of the profession who get engaged in Jane Austen's novels, only one, Mr Elton, is greatly concerned about wealth. Of the four already married, Dr Grant is the only one likely to have regarded it as a major consideration. Elton and Grant are not supposed to be very admirable characters but they are not wholly despicable either; nor was it at the time considered amiss, even in a clergyman, to give some thought to the lady's fortune. Mr Knightley regarded it as a point in favour of Elton, rather than against, that he was not likely to make an 'imprudent match'. 'He knows the value of a good income as well as anybody', he said. 'Elton may talk sentimentally, but he will act rationally.'[37] Money was not in itself a thing to be ashamed of. Even the Evangelicals realized that a clergyman's wife with a good dowry could free her husband from many a financial worry and enable him to concentrate on his work. Hannah More, in her novel *Coelebs*, listed as the first of many valuable contributions made by Mrs Barlow, the wife of the Evangelical parson featured in the story, the fact that she brought her husband 'a considerable fortune' and thereby greatly enhanced his power of doing good. Even to Jane Austen, Elton's fault was not that he married a wealthy women but that she turned out to be vulgar.

A parson's wife remained a part of neighbourhood society whatever she was like. Even a vulgar one could give a certain amount of satisfaction, if only to the gossips. The wife of the Rev. Charles Powlett was 'discovered to be everything that the Neighbourhood could wish her, silly & cross as well as extravagant'.[38] One who was approved could enhance her husband's position a good deal by sharing the interests of her fellow housewives. Women were expected to like flowers, as Henry Tilney pointed out to Catherine Morland, and much exchanging of seeds and roots of plants went on in country neighbourhoods (Miss Benn was given mignonette seeds by four different people).[39] Few women did their own digging like Mrs Austen but, generally speaking, the flower beds in a garden of any size were regarded as the woman's domain. She might also show an interest in the fruit in a kitchen garden and order the movement of potted plants from the greenhouse to the verandah – a matter of much concern to Mrs Grant.[40]

A wife who could entertain visitors graciously was an asset, though housekeeping to any standard was not easy in a village, as Mrs Grant pointed out to her sister from London.[41] Not only were butchers a rarity and poulterers virtually unknown; cooks capable of serving anything but the homeliest of meals and servants capable of waiting at table were hard to come by. The Austens at Steventon frequently had to make do with charwomen coming in daily: 'John Steevens' wife undertakes our purification', wrote Jane on 27 October 1798. 'She does not look as if anything she touched would ever be clean, but who knows?' They were fond of 'Nanny', who had been with them a long time and done everything from cooking to combing Jane's hair, but when they were about to leave Steventon and Jane tried to think of a suitable position for her, the best she could suggest was that of maid-of-all-work to Lucy Lefroy, newly married to the Rev. Henry Rice: 'Mrs H. Rice's place would be very likely to do for her', she wrote. 'It is not many, as she is herself aware, that she is qualified for.' Unmarried women, who were more mobile than someone like Nanny with a husband working in the area, could look further afield for better-paid posts in gentry houses. James's wife at Deane employed a young girl from Ashe to be her 'scrub', but although the girl had never been out to service before, and James doubted whether she would be 'strong enough' for the place, she very soon 'jilted' Mary and hired herself elsewhere. Problems of this kind were naturally a frequent topic of conversation amongst women whilst awaiting the entry of the men-folk after dinner, but a line had to be drawn: Mrs Elton confirmed the neighbourhood's poor opinion of her when she reported the views of her housekeeper concerning Mr Knightley's Mrs Hodges, thus revealing that she herself gossiped with her servants.[42]

The position of parson's wife had come into being with the Reformation. In the Thirty-Second of its Thirty-Nine Articles of Religion the Church of England rejected celibacy as a necessary qualification for the clergy:

> Bishops, Priests, and Deacons are not commanded by God's law, either to vow the estate of the single life, or to abstain from marriage: therefore it is lawful also for them, as for all other Christian men, to marry at their own discretion, as they shall judge the same to serve better to godliness . . .

'Serving better to godliness' by no means meant that the parson's wife was expected to pursue an independent ministry: even in Jane Austen's day the typical parson's wife of the Victorian era – teaching in Sunday School, running Bible classes and organizing women's societies – was still a long way off. Hannah More's exemplary Mrs Barlow was a pious woman but she was described as attentive to the *bodies* of the parishioners as distinct from their *souls*, which presumably meant that she distributed charity and medicines to the needy and practised her teaching abilities only on her own children.[43] It would nevertheless seem to have been obvious that a clergyman needed a wife who at the very least attended church regularly, accepted its doctrine and strove in some measure to carry out its teachings. An eighteenth-century clergyman was more fortunate than his modern counterpart in being able to rely on a basic acceptance of religion among the classes of womenfolk he was likely to meet. Edmund Bertram was singularly unlucky in becoming attached to a woman like Mary Crawford: it is understandable that he could not believe her cynicism to be as deeply engrained as she made out. Only occasionally can a clergyman have found himself in so anguished a quandary as the Rev. William Jones, who when newly ordained found himself attracted to a lady who gave no thought to religion. She was charming and beautiful, and was said to be wealthy, 'But what am I doing?' he asked the pages of his journal.

> Am I, as they call it, in love? With what? with my own folly and, it may be, my own misery. I fear there is something very mean and base in my attachment to my present object. She seems to be an utter stranger to God; and yet I fondly think I could be happy with her. But how can two travel together, except they be agreed? Were I (as I now think happy enough) to marry her, what distress might it not occasion? the more I loved her, the more would it pierce my soul to think that I was embracing in my bosom one who, perhaps, must be after this life everlastingly separated from me. With respect to the training of children, if we had any, and the management of other parts of our family, how distinctly opposite must our sentiments be! . . . Is it not time to awake? When I consider matters soberly, I must needs be ensured of enjoying more true happiness in marriage with a pious woman, tho' possessed not of a farthing, than with a graceless, gay, dissipated lady, who has a million a year at her command. Guide me, O my heavenly Father!

He ultimately married a woman whose principles he greatly admired but of whose sharp tongue he stood in considerable awe.[44]

In addition to a general sympathy with his religious outlook, a sensible man might well wish for someone intelligent enough to supply him with companionship in his country parish. In respect of education, parsons' daughters were not always a safe bet. George Austen was lucky in that his wife, Cassandra Leigh, came from a particularly academic family: what kind of formal education she had received we do not know, but she prided herself on having inherited the native intelligence which secured her father an Oxford Fellowship when so young he was nicknamed 'Chick' Leigh, and gave her uncle, the Master of Balliol, so sharp a tongue that his witticisms were remembered in the university long afterwards.[45] Her letters are written in a precise, epigrammatic style, and she remained interested throughout life in reading both novels and serious works. Many parsons' daughters were educated by their mothers at home, where the standard was often that of Mrs Morland, whose daughter Catherine by the age of ten had learnt a few poems by heart, read a few moral tales, gained a smattering of French and reached a modest proficiency in writing and accounts – after which, she was left to her own devices. Jane Austen implied that for a sensible and intelligent girl this was not necessarily a bad thing. Catherine went on to read a certain amount of history and a few extracts from literature, among the many Gothick novels that absorbed the greater part of her attention, and showed signs of improving as time went on.[46] Some girls improved a great deal, others not at all. The Lloyd sisters, daughters of the Rev. Noyes Lloyd of Enborne, received rather less education than Catherine Morland: their mother taught them to read, but only by guiding them through the Psalms and through daily portions of Scripture – no other books were thought of. Peripatetic masters came to the house to teach them writing and arithmetic. They learnt no French. The result could hardly have been predicted, for Martha Lloyd became interested in reading and looked forward to discussing books with her friend Jane Austen, whereas it was the latter's view that Mary Lloyd, who became her sister-in-law, never willingly read a book in the whole of her life.[47]

In wealthy homes such as Mansfield Park and Rosings (and in Jane Austen's actual experience Godmersham) a governess was usually employed to give the younger children an education, after which much emphasis was placed on taking girls to London to study music and drawing with 'masters'. Jane tended to regard the latter as at best unnecessarily expensive and at worst fraudulent.[48] By comparison she was only mildly critical of the fashion among gentry families, and others which aspired to gentility, of sending girls away to school. It was possibly Mrs Austen's determination to keep up with her wealthier relations, as much as her need to get her daughters out of the way, which prompted her to send Jane and Cassandra for two brief spells of time to school. They were not happy with Mrs Cawley at Oxford and when, after being taken by their preceptress to Southampton, they almost succumbed to an epidemic (a common hazard of the times) they were brought home. The next experiment was happier. The Abbey School at Reading was run by a woman who had been given by her employers the name of Mrs La Tournelle but whose real name was Sarah Hackitt. She was pleasant, easy-going and mildly eccentric. Her job was to see that the girls were properly fed and looked after, whilst two or three young teachers, assisted by visiting masters from the nearby grammar school, gave lessons. The girls were taught writing, spelling, French, needlework, drawing, music and dancing, but the regime was not exacting. Provided they attended lessons in the morning, they were free in the afternoons to roam around the charming old building and its grounds and to laugh and chat amongst themselves. Jane remembered her days there with affectionate amusement: 'I could die of laughter at it, as they used to say at school', she once wrote to Cassandra.[49]

She and her sister stayed there for possibly eighteen months – Jane was back home for good by the time she was eleven; but it was common for girls from more affluent homes to remain well into their teens and return home, like Mrs Jennings's daughter, with landscapes which they had embroidered in silks 'in proof of . . . having spent seven years at a great school in town to some effect'.[50] Mrs Musgrove's daughters, we are told, had 'brought from a school at Exeter the usual stock of accomplishments', and it is tempting to wonder what sort of a wife Henrietta Musgrove was likely to have made for the scholarly Charles Hayter in his country parsonage. Jane Austen would doubtless have treated such a question much as she treated that arising from the match between Henrietta's sister and the studious Captain Benwick: 'they would soon grow more alike'.[51] Until they did so, Henrietta's skills in petit point and water colours would at least enable her to converse amiably with gentlemen's daughters in the neighbourhood, most of whom could be relied upon to have had the same sort of education. Her ability to play the harp, in particular, might have created the right impression in the more fashionable quarters (Fanny Knight at Godmersham played the harp). Jane Austen had mixed feelings about musical accomplishments but when she heard that the new curate's wife at Godmersham was 'musical' she at least hoped that it would make her acceptable to Fanny as a friend.[52]

A clergyman who married a gentlewoman had reason to take care that she would not require him to live above his income. James Austen's choice of partner for his first marriage was fraught with problems. James had always been susceptible to elegant, aristocratic ladies, and Anne Mathew was the daughter of General and Lady Jane Mathew, sister to the Duke of Ancaster. Jane remembered Anne as a pretty woman with 'large dark eyes and a good deal of nose';[53] but she was thirty-three when James offered for her and she perhaps saw him as her last chance of matrimony. Her family, however, thought that she had married beneath her: it was perhaps for this reason that James as curate of Deane embarked on a ridiculously extravagant lifestyle. Anne had in fact very little money – a mere £100 a year to add to James's £200. The two of them nevertheless spent £200 on refurbishing their small house; Anne kept her own 'close carriage' for travelling about the neighbourhood and James indulged the passion for hunting he had acquired at Oxford and bought a pack of harriers. Where this would have led them can only be conjectured, for Anne died suddenly after only three years of matrimony and was buried under the chancel of Steventon church, where she was commemorated with a fashionable stone tablet on the south wall. James was left disconsolate with a little daughter, Anna, two years old. The General remained interested in his granddaughter to the day of his death, but the money he had hoped to settle on her went to pay a debt he owed to the Treasury and James suffered a good deal of frustration in vain attempts to recover it.[54]

This moral tale increases the general air of good sense in the advice which Lady Catherine de Bourgh too haughtily gave to her protégé:

> Mr Collins, you must marry. A clergyman like you must marry. – Chuse properly, chuse a gentlewoman for *my* sake; and for your *own*, let her be an active, useful sort of person, not brought up high, but able to make a small income go a good way. This is my advice.[55]

He could not have done better than choose Charlotte Lucas.

Even when it was not necessary 'to make a small income go a good way', Mrs Norris was probably right in saying that 'a fine lady in a country parsonage was quite out of place'. She was referring cattily to Mrs Grant, who in order to cater for her husband's gourmet tastes gave her cook as large a salary as they paid at the manor house and was seldom seen in the kitchen quarters herself. The result was that she had too little to do, as we are told later in the novel:

> Mrs Grant, having by this time run through the usual resources of ladies residing in the country without a family of children; having more than filled her favourite sitting-room with pretty furniture, and made a choice collection of plants and poultry – was very much in want of some variety at home.

Welcoming her half-sister and half-brother into her house for as long as they wished to stay, she eagerly set about the task of match-making for them in the neighbourhood.[56]

These are not problems that would have arisen at any earlier time, the Reformation notwithstanding. Henry VIII strongly disapproved of the idea of clergy being allowed to marry, fearing that they would have more children than they could support. His son Edward VI allowed them to marry whilst making it plain that he preferred them to remain celibate; a quarter of the clergy took advantage of his grudging permission to break their vows, only to find when Catholic Mary came to the throne that they must either hide their wives or find themselves dispossessed of their livings. Elizabeth I refused to reinstate those who had been deprived and, although she winked at the sudden appearance of 'hidden' wives and turned a blind eye upon further clergy marriages, she made clear her disapproval in principle and refused to establish clergy marriage by law. Under these doubtful circumstances, no gentleman was going to encourage his daughter to marry a clergyman.[57] The advent of the Stuarts hardly brought more certainty as to the future of Protestantism, and it was not until the Hanoverian dynasty was safely installed that the prospects for married clergy began to improve. By March 1817 the Rev. Benjamin Newton of Wath could write confidently in his diary:

> It has occurred to me that one of the strongest parts of our Constitution, at least one which is the greatest security against revolutions, is that which merges all the younger sons of the Nobles into the mass of the people, by which the Nobles and Commoners are linked in the strongest possible manner together, and the marriage of the clergy not allowed in Catholic countries cements that body to the laity and in the present times to the most powerful and respectable part of the laity, the great merchants or the country gentlemen from whose families the clergy and their wives (with very few exceptions) are now almost universally taken.[58]

James Edward Austen-Leigh – writing in 1869 when he was himself a clergyman, married and in fairly affluent circumstances – believed that the social standing of parsons' wives was higher in his own Victorian times than when his grandfather was rector of Steventon in the 1760s and 1770s.[59] He could not have been thinking of the social class from which the wives came; for his own wife, though a niece of Mrs Chute of The Vyne, could hardly have outshone his grandmother when it came to lineage, Mrs Austen having been descended from the same Lord Mayor of London as the titled Leighs of Stoneleigh and named Cassandra in honour of her great-aunt Cassandra, Duchess of Chandos. He was thinking, rather, of the way of life they adopted when they were married. 'It is probable that their way of life differed a little from ours, and would have appeared more homely', he wrote. His step-sister Anna Lefroy had told him how their grandmother used to sit sewing and mending in the little parlour to which visitors were admitted at Steventon parsonage. He had seen for himself the practical concern for household affairs which she handed on to her elder daughter at Chawton. It is doubtful, however, whether she would have regarded these practices as a sign that she had down-graded herself. She remained proud of her aristocratic cut of countenance, long-nosed and handsome rather than pretty, and she retained a number of lordly characteristics such as an unsentimental attitude to her children. In her day, a great lady equally with the parson's wife was interested in household affairs. Neither of them did the actual cooking (Mrs Austen employed a cook even when she was widowed) but both prided themselves on their needlework, which might take such useful forms as shirt-making: when Jane visited her brother Edward and his wife at their first home in Rowling she found the whole party of ladies engaged in making Edward's shirts.[60] Mrs Austen's sewing and mending in front of visitors was as much a sign of her aristocratic disdain for appearances as of her need to make ends meet. Later, when useless embroidery was the only stitching that could elegantly be carried on in company, Jane and Cassandra tried to break their mother of former habits but could never be sure of success: 'Mrs Armstrong sat darning a pair of stockings the whole of my visit', Jane reported disapprovingly to Cassandra after calling on that old lady at Lyme, 'But do not mention this at home, lest a warning should act as an example.'[61]

Mary Lloyd, who succeeded her mother-in-law as mistress of Steventon parsonage, was much more concerned about appearances, even when her husband James was merely a curate at Deane. This may have been due in some degree to personality. Although Mary had her own aristocratic forbears (her grandfather was the Honourable Charles Craven, youngest brother of the second earl) she had none of her mother-in-law's self-confidence; she was always jealous of James's first wife and conscious that he had once wanted to marry his cousin, the widowed Comtesse de Feuillide. There are signs that it was also a trend of the times, however, for she continually cried out poverty, as though she regarded her various extravagances as necessities rather than as luxuries. She attempted in a number of ways to put on a show. Mrs Austen had been endlessly hospitable to members of the family but there are no reports of her entertaining widely in the neighbourhood; Mary in 1799 announced that she and James were going to 'enter more into dinner parties' and Jane was invited to Deane to help entertain Mr Holder of Ashe Park and the Biggs of Manydown. At about the same time Mary acquired a closed carriage and a five-year-old horse, 'used to draw, and thought very pretty'. When her second baby was born she christened one of the bedrooms at Deane 'the nursery' and employed a nursemaid especially to take the child out for airings; earlier, she had been found borrowing sewing patterns from Godmersham that her little boy might be dressed like his wealthier cousins.[62]

Jane was not always polite about Mary's efforts. Visiting her after the birth of her first baby she wrote critically:

> Mary does not manage matters in such a way as to make me want to lay in myself. She is not tidy enough in her appearance; she has no dressing-gown to sit up in; her curtains are all too thin, and things are not in that comfort and style about her which are necessary to make her situation an enviable one. Elizabeth was really a pretty object with her nice clean cap put on so tidily and her dress so uniformly white and orderly.[63]

It was perhaps a little unfair to compare Mary with her sister-in-law at Godmersham, who had everything that money could buy; yet Mary's two sisters, neither of whom was wealthy, managed to carry things off better: Jane thought Martha elegant and Eliza (wife to the Rev. Fulwar Fowle) really beautiful.[64] Mary went on trying. She moved almost too eagerly into the larger accommodation afforded by Steventon parsonage, several years before James secured the tithes, and at once began increasing the number of her servants. When James received an annuity from his Aunt Leigh-Perrot and announced that he was going to keep two more horses on the strength of it, far from trying to dissuade him from the extravagance, she asked him to choose two that could carry ladies.[65] In 1811 she agreed to have her portrait painted although (unlike her sister-in-law at Godmersham, who had sat for Cosway) she had to make do with an itinerant artist who appeared in the neighbourhood and doubtless did the job for a small fee and a couple of meals in the kitchen. In the same year she surprised her mother-in-law by purchasing a pair of coloured shoes.[66]

In spite of all this finery, she retained her mother-in-law's interest in the dairy. Earlier in the century it had not been uncommon for the parson's wife, like Fielding's Mrs Trulliber, to help with milking the cows and churning the butter. While there is no evidence that Mrs Austen performed such menial tasks, she certainly supervised the work and could discuss dairy matters with the frankness of any farmer's wife.

> My little Alderney . . . turns out tolerably well, and makes more butter than we use, and I have just bought another of the same sort, but as her calf is but just gone, cannot say what she will be good for yet . . .

she wrote to her sister in 1770; by 1773 she was describing herself as 'worth a bull and six cows' as well as 'jackies and ducks and chicken'. In retirement she was interested in receiving such news as that of the calving of a cow at Steventon and in discussing with Mary the sharing out of the pork when a pig was killed.[67]

Jane Austen in her earliest novels more or less took it for granted that a parson's wife was involved in farming. There is no evidence that Elinor

Dashwood was at all interested in such matters before her marriage, yet she had not long been established in the parsonage at Delaford when she was looking for better pasturage for her cows. Charlotte Lucas, brought up to be a gentlewoman, acquired upon marriage to Mr Collins the care of cows and poultry. Even Mrs Grant kept poultry as a pastime.[68] It was an occupation that had its advantages in integrating the parson's wife into a wider cross-section of the female society of the neighbourhood than the social elite, for women of all levels were interested in the production of food. Dairy farming connected the parson's wife with the lady of the manor, for whom it was traditionally a source of pin-money; with the retired gentlewoman, such as Mrs Weston in *Emma*, and Mrs Clement at Chawton who kept a cow as a hobby;[69] and also with the farmer's wife, for whom it was work.

Not all parsons' wives were passionately absorbed by farming. Mrs Lefroy at Ashe seems to have had quite different priorities. It is a moot point as to what extent Jane Austen in *Mansfield Park* deliberately tried to break away from the farming image and present Fanny Price as a better type of parson's wife. It is difficult to imagine Fanny engaged with poultry, or supervising apple-picking like Mrs Fowle of Kintbury; her role as suggested by Jane Austen was to be a gently moralizing one. She would strengthen Edmund's moral purposes and supply the shrewd assessment of the people around him which he clearly lacked. Without appearing to assert herself, she would be an influence for good among the people who got to know her well, as Henry Crawford realized she would have been upon him. It was a role in keeping with the mission Jane Austen had outlined for the clergyman himself: that of living quietly and influencing his neighbours by the example of his domestic life. It was not necessarily incompatible with a more practical approach provided the latter did not result in bustle. Fanny had always been quietly useful to Lady Bertram; Mrs Norris, by contrast, did her best 'to be in a bustle without having anything to bustle about, and . . . nothing was wanted but tranquillity and silence'. Interestingly, Mrs Austen thought Fanny insipid and was amused rather than irritated by Mrs Norris.[70]

In real life, Jane Austen never detailed any qualities that she regarded as essential in a parson's wife. She frowned on one or two instances of flightiness: on Eliza Fowle, after she was married, for wearing her cap too jauntily on the back of her head; on Lucy Rice, before she was married, for showing too much interest in army officers; on Charles Powlett's bride for appearing at a dinner party 'at once expensively & nakedly dressed'.[71] These were impish remarks rather than serious criticism. Few young women could have been flightier than her niece Anna, but it did not prevent Jane from hoping that Anna's husband would take Orders. She was more serious in her criticisms of her sister-in-law Mary for showing some of the faults she condemned in Mrs Norris: for pleading poverty when it was unjustified; for economizing sometimes to the point of meanness; for sententious and ill-judged opinions and for trying to organize everybody.[72] She never specifically related them to Mary's role as a parson's wife, however. Among the clergymen's wives that she knew, she wrote most admiringly of Catherine Bigg and Jane Buller, wife of the Rev. Richard Buller – in both cases because of their habitual air of calm composure.[73] It was a quality which she gave to Elinor Dashwood, prospective wife of the Rev. Edward Ferrars. She also appreciated the warmth and friendliness of Harriot Bridges and in *Mansfield Park* forgave Mrs Grant many failings on account of her 'temper to love and be loved'.[74]

In several of her early letters, Jane teased her sister Cassandra about the possibility of a future relationship with their old playmate, the Rev. James Digweed.[79] Cassandra had recently suffered the loss of her fiancé, and Jane's remarks now seem as misplaced as those of Mrs Jennings to Elinor Dashwood when the latter seemed doomed to spinsterhood. They were no doubt equally well-meant, as an attempt to encourage Cassandra to think positively of the future. Jane cannot seriously have believed that Digweed was in love with her sister, for she was at the same time reporting him to be interested in Jane Lyford. There can be no doubt, however, that she would have recommended Cassandra wholeheartedly as a parson's wife. She admired her sister enormously, not least for her organizing abilities. It was Cassandra who was in charge of the family's charitable efforts, Jane reporting to her on such matters when she was away. It was Cassandra who shared Mrs Austen's interest in farming, to the extent that from Chawton she wrote nostalgically to her cousin Philadelphia Walter:

> I quite envy you your farm; there is so much amusement and so many comforts attending a farm in the country that those who have once felt the advantages cannot easily forget them. We have not now so much as a cow.[76]

It was Cassandra who planted seeds in the garden and looked after the potted plants; Cassandra who was always in demand to assist when brothers' wives were having babies; Cassandra who took over the control of the household at Chawton with such apparent ease that Jane wondered how she found time to accomplish so many other things – for

Cassandra also emerges from the letters as a lively and intelligent woman, popular in the neighbourhood and sharing literary interests and artistic tastes with Jane. Her moral sense made her seem to Jane a model of proper behaviour, while her Christian faith remained staunch in every adversity. Although she had none of Fanny Price's saintly airs, she could hardly have failed to be an influence for good on all who knew her.

PRACTICAL AND FAMILIAR

SERMONS,

DESIGNED FOR

PAROCHIAL AND DOMESTIC INSTRUCTION.

By the Rev. EDWARD COOPER,

RECTOR OF HAMSTALL-RIDWARE AND OF YOXALL IN
THE COUNTY OF STAFFORD, AND LATE FELLOW
OF ALL-SOULS' COLLEGE, OXFORD.

VOL. I.

THE THIRTEENTH EDITION

LONDON:

PRINTED FOR T. CADELL, IN THE STRAND.

1824.

Sermons by Jane Austen's Evangelical cousin, which she greatly
disliked when they were first published in 1809, ran into many
editions in the course of the century.
(*Dr Williams's Library*)

Chapter 9

Manners and Morals

When Edmund Bertram referred to the clergy's control over 'religion and morals, and the manners which result from their influence', he was touching upon a subject which had been much discussed in England during Jane Austen's lifetime. 'Religion and morals' was assumed by the majority of Anglican clergymen (as distinct from the Evangelical minority) to be an undivided subject: it was the nature of the connection, if any, which existed between manners and morals that exercized most minds. Typically, therefore, it was this part of his statement that Edmund saw fit to enlarge upon.

If morals were the inner principles which distinguished right from wrong in the relationship between individual human beings, manners were the code of practice which governed the outward conduct of those relationships. In a society which attached supreme importance to direct personal contact, in all public affairs both national and local, it is not surprising that attention should have been paid to this code. 'Manners are more important than laws', Burke pointed out:

> The law touches us but here and there, and now and then. Manners are what vex and soothe us, corrupt or purify, exalt or debase, barbarize or refine us, by a constant, steady, uniform, insensible operation, like that of the air we breathe in. They give their whole form and colour to our lives.[1]

In accordance with this view, elaborate rituals were formulated and set forth in books of etiquette; gentlemanly conduct was defined in clubs and enforced by rigorous sanctions such as blackballing and duelling. But could any number of rules guarantee politeness in every situation? Was it not better to accept the principles that lay behind the rules rather than the rules themselves? Would not the most rigid of rules be likely to break down under provocation unless backed up by firm adherence to principle?

In 1787 William Wilberforce, dismayed by the debauchery he saw everywhere around him, believed that he could bring about an improvement in society by governing people's outward behaviour. 'God', he decided, 'has set before me as my object the reformation of manners.' Through his privileged access to the Archbishop of Canterbury he persuaded George III to issue a proclamation enjoining the enforcement of laws, already in existence but long in abeyance, against sabbath-breaking, swearing, drunkenness, licentious publications, unlicensed places of public amusement and the misuse of licensed places. He probably knew that this in itself was unlikely to have much effect: clergy had long been supposed to help the magistrates to enforce such injunctions but, apart from a few fanatics like Grimshaw of Haworth and Skinner of Camerton, there were few who did so. There are certainly no reports of George Austen or any of the clergy Jane Austen knew patrolling the lanes on a Sunday to make sure their parishioners were obeying the law.[2] However, it gave Wilberforce the opportunity to form a society (later known as the Vice and Immorality Society) to win open support from persons in high places for a campaign to promote the cause of good behaviour throughout the nation. 'I know that by regulating external conduct we do not change the hearts of men', he wrote to a friend,

> but even these are ultimately wrought upon by these means, and we should at least so far remove the obtrusiveness of temptation that it may not provoke the appetite which might otherwise be dormant.[3]

In the course of the next ten years, Wilberforce moved on from his original position. He decided that neither manners nor morals – neither rules nor principles – could be effective without the religious beliefs which lay at their foundation. In his *Practical View of the Prevailing System of Professed Christians in the Higher and Middle Classes of this Country Contrasted with Real Christianity* (1797) he attacked those who thought they could either cultivate 'amiable tempers' or lead 'useful lives' without wholehearted faith in Christ. In other words, men's relationship with God was more important, even as a starting-point, than their relationship with each other. Thereafter, Wilberforce felt it his duty to rebuke even the most casual acquaintances if their conversation or behaviour revealed the slightest lack of Christian fervour. We are assured by his immediate biographers that he lost none of his well-known charm of manner in the process. The same could not always be said of his followers: Jane Austen thought that her Evangelical cousin Edward Cooper was downright rude. Some Evangelicals even thought that they were under obligation to be so: Wilberforce himself was worried about his social graces, lest they were a sign that he lacked zeal.[4]

Meanwhile Hannah More had begun where Wilberforce left off. In her first book, *Thoughts on the Importance of the Manners of the Great to General Society* (1788), she denounced the lukewarm Christianity which she believed to be the practice of the majority of members of the upper classes – 'good kind of people, who live within the restraints of moral obligation and acknowledge the truth of the Christian religion', but who forget God most of the time. She warned against the belief that charitable works were sufficient to secure entry to the Kingdom of Heaven. She nevertheless deplored too much soul-searching. Once people had eradicated worldly considerations from their minds they must turn again to live in the world: love of Christ must show itself in love of others. This brought behaviour once more into the limelight – but not the codes of behaviour to be found in such works as Castiglione's *The Courtier*, Hannah More hastened to point out. Principles, she insisted, were more important than codes; the writings of St Paul produced finer gentlemen than the letters of Lord Chesterfield. At the back of Hannah More's mind, always, was the fear that polished manners could hide not only inadequate virtue but downright wickedness: the smooth villain of melodrama was forever lurking in the wings.[5]

Manners of the Great rapidly became one of the most widely read books of the time and anything written by the same author was thereby assured of publicity. Hannah More reached a position where her works, even if published anonymously, were easily recognized as hers and much discussed. Her ideas were common currency and Jane Austen could not have avoided being acquainted with them. She never admitted having read any of Hannah More's books: when Cassandra tried to interest her in *Coelebs in Search of a Wife* (1809) she wrote back: 'You have by no means raised my curiosity after Caleb' (she refused to believe that anyone could have called the hero of a novel Coeleb).

> My disinclination for it before was affected, but now it is real; I do not like the Evangelicals. Of course, I shall be delighted when I read it, like other people, but till I do I dislike it.

She regarded it as typical of the Miss Webbs, a trio of spinster ladies at Chawton whom she found particularly tiresome, that she should have

C Œ L E B S

IN SEARCH OF A WIFE.

COMPREHENDING

OBSERVATIONS

ON

DOMESTIC HABITS AND MANNERS, RELIGION
AND MORALS.

For not to know at large of things remote
From ufe, obfcure and fubtle, but to know
That which before us lies in daily life,
Is the prime wifdom.   MILTON.

IN TWO VOLUMES.

VOL. I.

LONDON:

PRINTED FOR T. CADELL AND W. DAVIES,
IN THE STRAND.
1808.

Title page to the first edition of Hannah More's novel, whose
hero Jane Austen insisted on calling 'Caleb'.
(*British Library*)

found them 'reading with delight Mrs H. More's recent publication' (probably *Practical Piety*) when she called on them in 1811.[6]

In spite of all this, Jane Austen's standpoint on manners and morals was not wholly different from that of Hannah More. Indeed she even included, in her last complete novel, a character whose deliberate hypocrisy could be said to fit exactly Hannah More's dark hints about men whose 'evil designs' were 'spangled over' with pleasing qualities.[7] Mr Elliot succeeds in presenting a gentlemanly appearance to almost everybody he meets: only the unusually perceptive Anne realizes from the start that there is something wrong with him.[8] In the earlier novels there are characters who, without being deliberately villainous, succeed in creating a fair amount of havoc; and all of them – Willoughby, Wickham, Frank Churchill, Henry and Mary Crawford – are noted for a charm of manner which turns out to be in excess of their moral principles. Unlike Mr Elliot they do not have to work at it: their charm comes naturally to them. It gets them a long way. Jane Austen was not particularly concerned to bring them to their deserts: only Willoughby comes to an unhappy end. Her aim was to show that people are often judged by their manners and that manners are often misleading. In each of the characters concerned there are tell-tale signs of unworthiness: Willoughby's too-ready opinions; Wickham's improper disclosures; Henry Crawford's flirtations with an engaged woman; Mary Crawford's disrespectful remarks about her uncle; Frank Churchill's lack of atten-tion to his stepmother. These are not widely noticed by their acquain-tance: the truth only becomes apparent when some tougher yardstick, such as loyalty, integrity, self-sacrifice or self-discipline, is employed instead of mere charm to judge them by. Jane Austen was aware that circumstances do not always make such yardsticks immediately available – in such cases she recommended that judgement should be reserved. Elinor Dashwood's caution with regard to Willoughby, and Fanny Price's reluctance to enter unreservedly into friendship with Mary Crawford, may not seem very endearing characteristics but they are proved to have been wiser than Marianne's effusive acceptance and Edmund Bertram's naive susceptibility. Mr Weston in *Emma* is criticized for being on friendly terms with everybody he meets. In real life Jane Austen wrote warily of Miss Armstrong, a woman she met at Lyme and found on the whole to be sensible and engaging but who seemed 'to like other people too easily'.[9]

If the dangerous characters were those whose demeanour gave a false impression of goodness, hardly less reprehensible in Jane Austen's eyes were those who displayed elegant manners with the sole purpose of

advertising their social status. Sir Walter Elliot and his eldest daughter
Elizabeth are the most obvious case in point: they pay meticulous
attention to every rule of outward behaviour in order to be known as
'models of good breeding'. Having always moved in gentry circles they
do it very well: even Anne can seldom find occasion to blush for them.
(Jane Austen took it for granted that persons of lowlier station were
unlikely to achieve the proper style. Although their gaffes were sometimes entertaining, as in the case of Mrs Britton of Godmersham with
her 'would-be genteel manners', they could also be extremely irksome,
like those of Mrs Elton, whose efforts to achieve well-bred ease of
manner resulted in vulgar familiarity.)[10] The Elliots prove, however,
that even the most successfully polished behaviour has unhappy results
if it is unaccompanied by genuine good feeling. It fails to put other
people at their ease and cannot, therefore, be regarded as constituting
true refinement. Sir Walter and his daughter may know how to enter a
drawing-room in precise conformity to etiquette, but their entry invariably casts 'a general chill' over the assembled company. Lady Middleton
of *Sense and Sensibility* may give superbly stylish dinner parties, but she
can contribute nothing to her guests' enjoyment because she lacks
interest in them and has therefore nothing to say to them. Another
drawback was that decorum may break down under provocation. Emma
Woodhouse, whose chief pride is in commanding all the social graces
appropriate to a great lady, finds to her own horror that on one
particularly trying occasion she proves to be capable of outrageous
behaviour towards Miss Bates, an elderly gentlewoman whose stricken
fortunes make her as deserving of consideration as she is vulnerable to
insult.

In *Mansfield Park* Jane Austen seemed anxious to make it clear once
and for all that she too, like Hannah More, could not approve of what
the latter called 'mere manners'. Julia and Maria Bertram have been
taught all the rules of good behaviour and none of the principles which
would have made those rules congenial to them. Julia accepts the
obligation to walk politely with Mrs Rushworth when she encounters her
in the garden at Sotherton, but 'the want of that higher species of self-
command, that just consideration for others, that principle of right
which had not formed any essential part of her education made her
miserable under it'. Maria's feelings of frustration are vented in
annoyance when she finds locked gates between the formal garden and
the freer world beyond: 'I cannot get out, as the starling said,' she
complains to Henry Crawford.[11] When, eventually, the two young

women abandon all restraint and both elope, their father realizes that there has been some 'direful mistake' in their upbringing:

> He feared that principle, active principle, had been wanting, that they had never been properly taught to govern their inclinations and tempers, by that sense of duty which can alone suffice . . . To be distinguished for elegance and accomplishments – the authorised object of their youth – could have had no useful influence that way, no moral effect on the mind. He had meant them to be good, but his cares had been directed to the understanding and manners, not the disposition; and of the necessity of self-denial and humility, he feared they had never heard from any lips that could profit them.[12]

Yet Jane Austen was by no means ready to underestimate the importance of good manners. In the absence of good feeling, good behaviour was better than nothing. In an earlier novel, *Pride and Prejudice*, she had noted with approval the training in courtesy which enabled Sir William Lucas (who had been received at St James's) to listen with forbearance to Mrs Bennet's impertinent remarks on his daughter's engagement; in a later novel, *Emma*, she was to express equal appreciation of the education in civility which Miss Woodhouse received from the genteel Miss Taylor, an education without which Emma would undoubtedly have behaved throughout her early adult life like the spoilt child that she really was. Jane Austen herself was always likely to be put out by rowdy behaviour: she could fully sympathize with the feelings of Fanny Price, whose dismay at the unbridled conduct which reigned in her parents' home at Portsmouth caused her to exaggerate the charms of Mansfield Park:

> At Mansfield, no sounds of contention, no raised voice, no abrupt bursts, no tread of violence was ever heard; all proceeded in a regular course of cheerful orderliness . . . If tenderness could be ever supposed wanting, good sense and good breeding supplied its place . . . Here [at Portsmouth] everybody was noisy, every voice was loud . . . Whatever was wanted was hallooed for, and the servants hallooed out their excuses from the kitchen. The doors were in constant banging, the stairs were never at rest, nothing was done without clatter, nobody sat still, and nobody could command attention when they spoke. In a review of the two houses, as they appeared to her before the end of a week, Fanny was tempted to apply to them Dr Johnson's celebrated judgment as to matrimony and celibacy, and say, that though Mansfield Park might have some pains, Portsmouth could have no pleasures.[13]

Fortunately, manners and morals were not such separate issues as matrimony and celibacy; to Jane Austen both had their value. She is prepared, though with some reluctance, to see the minor rules of

etiquette ignored when there is genuine good feeling: Mr and Mrs
Harville, for instance, can be allowed to hold a dinner party in rooms so
cramped that an invitation to attend might normally be regarded as an
insult; but on the whole she prefers even the most superficial rules to be
kept. When Admiral Croft, in spite of his good nature, seems in danger
of causing unnecessary embarrassment by his unconventional behaviour, his wife is quite right to check him.[14] If there are exceptional
reasons why a rule should be broken, as when Catherine Morland
knocks on General Tilney's door without previous announcement by the
servant, well and good; but otherwise the rules are better observed than
not.

Certainly there seemed to Jane Austen to be good sense in obeying the
conventions which governed relationships between the sexes, for these
were based on society's experience of the pitfalls involved. She was
always critical of parents, however well-meaning, if like the Musgroves
they failed to point out these rules to their young people. Both Captain
Wentworth and the two Musgrove daughters should have been told that
it was not proper for him to be receiving attentions from both of the
young ladies at once, since he could not possibly be true to them both.[15]
Jane Austen's novels are love stories; it is with the conventions surrounding courtship that they are necessarily much concerned.

Jane Austen had few old-maidish inhibitions. A certain lack of confidence in her own personal attributes made her reluctant to frizz her hair
in the latest fashion and caused her to rejoice when she heard that low-
cut dresses were no longer the mode, but she was fully prepared to see
young ladies setting out to be admired.[16] The extremely modest dress
which Fanny Price chose to wear at her first ball is more reminiscent of
the attire favoured by the pious Mr Stanley's daughters in *Coelebs* than of
anything Jane Austen ever selected.[17] Fanny's distress at hearing herself
praised also demonstrated a degree of self-effacement which Jane
Austen did not normally expect: the more natural reaction, in her view,
was the humble pleasure which Catherine Morland took in overhearing
two unknown gentlemen pronounce her to be a pretty girl. She was glad
when she heard from Cassandra that the seventeen-year-old Harriot
Bridges 'goes on now as young ladies of seventeen ought to do, admired
and admiring'.[18]

It went without saying that girls should not be allowed to think of
nothing but young men, as Lydia Bennet had done ever since a militia
regiment was quartered near her home. Again, parents were often to
blame: in Lydia's case it was her mother who had encouraged her to fill
her head with vain and frivolous thoughts from the moment she left the

schoolroom.[19] Alternatively, the fault might lie with some foolish companion such as Isabella Thorpe, who transposed into real life the
conventions gleaned from romantic novels: in *Northanger Abbey* Jane
Austen was as critical as Hannah More of the fashion for confiding in an
'intimate friend'.[20] The most sensible of young women might need to be
warned against paying particular attention to any one gentleman until
he had proposed marriage. This did not mean that a young lady could
not dance more than once with the same partner (Isabella Thorpe's
reference to some supposed rule of this kind was designed merely to
draw attention to James Morland's interest in her); but she must not
throw all restraint to the winds, as Marianne Dashwood did with Willoughby. 'When he was present', we read,

> she [Marianne] had no eyes for anyone else. Everything he did was right,
> everything he said was clever. If dancing formed the amusement of the night,
> they were partners for half the time; and when obliged to separate for a couple
> of dances, were careful to stand together and scarcely spoke a word to anybody
> else. Such conduct made them of course most exceedingly laughed at; but
> ridicule could not shame, and seemed hardly to provoke them.[21]

Reading between the lines of an early letter, it seems that Jane Austen
herself was once warned by her elder sister against 'exposing herself' at
dances by being 'too particular' in her attentions to Tom Lefroy, a visitor
at his aunt's house at Ashe. She had taken it in good part – unlike
Marianne, who, when Elinor ventured to suggest 'the propriety of some
self-command', could see no good reason to restrain feelings which were
not in themselves reprehensible.[22] The conventions had been formulated, however, to safeguard women from the pain of becoming attached
to men who were not serious in their intentions and from becoming
laughing-stocks by allowing themselves to be taken in: on both counts
Marianne would have done well to pay heed to Elinor's advice.

For gentlemen also there were rules of courtship, designed to safeguard them from being trapped into matrimony against their better
judgement. The self-assured Captain Wentworth, believing that he
needed no such protection, found that his persistent attentions to Louisa
Musgrove caused his friends to assume that he intended to marry her;
he would have been in honour bound to do so had he not been rescued
by an extraordinary turn of events. Because it was inadvisable for a man
to show a greater degree of interest than he felt, it was regarded as
altogether improper for him to do so: Frank Churchill was wrong to
shower attentions upon Emma Woodhouse when he was secretly

engaged to someone else, even though she was not misled by them. Colonel Fitzwilliam behaved more properly when he prefaced his frequent visits to Elizabeth Bennet with an indication that he was in no position to marry her. Persons with easier, or what Jane Austen called 'lively', manners in regard to relationships between the sexes were in her view unlikely to be moral: 'a family of lively, agreeable manners, and probably of morals and discretion to suit' was how she categorized the fashionable friends in whose company at Twickenham Maria Bertram was led astray.[23]

Relevant as the conventions surrounding romance and courtship may have been to the novels, the subject of manners and morals was too important to Jane Austen for her to confine her opinions to the one context. In more general terms her ideas were in line with those of Edmund Burke, who throughout his career defended manners as an essential component of civilized existence. For one thing they expressed, in his view, the accumulated wisdom of the ages, which he believed to be more trustworthy than individual judgement.[24] Likewise Jane Austen, although she could imagine an exceptionally perceptive person such as Anne Elliot being able to do without convention, recognized the value of the 'old world courtesy' which enabled even the feeble-minded Mr Woodhouse to win the respect and affection of the neighbourhood.

Manners, Burke also believed, were necessary to make morality acceptable: 'There ought to be a system of manners in every nation which a well-formed mind would be disposed to relish. To make us love our country, our country ought to be lovely.' Just as patriotism could be rendered easier by sheer delight, so would other virtues be likely to win more hearts if they were attractively presented.[25] This was the lesson that Jane Austen illustrated by the progress of Fanny Price at Mansfield Park: the influence of the once awkward little girl increased as her social grace matured. Sir Thomas Bertram, by contrast, was hampered in his desire to instill right conduct into his daughters by a sombre and forbidding manner – 'a most untoward gravity of deportment'.[26] Even the mutual respect that should exist between man and wife was more likely to be achieved, Jane Austen thought, if there was graciousness on both sides. For this reason she urged her niece Fanny Knight not to marry the estimable John Plumptre if his virtues, outstanding though they seemed to be, were unable to make her forget his awkwardness. Her ideal of perfection, she confessed, was one in which 'Grace and Spirit are united to Worth' and 'the Manners are equal to the Heart and Understanding'. Mr Darcy's education, she thought, had been as blameworthy as that of the Bertrams, but for the opposite reason: he had been taught not manners without morals but morals without manners.[27]

Whilst admitting that some people were born with more charm than others, Jane Austen did not believe that an attractive manner was beyond anyone's reach. Shyness she represented as a fault in Edward Ferrars – a fault which it was incumbent on him to overcome; and Mr Darcy was told by Elizabeth Bennet that recommending oneself to strangers was an art, and one that like her own piano-playing could be improved by practice. Indeed there was little merit in natural charm: Elinor Dashwood came to think that she had read too much goodness into Willoughby's graceful manners, which after all were second nature to him and cost him nothing.[28]

Burke had further defended manners on the grounds that they facilitate social intercourse, and that it is social intercourse which gives a moral quality to human nature. This was Rousseau's argument also: only when individuals become responsible members of a community can they achieve the balance between self and others which nature requires and conscience demands. Jane Austen's particular concern was to show that it is true knowledge of ourselves that makes us aware of our obligation to others and conditions our manner of dealing with them. As Wittgenstein was to state long afterwards:

> Lying to oneself about oneself . . . must have a harmful effect on [one's] style, for the result will be that you cannot tell what is genuine in the style and what is false.

Emma Woodhouse had to find out that she really cared less about her reputation as a great lady than about the good opinion of Mr Knightley: only then did she have the understanding to treat Miss Bates with genuine kindness. The Bertram girls were never taught to recognize their own limitations. Encouraged by their Aunt Norris to believe that their social status made them naturally gracious, they failed to acquire the true elegance of manner which would have embraced not only the rich Crawfords but their poor cousin Fanny. Their brother Tom, who assumed throughout his early life that he had been born simply to enjoy himself, needed a bout of severe illness to halt him in his tracks:

> He had suffered, and he had learnt to think, two advantages that he had never known before. He became what he ought to be, useful to his father, steady and quiet, and not living merely for himself.

Edmund Bertram hoped in vain that Mary Crawford 'might soon learn to think more justly, and not owe the most valuable knowledge we could any of us acquire – the knowledge of ourselves and of our duty, to the lessons of affliction'.[29]

A proper assessment of ourselves would, in Jane Austen's view, enable us to behave 'naturally' instead of 'artfully'. This by no means meant that she admired uninhibited behaviour. In keeping with views widely held in the eighteenth century, she admired nature not as it sometimes turned out to be when allowed to run wild but as it had presumably been intended to be. What she wanted in children, for instance, was the kind of training that brought out their naturally good qualities. They must not be allowed to behave boisterously, like Lady Middleton's children, monopolizing the conversation as though the world revolved around them; but equally they must not be repressed into unnatural timidity. Not all children were alike: parents should show discretion in deciding when to give a child free rein and when to hold it back. In the case of Anna Lefroy's two little girls, the one needed more restraint than the other, Jane thought.[30]

Young ladies, Jane Austen believed, were meant by nature to be modest, but not excessively so. Whilst disapproving of Mary Crawford's vulgar witticisms about 'Rear Admirals', she had no time for prudery. 'Your Anne is dreadful', she wrote to her niece Caroline when the latter was attempting to write a romantic novel:

> But nothing offends me so much as the absurdity of not being able to pronounce the word *Shift*. I could forgive her any follies in English, rather than the Mock Modesty of that French word.

(Caroline had presumably copied the latest fashion and referred to a *chemise*.)[31] In their dealings with young men young ladies should behave like Catherine Morland, who in a modest but straightforward way managed to convey to Henry Tilney her admiration of him; Jane Bennet could usefully have studied such an example.

Young men won approval from Jane Austen if they too were 'natural', which in their case meant being 'manly' without being coarse and domineering. 'William & I are the best of friends', she wrote in 1817 of her nephew, aged nineteen: 'Everything is so *natural* about him, his affections, his Manners & his Drollery.'[32] John Thorpe in *Northanger Abbey* would have done much better to be his natural self: nobody of sense was likely to be impressed by the swaggering, hard-drinking, devil-may-care fellow he pretended to be.

Natural behaviour took the form, even in children, of a capacity to engage in open and friendly conversation with others. Commenting on a visit from a young relative in 1807 Jane wrote:

> What is become of all the Shyness in the World? Moral as well as Natural Diseases disappear in the process of time . . . Our little visitor has just left us, & left us highly pleased with her; – she is a nice, natural openhearted, affectionate girl, with all the ready civility one sees in the best Children in the present day; – so unlike anything that I was myself at her age, that I am often all astonishment & shame.[33]

The ability to communicate openly and easily was an asset by which she set great store. Deeds of kindness were of course important but in most of the circumstances of life it was friendly converse that mattered. Eleanor Tilney and Catherine Morland cemented a true companionship with each other when they spoke unaffectedly together in the Pump Room at Bath:

> and though in all probability not an observation was made, nor an expression used by either which had not been made and used some thousands of times before, under that roof, in every Bath season, yet the merit of their being spoken with simplicity and truth, and without personal conceit, might be something uncommon.[34]

The people Jane Austen admired in her novels were all able to speak effectively, whether they were high in their particular social scale, like Mr Knightley, or comparatively humble, like Robert Martin the farmer and William Price the sailor. Even in awkward circumstances they can find appropriate words. Shyness, embarrassment and 'reserve' (a term which Jane Austen equated either with selfishness or with guilty secrecy) are banished where there is genuine feeling for others.

At the same time, openness of address was different from the flow of words that came to the heedless – to Tom Bertram, for instance, who had 'easy manners, excellent spirits, a large acquaintance, and a great deal to say'.[35] It was different, too, from the effusive language popular with devotees of sensibility. Hannah More, in her *Strictures on a Modern System of Female Education*, warned young ladies against the excessive sensibility which could prevent them from distinguishing between sentimentality and real feeling: Jane Austen demonstrated in her first novel how Marianne Dashwood was misled by Willoughby's fervent appreciations of poetry into judging him to be a man of genuine sensibility, and into comparing him unfavourably with Edward Ferrars who was more thoughtful and hence more restrained.[36] Similarly, the openness that

Jane Austen admired did not mean that people were to be forever expressing their concern for others: Elinor Dashwood, at the height of her sorrows, found herself beginning to appreciate Lady Middleton's coldness of manner by comparison with Mrs Jennings's 'officious condolence' and the 'clamorous kindness' of Sir John Middleton and Mrs Palmer.[37] Proportion was required in all things. The genuinely thoughtful person had that capacity to know how to behave appropriately in all circumstances which was referred to at the time as 'sense' or 'taste'. The gentlemen whom Jane Austen puts forward as models of behaviour in her novels – Colonel Brandon, Mr Gardiner, Mr Knightley – are preeminently men of 'sense', introduced as such on their first appearance. Mr Collins, on the other hand, arouses Elizabeth Bennet's suspicions as soon as she hears his introductory letter read out. His pomposity and his futile apologies for being next in the entail lead her to enquire of her father, 'Can he be a sensible man, sir?' – and to receive the prompt reply, 'No, my dear, I think not'.

Colonel Brandon and Mr Knightley (we see less of Mr Gardiner) have a delicacy in broaching sensitive subjects which Mr Collins wholly lacks. They know, also, how to approach especially sensitive persons: Mr Knightley's attitude to Mr Woodhouse is gently bracing and entirely understanding of his frailties, real and imagined. This proper consideration for the feelings of others does not involve any loss of integrity, as Elinor is at pains to point out to Marianne. It does not mean that one's own opinions have to be abandoned and other people unduly flattered:

> My doctrine has never aimed at subjection of the understanding. All I have ever attempted to influence has been the behaviour . . . I am guilty, I confess, of having often wished you to treat our acquaintance in general with greater attention; but when have I advised you to adopt their sentiments or conform to their judgment in serious matters?

Mary Crawford, accustomed to the artificiality of sophisticated town manners, is surprised by this distinction when she first meets with it in Edmund Bertram, who manages to make himself attractive to her although he pays no false compliments, talks no nonsense and sticks to his opinions unswervingly.[39]

Needless to say, the characters whom Jane Austen admires are noticeably intelligent. The 'knowledge of ourselves and of our duty', which Edmund Bertram valued above all other acquisitions, would seem to place more emphasis on the mind than on the heart as a source of goodness. It is indeed true that the kindhearted but blundering Mrs

Jennings, a type so often referred to as 'good-natured', is rated less highly in the novels than persons with a more intelligent approach. Colonel Brandon, Mr Knightley, Mr Gardiner and Anne Elliot are distinguished by qualities of mind. Colonel Fitzwilliam, introduced into *Pride and Prejudice* to help open Elizabeth Bennet's eyes to the unworthiness of Mr Wickham, is described as having 'the best informed mind'.[40] A kindly disposition is treated as something which some people – Catherine Morland, Harriet Smith, Willoughby, Henry Crawford, to name a miscellaneous few – are simply born with. It gives them a good start in life but the gift can be ruined if the mind is wrongly affected: Willoughby's mind is led into vanity by his early expectations of wealth; Henry Crawford is never encouraged to use his mind to direct his feelings, and deplorable conduct follows. When Edmund Bertram begins at last to have doubts about Mary Crawford's moral worth, he fears that it is her mind that has been tainted by evil influences.[41]

The emphasis on mind would seem to place the majority of mankind at a disadvantage in the pursuit of morality but Jane Austen (whilst admitting in *Mansfield Park* that 'knowledge of ourselves and of our duty' was not a common acquirement) did not think so.[42] The fact that she most frequently used the term 'mind' and 'understanding' rather than 'brain' and 'intelligence' indicates that she accepted the ideas of John Locke, who had argued in the late seventeenth century that reasonable behaviour, which to him was the same thing as moral behaviour since it meant living in accordance with God's laws for the universe, was open to everybody. Reasoning powers, which have been given to 'all mankind who will but use them', operate by a process of deduction based on experience.[43] The latter can be widened (Colonel Brandon, Elinor points out, 'has seen a great deal of the world, has been abroad, has read . . . ') but the mechanism can operate equally well in humbler circumstances. Catherine Morland, with a mind 'about as ignorant and uninformed as the female mind at seventeen usually is', can nevertheless use her native wit not only to enable her to travel about the country safely when thrown upon her own resources but to detect that John Thorpe, whatever Isabella said in his favour, was not altogether desirable as a companion, and that General Tilney, in whatever light his loyal family presented him, was not entirely amiable. Provided that a person's reasoning power was not altogether blunted, faults that had developed in the character could be rectified – as in the case of Lucy Steele, for instance, who in spite of an early proclivity for fortune-hunting did not 'lack sense, and that is the foundation on which every thing good may be built'.[44]

The ideas of John Locke were fashionable in the universities in the eighteenth century. Jane Austen may well have found copies of his *Essay concerning Human Understanding* and his treatises on education and political thought in her father's library. Whether she had read his books or not, she could have imbibed his attitudes from her acquaintances, for they were popular among the clergy. They placed a premium on the thoughtful, gentlemanly type of parson that she saw in her father and that she designed Edmund Bertram to become. It was her hope that this type would ultimately have more influence than the proselytizing Evangelicals.

Wilberforce had long recognized the importance of recruiting the clergy as front-rank fighters in his conversion campaign. He doubted whether many of them would be fit for the task, denouncing the typical clergyman of his day as 'a sensible, well-informed and educated, polished, old, beneficed, nobleman's and gentleman's house-frequenting, literary and chess-playing divine', useless for his purpose. Jane Austen did not regard any of the characteristics listed as drawbacks. Her worry was lest some of the clergy should lack the moral perception necessary to detect any but the grosser errors (Mr Collins) and the moral integrity to set the right example (Mr Elton). Just how a sensitive and upright man like Edmund Bertram was to succeed in making his presence felt, without engaging in the officious practices she so much deplored, is a question she never answered in any great depth or detail. He would not have been the last clergyman to have had to tackle it.

Chapter 10

Morals and Society

In the last years of the eighteenth century, a well-placed observer of influential society highlighted as the major evil of the times the fact that 'so little sense of responsibility seems attached to the possession of high rank, or splendid abilities, or affluent fortunes, or other means or instruments of usefulness'.

> The instructive admonition, 'give an account of thy stewardship', or 'occupy till I come', are forgotten . . . Accordingly we find that the generality of mankind among the higher orders, in the formulation of their schemes, in the selection of their studies, in the choice of their place of residence, in the employment and distribution of their time, in their thoughts, conversation, and amusements, are considered to be at liberty, if there be no actual vice, to consult in the main their own gratification.

The words are not Jane Austen's, although they express her own fundamental view of the evil of her times, but Wilberforce's, published in 1797 in his *Practical View of the Prevailing System of Professed Christians*. Ten years earlier, Wilberforce had given the impression that his main concern was with the grosser sins of drunkenness, licentiousness and profligacy. These are not entirely overlooked in the *Practical View* – there are sinister references to the large number of people who indulged in 'sensual pleasures' and 'animal gratification' – but they were relegated to the margin, as not likely to form a part of the habitual behaviour of the readers now being addressed, namely the vast majority of middle-and upper-class persons who were at least nominal Christians and regarded themselves as respectable citizens. While these people were not dissolute or criminal, their lives were nonetheless unworthily absorbed either by love of riches, or by a desire for worldly estimation, or by the pursuit of pleasure.[1]

Many thoughtful members of Wilberforce's generation were frightened by the example of the French Revolution into thinking that a situation similar to that of the last days of the Roman Empire had been reached, and that a thoroughly immoral civilization was likely to come crashing about their ears. 'Gloom and misanthropy have become the characteristics of the age in which we live', wrote Shelley,[2] and it was not mere Romantic affectation but genuine foreboding that made them so. In *Mansfield Park* Jane Austen herself gave the impression that she believed that the whole of English society was corrupt: religion was regarded as out of date and morality had become unfashionable. On the whole, however, she was not a prophet of doom. The fact that her one deliberate hypocrite, Mr Elliot in *Persuasion*, made a pretence at honouring moral standards, was some kind of testimony to surviving virtue. All in all, Jane Austen had faith in her fellow countrymen and resisted extreme denunciations: after reading Southey's bitter criticisms, published under the pseudonym of Dom Manuel Alvarez Espriella (which she read out to her mother and sister-in-law at Southampton), she commented to Cassandra: 'The Man describes well, but is horribly anti-English. He deserves to be the foreigner he assumes.'[3] She nevertheless saw in society much the same faults as Wilberforce and pilloried them in her novels by illustrating their role in everyday life. If the clergy were to exert the moralizing influence on the nation that Edmund Bertram assumed they possessed ('as the clergy are or are not what they ought to be, so are the rest of the nation'), these were the faults they would need to address.

In Jane Austen's view, the prevailing love of money seldom manifested itself in crude avarice: John Dashwood in *Sense and Sensibility* is the only one of her characters who grasps at wealth for its own sake. The more common form of the evil was a mercenary caste of mind which distorted people's sense of values and made them incapable of recognizing true worth. Like Mr Collins, they reduced the beauty of the rural scene to the number of trees in each clump and the elegance of a Regency mansion to the cost of glazing the windows on the main front.[4] Since her novels are mainly love stories, it is in the arranging of marriages that she finds most occasion for criticism. She realized that, in a society which gave little or no relief to hardship, financial considerations could not properly be ignored when contemplating matrimony. She was inclined to accept the convention whereby parents and others in a position to guide the young took it upon themselves to warn them against 'imprudent' matches (as Aunt Gardiner did Elizabeth Bennet when she believed her to be in love with Wickham);[5] but to regard money as the main criterion of a suitable marriage seemed to her wholly deplorable. She realized that for women without independent fortune the pressure to marry someone – anyone – who could look after them was very great, for they would otherwise become a burden to their family; she had herself, presumably for such a reason, accepted briefly a proposal of marriage from her neighbour of Steventon days, Harris Bigg Wither, a young man she could not love. Even for men the pressures were not wholly absent. Until it was taken for granted that men worked for a living, there were bound to be those who, like Edward Ferrars and Frank Churchill, found it difficult to resist a marriage that would please a mercenary parent or guardian. Jane Austen nevertheless remained convinced, to the end of her days, that it was wicked (the word was Fanny Price's) to marry without affection.[6] While she could understand the desperation which drove the penniless Isabella Thorpe and Lucy Steele to set their caps at any promising young gentleman who came their way, she could not approve of the endeavour. And if it was wrong to marry for security, how much more reprehensible was it to marry for actual riches. The fact that Mrs Bennet regarded Elizabeth's engagement to Mr Darcy as more satisfactory than Jane's to Bingley, simply because the former gentleman was 'worth' £10,000 a year and the latter £5,000, reduced the union of true hearts and minds to the level of the cattle market.[7] We learn from the novels that the marriage market was so well established that it had its own price list: when Miss Maria Ward, 'with only seven thousand pounds', had the good luck to captivate a baronet, 'her uncle, the lawyer, allowed her to be at least three thousand pounds short of any equitable claim to it'.[8] To indulge in a marriage less lucrative than might have been expected was regarded as 'throwing oneself away', and someone like Mary Crawford, who prided herself on her realism, could not bring herself to do it.[9]

Jane Austen was perceptive enough to see that the importance which England had come to place on a market economy could lead to a pride and zest in the making of money which could be rewarding quite apart from the profits involved. She herself was intrigued by the new game of 'Speculation', which she introduced to her nieces and nephews.[10] In *Sanditon*, Mr Parker, a kind-hearted family man, is described as entering into the business of developing his seaside village into a thriving health resort for the sheer satisfaction of achieving what he regarded as progress.

'Civilization, Civilization indeed! – cried Mr P. – delighted. 'Look my dear Mary – Look at William Heeley's windows. – Blue shoes, & nankin Boots! – Who wd have expected such a sight at a Shoemaker's in old Sanditon! This is new within the month. There was no blue shoe when we passed this way a month ago. – Glorious indeed! Well, I think I *have* done something in my Day.'[11]

As in this case, the end product was often of little value – the public was being defrauded by being made to believe that progress and necessity were at issue.

Whilst many people devoted their entire attention to the acquisition or making of money, others set particular store by being able to show off their rank and status to the world at large. 'Magnificent houses, grand equipages, numerous retinues, splendid entertainments, high and fashionable connections, appear to constitute, in their estimation, the supreme happiness of life', wrote Wilberforce.[12] It is unlikely that Jane Austen saw much conspicuous consumerism in the course of her life, for even before her father's retirement and death she was complaining that 'People get so horribly poor & economical in this part of the World, that I have no patience with them'. The age-old addiction to what the Book of Common Prayer called 'the pomps and vanities of this wicked world' could be seen as much in small purchases as in large, however: General Tilney at Northanger Abbey displayed his overweening ego in both. There was nothing wrong with his acquisitions in themselves: his improvements to the kitchens, we are told, 'might at any time have placed him high among the benefactors of the convent' – it was his attitude towards them that was at fault. He showed Catherine around what he regarded as the most impressive parts of his house for his own satisfaction rather than for her pleasure (she would have chosen to see quite different areas if she had been consulted); and it was to display his own taste that he pretended to apologize for a slightly out-of-date tea service (which she, in fact, thought charming).[13]

A show of wealth, or status, or learning, or anything else, might have been considered by Jane Austen comparatively harmless had it not often been an empty show. Mr Rushworth, who is determined to appear on stage in the amateur theatricals at Mansfield Park in a series of the most magnificent costumes, has really nothing worthwhile to offer his audience: the chances of his ever being able to learn the 'two and forty speeches' of which he boasts are remote.[14] Empty-headed and vain, he is not the man to restore new life to the great estate of which he has become master. All he can think of doing is to employ the fashionable Repton at the considerable sum of five guineas a day to effect a few ostentatious changes. Repton would devise a grander approach to the house (perhaps by pulling down a row of labourers' cottages and replacing them with model terraces as he had proposed to do at Tatton, for were not the cottages on the approach to Sotherton Court described by Maria Bertram as 'a disgrace'?). Repton would create an open prospect from the windows so that guests could appreciate the full extent of the grounds (which were much more extensive than his friend Smith's at Compton – 'a good seven hundred [acres], without reckoning the water meadows'). No matter if this meant chopping down an avenue of oak trees a mile and a half long: Repton had decreed that avenues were permissible if they led up to the gates of a house, and thereby enhanced the approach, but not if they impeded the panoramic view from the windows of the main front as they apparently did at Sotherton (where 'every room on the west front looked across a lawn to the beginning of the avenue').[15]

The satisfaction with which Sir Walter Elliot and his daughter Elizabeth describe their lifestyle at Bath is equally hollow:

> Their house was undoubtedly the best in Camden Place; their drawing-rooms had many decided advantages over all the others which they had either seen or heard of; and the superiority was not less in the style of the fitting-up, or the taste of the furniture. Their acquaintance was exceedingly sought after. Everybody was wanting to visit them. They had drawn back from many introductions, and still were perpetually having cards left by people of whom they knew nothing.

Listening to this recital, Anne can only sigh over the fact that her father sees nothing to regret in having left behind 'the duties and dignity of the resident land-holder', and that he should find so much to be proud of in 'the littlenesses of a town'. There was worse to follow, for the pair are soon to be found fawning upon their titled cousins, the Dowager-Viscountess Dalrymple and the Honorable Miss Carteret, who have nothing to commend them except their rank and a house in Laura Place. Characteristically, Sir Walter, whose judgement is always based on superficial criteria, assesses the value of any new acquaintance on the social standing of the part of the town in which they lived. 'Westgate-buildings! and who is Miss Anne Elliot to be visiting in Westgate-buildings?' he asks scornfully, when Anne befriends a former school-fellow who has fallen on hard times. Camden Place, needless to say, is considered a lofty situation, befitting a man of consequence.[16]

Jane Austen had first become acquainted with Bath in the 1790s, when she visited it – probably several times – as a guest of her Aunt and Uncle Leigh-Perrot who rented an apartment at No. 1 The Paragon. In *Northanger Abbey* she wrote of the delight which Bath afforded an unsophisticated girl in the days when public assemblies were still the vogue. By the time she wrote *Persuasion* she had experienced, as an older woman, a few years' residence in the town; assemblies had given way to private parties and the social life of the place had come to seem tedious and shallow. In both its manifestations, Bath was symbolic to her of a life given over to the pursuit of pleasure. Though ostensibly a spa, to which many people went for health reasons, the business of filling in their time between taking the waters, and the task of providing entertainment for their families during a lengthy sojourn, had rapidly become the main concern of the town. A foreign traveller who arrived there in 1810 noted of it:

> No trade, no manufactures, no occupations of any sort except that of killing time, the most laborious of all. Half the inhabitants do nothing, the other half supply them with nothings.[17]

Jane Austen was no kill-joy; unlike the Evangelicals she disapproved of no diversion that was entered into innocently and in moderation; but, like Wilberforce, she deplored living for pleasure. This was not only because there were better things to do but because pleasure as an end in itself was addictive: the palate became jaded, bigger and bigger doses were needed to satisfy it, and the victim went from bad to worse. In all probability he or she lived beyond his or her income and was driven to unworthy courses (such as marriage without affection) to obtain money for more pleasures. This was the trouble with Willoughby, who wins the love of two women, both of whom he abandons because they are poor, although either of them would have made him happier than the wealthy woman he eventually marries. The second, Marianne Dashwood, he loves with all the sincerity of which he is capable, but his affection for her cannot rescue him from his love of pleasure. Mrs Jennings, in her simple way, comments on the matter with some truth:

> Why don't he, in such a case, sell his horses, let his house, turn off his servants, and make a thorough reform at once? I warrant you, Miss Marianne would have been ready to wait till matters came round. But that won't do now-a-days; nothing in the way of pleasure can ever be given up by the young men of this age.[18]

Even if money was not at issue, boredom and restlessness could drag the victim down. When Henry Crawford has exhausted every legitimate pleasure that society in both town and country had to offer, his 'sated mind' turns to less legitimate pursuits,[19] namely those of making love to young ladies for the sheer excitement of the chase. This, too, proves boring whenever conquest was in sight; hence he turns his attention away from the receptive Miss Bertrams to the elusive Fanny Price. Like Willoughby in the earlier novel, he finds himself caught in the toils of true love, and like Willoughby also he cannot break with former habits. Meeting again with the elder Miss Bertram, now married and in a less welcoming mood than before, his vanity succumbs to the temptation of seducing her in spite of her married state.

It was after an assembly in the Upper Rooms at Bath that Jane Austen wrote to Cassandra in 1801:

> I am proud to say that I have a very good eye at an Adultress, for tho' repeatedly assured that another was the *She* I fixed upon the right one from the first . . . Mrs Badcock & two young women were of the same party, except when Mrs Badcock thought herself obliged to leave them and run round the room after her drunken Husband.[20]

Her exposure to sexual immorality and drunkenness was not confined to Bath, however; even the secluded village of Steventon provided the setting for an elopement similar in circumstance to that of Maria Bertram in *Mansfield Park*. Drunkenness Jane Austen was bound to have come across, for gentlemen cooped up in their country houses, or convivial after a day's sport, drank hard in her day. Like Wilberforce, she was not particularly concerned with such offences, and mentioned them in her novels only in so far as they were necessary to the plot. Mr Elton, for instance, had to be given a degree of Dutch courage to enable him to carry out his intention of proposing to Emma; we are told, therefore, that he drank 'wine enough to elevate his spirits, not at all to confuse his intellects'.[21] Jane Austen's intention in recounting the episode was not to give the impression that Mr Elton was too fond of the bottle but to show that he was full of an over-weening self-esteem which made him think that he had only to propose marriage to be immediately accepted. To Jane Austen all faults, from Henry Crawford's sexual misdemeanours to General Tilney's acquisitiveness, resulted from an overestimation of the attention due to self and too little consideration of the duty owed to others. The remedy lay in promoting on the one hand a greater degree of self-knowledge and on the other a stronger sense of community. Education and private study might help in both cases but they needed assistance from the experience of living together with other people engaged in a common endeavour.

More than one eighteenth-century writer pointed out that our first experience of community life comes from the family. Edmund Bertram's hopes that his private life would set a good example were clearly enhanced when he married Fanny Price. His prospect of happiness with Fanny, we are assured, was as certain as human happiness can ever be. At the same time his family life beyond his own parsonage had improved in moral purpose, for Sir Thomas, having failed abysmally in the training of his own children, established a much better relationship with his adopted nieces and nephews.[22]

Jane Austen was obviously aware that, whilst family life at its best had much to recommend it, the best was not everywhere achieved. It was common enough for parents to stress the duty which their children owed them, but less common, and to Jane Austen equally important, for parents to recognize that they in their turn had a duty to love and cherish their children. Mary Musgrove, pettishly concerned for her own comfort, perpetually seeks to confine her children to proper behaviour by querulous admonition and finds that they will not obey her; her husband Charles, who was more fond of them, manages them better.[23] This did not involve indulging children in everything – the Rev. George Moore and his wife won Jane's approval for not 'spoiling' their little boy – but appreciating them as individuals and giving them affectionate guidance.[24] Jane Bennet, left in charge of the Gardiner children, was 'exactly adapted' by her 'steady sense and sweetness of temper' for 'attending them in every way – teaching them, playing with them, and loving them'.[25]

Jane Austen was in no doubt that moral training should begin in the home. She had no great faith in the moral literature that parents could buy for the purpose: she herself as a child had apparently been instructed in articles from *The Mirror*, and it was with mild amusement that she recounted Mrs Morland's offer of a wholly inappropriate essay from its pages when Catherine returned home from Northanger Abbey with a broken heart.[26] As usual, Jane believed sound common sense to be the surest guide. Unlike Hannah More, who placed the whole burden of bringing up children in proper principles upon the mother, Jane Austen gave the father an equal role. It was to 'the guidance of an illiterate and miserly father' that she attributed many of Mr Collins's moral defects.[27] If Lady Bertram was to blame for her lethargy in not instructing her children properly, Sir Thomas was equally to blame for not winning their confidence sufficiently for him to be able to detect their shortcomings.[28] Mrs Bennet was largely to blame for filling her daughter's head with silly ideas, but Mr Bennett was made to recognize that he, with his greater intelligence, was at fault in not having curbed Lydia's injudicious behaviour early enough.

In adult life, relationships between parents and children continued to be important to Jane Austen. Grown-up sons and daughters should continue to show respect for parents and guardians – John Thorpe and Mary Crawford are both at fault in this matter – but they could not rightly be required to obey unjustifiable commands. Jane Austen had no time for domestic tyrants like General Tilney, who not only insisted on having the entire routine of the household established to suit his pointless requirements but expected to be obeyed in all things, right or wrong. While Henry Tilney is justified in opposing his father's injunction to abandon Catherine when he feels himself bound in honour to her, it is nevertheless right that he should maintain an outward show of filial respect by refraining from marrying her without his father's consent.[30] Parents, in Jane Austen's view, should continue to do their best to promote their offspring's happiness, giving the necessary attention to worldly considerations but not regarding the latter as paramount. The elder Musgroves are exemplary in this respect. They would have liked their daughters to have chosen wealthier partners, but are content that each is assured of at least a modest income. They themselves do what they can to provide extra security and comfort by giving their daughters as much dowry as they can possibly afford, rather than saving all their money for their eldest son – a common practice which Wilberforce thought a mere cloak for selfishness. Charles Musgrove, who is a good son and brother, is grateful for the fact that his father had always been generous with him and feels he has no right to begrudge his sisters their share of the family inheritance. Duty and affection among siblings rank high on Jane Austen's list of virtues.[31]

The relationship between husband and wife was also something which concerned her deeply. She did not ask for romantic love so much as for mutual respect and consideration. These were not necessarily precluded from a marriage which had been made in the first place for convenience: Elizabeth Bennet's complaint against Charlotte Lucas was not that she had engaged herself to a man she did not love but that she was marrying a man she could not possibly respect.[32] There was an even greater problem where physical attraction had been the sole impulse. Mr Bennet, we are told,

> captivated by youth and beauty, and that appearance of good humour, which youth and beauty generally give, had married a woman whose weak understanding and illiberal mind, had very early in their marriage put an end to all

real affection for her. Respect, esteem, and confidence, had vanished for ever; and all his views of domestic happiness were overthrown.[33]

This was apparently a common experience – too common for Elinor Dashwood to accept it as a reason for Mr Palmer's ill-humour.[34] In such circumstances it was the duty of the husband to show at least an outward respect for his wife: Mr Bennet is seriously at fault in exposing Mrs Bennet to the contempt not only of their neighbours but of her own children. Even Darcy has to learn to treat her politely.

Jane Austen's advice for avoiding such calamitous situations was that couples should get to know each other properly before marriage – a difficult assignment when convention (in her opinion rightly) forbade 'too particular' a relationship before engagement. An important injunction, however, was that men and women should always be honest with each other and not set out to create a misleading impression – marriage should not be a 'take-in', as Mary Crawford feared so many were.[35] Couples should also regard marriage as a coming together of equal partners. Young men too often thought in terms of 'conquering' young women. Frank Churchill, Emma Woodhouse noticed, was too importunate in his demands that she should dance with him. Henry Crawford was determined to have 'the glory of forcing Fanny Price to love him', much to her disapproval. Her response was:

> Let him have all the perfections in the world, I think it ought not to be set down as certain that a young man must be acceptable to every woman he may happen to like himself.[36]

To be adopted into a home where there was proper respect between husband and wife and between parents and children was the remedy to which Jane Austen more than once turned for rescuing characters less successfully brought up. Kitty Bennet improved greatly on being transported to Pemberley, Susan Price on succeeding to Fanny's old place at Mansfield Park.[37] Not everybody could be adopted into model families, however, and Jane Austen was in any case aware that taking children from their natural home was never accomplished without pain.

Apart from the family, what other moralizing circles did she recommend? Later in the nineteenth century, writers were to promote the idea of the nation as a unit to which the individual might relate. Jane Austen, although she was as patriotic as anyone else in wartime, seldom mentioned her country except in direct contrast to other, less desirable, places overseas.[38] William Wilberforce, a friend of the Prime Minister and himself an influential Member of Parliament, might think in terms of reforming the nation by direct action at the centre of affairs, but when Edmund Bertram looked beyond his immediate family it was to the next, most immediate circles that he turned. In rural England the clergy were sufficiently thick on the ground to be able to concentrate on small areas. As William Cobbett wrote in 1802:

> The clergy are less powerful from their rank and industry than from their *locality*. They are, from necessity, *everywhere*, and their aggregate influence is astonishingly great. When from the top of any high hill, one looks round the country and sees the multitude of regularly distributed spires, one . . . is astonished that any such thing as disorder or irreligion should prevail. It is in the equal distribution of the clergy, their being in every corner of the country, which makes them such a formidable corps.[39]

Edmund Bertram mentions two units which came under their influence: the parish and the neighbourhood. Of the two it was the neighbourhood that figured the more prominently in Jane Austen's social consciousness, and to which she referred the more often in her novels.

In his *Reflections on the Revolution in France* Edmund Burke criticized the French for destroying their age-old provinces and dividing the country for administrative purposes into geometrical departments. Far from transforming Gascons, Picards, Bretons and Normans into Frenchmen, as the revolutionaries hoped, this artificial arrangement, Burke said, would deprive them of the very means by which they had formerly come to love their country. 'We begin our public affections in our families', he wrote:

> We pass on to our neighbourhoods and our habitual provincial connections. These are inns and resting places. Such divisions of our country as have been formed by habit, and not by a sudden jerk of authority, were so many little images of that great country in which the heart found something it could fill.[40]

If, in her general acquaintance with this most popular writer of her youth, Jane Austen ever noticed this particular passage, it must have struck a harmonious chord. Her love for her family, tiresome though she found some of its members to be, was unswerving. In childhood her family provided her with everything she needed, both for comfort and enjoyment. From the family she graduated naturally (there was no artificial 'coming out', a convention she despised) into the society of the neighbourhood. There she met her brothers' friends and her father's

AN

ENQUIRY

INTO THE

DUTIES OF THE FEMALE SEX.

By THOMAS GISBORNE, M. A.

THE SECOND EDITION, CORRECTED.

LONDON:

Printed for T. CADELL jun. and W. DAVIES
(Succeffors to Mr. CADELL) in the Strand.

M DCC XCVII.

Title page of Thomas Gisborne's essay of 1797, which Jane Austen
greatly appreciated when she was persuaded to read it in 1805.
(*Dr Williams's Library*)

fellow-clergy; she accompanied her mother on social calls upon the ladies round about; she attended parties and balls at which she flirted with young men, and joined the occasional shooting party at which she discovered that she was a bad shot. The neighbourhood of Steventon provided her with both entertainment and experience; when she was obliged to move away in 1801 she needed a little time to reconcile herself to the idea of leaving it. The supposedly more brilliant society of Bath, constantly shifting and with no roots other than those formerly established in a distant countryside, provided nothing comparable to engage her affections. Not until she reached Chawton did she feel at home again. There, albeit in a more limited circle than the one she had known at Steventon, she found neighbours who were interested in her doings and keen to entertain members of her family when they arrived on visits, thereby giving her status and identity in her spinsterhood.

Early in the century Addison had concluded, in a passage in the *Spectator*, 'the country is not a place for a person of my temper, who does not love jollity and what they call good neighbourhood'.[41] Judging by her letters, Jane Austen regarded socializing in the neighbourhood as a duty which could not be avoided without downright rudeness. From Steventon she wrote to Cassandra in October 1800:

> We have been obliged to take advantage of the delightful weather . . . by going to see almost all our Neighbours. On Thursday we walked to Deane, yesterday to Oakley Hall & Oakley, & today to Deane again . . . [42]

On another occasion she felt obliged to put off a visit to her friend Martha at Ibthorpe when she found it coincided with the date of a local assembly: 'I would not on any account do so uncivil a thing by the Neighbourhood as to set off at that very time for another place', she assured Cassandra.[43] At Chawton she courteously accepted an offer from the Clements of a lift in their carriage to the Papillons, although she knew that they had no real wish to pick her up and for her part she would rather have walked ('civility on both sides'); and she went on visiting the Miss Webbs, tedious though she found them, as long as they lived in the village.[44] She would undoubtedly have agreed with Burke that: 'There is a *Law of Neighbourhood* which does not leave a man perfectly master on his own ground.'[45] It was a lesson Marianne Dashwood had to learn from her sister in *Sense and Sensibility*.

Jane Austen was aware that neighbours could be insufferably nosy and gossipy. 'Mr Richard Harvey is going to be married; but as it is a great secret, & only known to half the Neighbourhood, you must not mention it', she wrote to Cassandra from Steventon; and at Chawton she felt herself persecuted by neighbours who called at the house on purpose to try and discover if, as rumour had it, she was the anonymous author of *Pride and Prejudice*.[46] She also knew that neighbourhood opinion could be ill-informed, sententious and even cruel. In *Mansfield Park* the neighbourhood jumped to the conclusion as soon as the wealthy Mr Rushworth arrived in the vicinity that he was a suitable match for Miss Bertram. It was partly this common assumption that made Sir Thomas loth to bring an end to the engagement which ensued, although his better judgement told him that it would be wise to do so.[47] Raised eyebrows among neighbours could be hard to bear: in 1812 Jane Austen confessed to feeling sorry for the newly-married Mrs John Butler of Ibthorpe, obliged 'to stand the gaze of a neighbourhood as the Bride of such a pink-faced, simple young Man'.[48]

She nevertheless believed that neighbourhood opinion played a useful part in enforcing moral standards, if only because thoroughly undesirable conduct was unlikely to remain uncensured. A little reflection tells Elizabeth Bennet that Darcy could never have behaved as badly to Wickham as she had been led to believe without his neighbours knowing all about it and shunning him for it. As Henry Tilney points out to Catherine Morland, neighbourhoods are composed of 'voluntary spies': was it likely that atrocious crimes of the kind Catherine suspected to have taken place at Northanger Abbey would have remained hidden?[49] It is in tacit acknowledgement of the restraints imposed by neighbourhood society that Jane Austen usually removes her fictional characters to London or Bath or the seaside whenever they are about to behave in an outrageous manner: it was in London that Maria Bertram succumbed to the blandishments of Henry Crawford; in Bath that Willoughby seduced Colonel Brandon's young protégée; in Brighton that Lydia Bennet eloped with Wickham. In *Mansfield Park*, Edmund Bertram implies that if he could improve the moral judgement of the neighbourhood he would have a powerful weapon for good in his hands.

In *Emma*, Jane Austen gave a picture of a neighbourhood which both helped and hindered individuals in the task of fulfilling their own Christian potential and living sociably with one another. Mrs Elton was encouraged by the snobbishness of Highbury to show all her worst characteristics. Mr Knightley, on the other hand, though he was no saint (he is not above feeling jealous of Frank Churchill), clearly finds the right milieu in which all his best characteristics are brought out. He works hard as a magistrate and stints neither the time needed to give advice to his tenant, Robert Martin, nor the patience needed to be courteous to the garrulous Miss Bates. He is polite and considerate to the tiresome but well-meaning Mr Woodhouse, quick to perceive an opportunity to do anyone a good turn, and generous (as the more worldly might say) to a fault. As a result of his influence, Emma comes to see her own priorities more clearly, Harriet Smith is guided towards her proper destiny, and Miss Bates is encouraged to think gratefully of her lot in Highbury.

Mr Knightley, we are given to understand, belonged to a long succession of English country gentlemen who had taken it for granted that privileges and status carried duties and responsibilities. He treated his house and lands not as private property which could be exploited to enhance his own wealth and prestige but as a trust which he must hand on to his heirs. His manor house, Donwell Abbey, had been enlarged over the years, but with more concern for comfort and hospitality than grandeur. No thought had ever been given to the fine 'prospect' which could have been afforded by gardens which stretched down to the nearby stream. Its many trees still stood 'in rows and avenues, which neither fashion nor extravagance had rooted up'. As Emma Woodhouse gazed out across the surrounding meadows she decided that it was a thoroughly English scene, one that she could be proud to belong to.[50]

In presenting this picture of Mr Knightley as the supreme moralizing influence upon the neighbourhood of Highbury and Donwell, Jane Austen has been accused both of worshipping a non-existent past and of believing that the rural society which she knew, with all its hierarchical associations, was sacrosanct and must be preserved at all costs. The first charge is to some extent true: the most that can be said in mitigation is that she was not alone in her fault. An idealized picture of the English past had received support from a number of quarters during the preceding decades. The Picturesque movement, of which Jane Austen was said by her brother Henry to have been 'enamoured', blurred any uncomfortable thoughts about the exploitative and tyrannical nature of England's abbeys and castles: covered now with moss and creeper, their stones mellowed with age, they appeared to have become part of England's organic growth, to be cherished for the future. Similarly the craze for visiting country houses (to which access could be gained, as at Pemberley, by ringing the doorbell and asking to be shown round) gave the impression that the mansions of the aristocracy were not so much private luxuries as a part of the cultural heritage of the nation: Jane Austen believed that such visits ought to be entered upon with proper taste and feeling, not mere curiosity such as impelled people like the

Miss Ballards, whom she met at Southampton, to go on tours.[51] Even the natural style in gardens, which owed much of its inspiration to the Italian gardens of the sixteenth and seventeenth centuries seen by generations of young men taking the Grand Tour, had come to be regarded as a peculiarly English style, expressive of the Englishman's love of liberty.

The fact that England escaped the contagious example of the French Revolution encouraged the English ruling classes to believe that they had behaved better than their counterparts across the Channel, while the patriotism engendered by the long wars against France similarly encouraged a belief in the English gentleman's innate qualities of character and breeding. Jane Austen could laugh at her own propensity to think in such terms: 'Monsieur the old Count, is a very fine looking man, with quiet manners, good enough for an Englishman', she wrote for Cassandra's amusement after meeting the émigré Monsieur d'Entraigues and his son in London in 1811;[52] but she knew she was speaking for many a stout-hearted English squire when she had Mr Knightley disagreeing with Emma Woodhouse over the charming but superficial Frank Churchill's amiable qualities:

> No Emma; your amiable young man can be amiable only in French, not in English. He may be very 'amiable', have very good manners, and be very agreeable; but he can have no English delicacy towards the feelings of other people: nothing really amiable about him.[53]

This is reminiscent of Bishop Porteus, who found that there existed in his neighbourhood of Kent

> that judicious mixture of society and refinement which constitute the true felicity of human life, and which so remarkably and so fortunately distinguish the gentry and nobility of England from those of almost all other countries of Europe.[54]

Even Wilberforce, who had led the assault on the immorality of the upper classes of his day, succumbed to the myth of the old English landed gentry to the extent of suggesting that tax concessions should be made to those who were prepared to continue living on their estates.[55] Cobbett, too, who railed persistently against England's post-war landowners, accused them of departing from former traditions: his ideal, like that which warmed the heart of Emma Woodhouse, was of a rural community presided over by a caring English squire of what he believed to be the old school.

As to imagining that many such communities existed in her own time, however, or that they could be preserved for the future, Jane Austen must be exonerated from blame. In *Sense and Sensibility* Elinor Dashwood realizes how false are her sister's illusions of continuity in the country-side: the 'dear trees' which Marianne imagines will stand for ever around the manor house at Norland are ruthlessly chopped down by her own step-brother to make way for his wife's latest fad, an up-to-date green-house.[56] There are countless indications in Jane Austen's novels that she knew rural society to be breaking up. Landowners were moving out of their manor houses and putting them up for rent, either because they had run into debt or because they preferred to live in town. Jane Austen refused to regard the financial difficulties widespread among the gentry as due to anything but mismanagement: Colonel Brandon can soon put to rights the encumbered estate he inherited from his profligate brother; and Sir Walter Elliot could have stayed at Kellynch if he had been prepared for modest retrenchment.[57] She nonetheless recognized that absentee landlords were becoming as common as absentee parsons. When Mrs Bennet thinks fondly of renting a country house for Lydia and Wickham, she can reel off the names of several that were available in the immediate neighbourhood.[58] When the Rev. John Harwood inher-ited from his father Deane House and an estate heavily encumbered by his father's secret gambling debts, his friends thought him mad to give up his own chances of a happy marriage and to beggar himself in an attempt to cling on to the property his family had owned for genera-tions.[59] The practice of letting out ancestral property was so common that when Sir Walter Elliot finally agrees to leave Kellynch Hall his lawyer can provide him with exact details as to what tenants might expect in the way of hunting and fishing rights on the estate and the use of the pleasure gardens surrounding the house.[60]

In *Emma* Jane Austen showed that, like Burke, she appreciated the feeling of security to be found in a hierarchical society: her sympathies as narrator seem to be on the side of Emma Woodhouse in thinking that the mixture of families the heedless Frank Churchill would have invited to a ball at Highbury was bound to result in embarrassment.[61] But there are also many indications that she was by no means hostile to change. Admiral Croft turns out to be a better tenant for Kellynch Hall than Sir Walter Elliot of ancient lineage – better for the grass, the sheep, the poor and the parish, as well as for the house.[62] One of the few lyrical passages Jane Austen wrote centres upon the outstanding economic development of her day, the enclosure of land, which she treated as a symbol of hope. Anne Elliot, walking through large enclosed fields towards Winthrop, had been inclined to sigh over her lost youth until 'the ploughs at work, and the fresh-made path spoke the farmer counter-acting the sweets of poetical despondence, and meaning to have spring again'.[63] In *Mansfield Park* Jane Austen might have given the impression that she was averse to any adaptation of an existing house, even to the moving of a bookcase from in front of the billiard-room door; but in *Northanger Abbey* it is Catherine Morland who is shown to be at fault for liking gloomy rooms and dark passages, not the General for building a new wing of the kind Jane and her mother had enjoyed at Stoneleigh.[64]

In describing houses and gardens, Jane Austen sometimes drew on examples she knew at first hand. Mr Knightley's Donwell Abbey, basically Elizabethan with a few extensions made over time, owed something to Chawton Manor, whilst Northanger Abbey, a medieval convent with a startlingly new wing, was remarkably like Stoneleigh. On the whole, however, her fictional houses owed little to her direct experiences. Most of the houses she visited, whether at Steventon or in Kent, were of the early Georgian period.[65] In her novels she was prepared to move well outside this period if it suited her metaphorical purposes to do so. If she wanted a symbol of homeliness, as when describing the elder Musgrove's manor house at Uppercross, or of security, as in Colonel Brandon's case at Delaford, she described an old-fashioned house with walled gardens, stew-ponds and yew trees.[66] If, on the other hand, she wanted to give an impression of taste and elegance she resorted to the vague and effusive terms used in current publications devoted to 'gentlemen's seats' (with one of which, W. Watts's *The Seats of the Nobility and Gentry*, published in 1779, she was likely to be well acquainted, since her brother's house at Godmersham featured in it). Pemberley and Mansfield Park, with their light and airy rooms and their landscaped gardens beautifully set on rising ground, were calculated to conjure up, in the minds of her readers, not the gentry houses commonly found in the countryside but the dream houses of Regency England.

Similarly her fictional neighbourhoods are not observed local units so much as moral entities. It was not, after all, places that mattered to her so much as the people living in them. Norland estate remains intact but, on the death of one owner and the advent of another, it is changed almost overnight from a caring community with a landlord respected by all who know him to an exploitative enterprise. Neighbourhoods were not exclusively found in the country: even London could provide a caring atmosphere when there were people like Mr Haden and the Tilsons living near to Henry Austen in Hans Place.[67] Nor are the characters in Jane Austen's novels divided into good country folk and bad townspeople: each one can display social instincts ('country' manners) and selfish instincts ('town' manners) at alternating intervals.

In *Persuasion*, Jane Austen's descriptions of the lifestyle of Captain and Mrs Harville and their seafaring friends suggest that she was willing to envisage quite different sorts of community from the ones she knew best.[68] On the whole, however, she preferred to stick to 'three or four families in a country village',[69] whether or not such communities were passing away, because she could use them to exemplify her ideas of social morality. The restlessness which caused Mrs Bennet to fear that Bingley would be 'always flying about from one place to another' was of a piece with the inability of Wickham and Henry Crawford to stay fixed in one place.[70] In describing such things, Jane Austen was less concerned with types of economy and social organization than with the self-centredness which prevented some people from putting down roots, because they gave no thought to others and no thought to the duty and service which as individuals they might owe to the community. These were the ideals which she hoped could be defended and promoted through the influence of the clergy and the pressure of right-minded opinion in the England of her day.

Section and plans of the Octagon Chapel (designed by
T. Lightoler, 1765-67), where it is thought Jane Austen worshipped
when she lived in Bath.
(*Bath City Library*)

Chapter 11

Worship and Belief

Churches built during the Georgian period and hence regarded as characteristic of Jane Austen's England were architecturally plain to the point of austerity. The soaring arches so beloved of previous centuries, the lengthy chancels and half-hidden choirs designed for the practice of the old religion, had been replaced by wide, unimpeded naves in which congregations gathered to hear the foundations of their beliefs explained and to receive moral instruction for the days ahead. Walls were often whitewashed and wainscoted and the round-headed windows filled with clear glass. If such churches appealed to any emotion at all, it was to a sense of taste, propriety and proportion. Jane Austen was familiar with one such church near to her brother Henry's house in London and imagined her sister Cassandra attending it when she visited him.[1] St Paul's Covent Garden, built in the 1630s, had had no immediate successor, but had become a prototype for the fashionable churches of the following century. Its architect, Inigo Jones, had referred to it as a barn; and it was indeed no more than a single rectangular room with no screen to divide it into chancel and nave, no arcades and no other sanctuary than an altar surrounded by a rail on the east wall. Externally, the purity of its classical façade, with a noble portico supported by Tuscan pillars giving on to a grand piazza in the Italian style, made it (again in the words of its designer) 'the handsomest barn in England'.

In all such churches the altar was required to share its importance with the pulpit, which was sometimes the most grandiose feature of the interior. Congregations no longer stood in the nave, or leant against cold stone walls, but sat comfortably in high box pews, sheltered from draughts. Jane Austen when at Bath is believed to have worshipped at the Octagon church, which greatly scandalized Parson Woodforde by allowing well-off members of the congregation to install fires at which to warm themselves during the services. Jane Austen's surviving letters make no reference to the church, but she seems to have appreciated the practice among members of the congregation of walking after the services in the Crescent Fields. It was a common custom, especially in towns, for families to parade the streets after attending church; in *Mansfield Park* Jane Austen expressed approval of it as a means of boosting the self-esteem of an otherwise ineffectual person such as Mrs Price.[2]

Most of the churches known to Jane Austen and to country-dwellers generally were in fact older than the neo-classical models found in fashionable areas. They had been built to cater for a form of worship in which the laity in the nave were separated from the clergy in the chancel, often by a wooden screen, and in which the daily celebration of the Mass at the altar took precedence over the occasional sermon. Even so, they were often small and bare, their Norman arches relying on simple dog-tooth decoration, their Early English windows only occasionally boasting stained glass. There was no heating: often rushes were still placed on the floor to soak up the damp. Chancels were still the property of the patrons, many of whom decorated the walls with elaborate stone tablets in memory of members of their family; but there was no longer a liturgical use for chancels and William Cobbett claimed to have seen many that had been allowed to fall into ruin.[3] The normal practice in less disreputable parishes was for the officiating clergyman to say Morning and Evening Prayer from his stall at the west end of the chancel and, at the monthly Eucharist, to lead such members of the congregation as had expressed their desire to communicate to partake of bread and wine at the altar rail at the east end. So little ceremony was observed that the vicar in George Crabbe's narrative poem *The Borough* could complain that even in the Ante-Communion service

> Not at the altar our young brethren read
> (Facing their flock) the Decalogue and Creed;
> But at their duty, in their desks they stand,
> With naked surplice, lacking hood and band.

Many ancient customs had been abandoned:

> Few sprigs of ivy are at Christmas seen
> Nor crimson berry tips the holly green.

Even marriage services were bleak in the villages: Caroline Austen, recalling in old age her sister Anna's marriage with Ben Lefroy, described how the immediate relatives gathered at the home of the bride and proceeded (the ladies in the same carriage as the bride, the gentlemen on foot) half a mile down 'the unfrequented road' to 'the lonely old church', where they found

> no stove to give warmth [it was November], no flowers to give colour or brightness, no friends, high or low, to offer their good wishes and so to claim some interest in the great events of the day – all these circumstances and deficiencies must, I think, have given a gloomy air to our wedding. Mr Lefroy read the service, my father gave his daughter away. The Clerk of course was there altho' I do not particularly remember him; but I am quite sure there was no one else in the church, nor was anyone else asked to the breakfast, to which we sat down as soon as we got back . . . Such were the wedding festivities of Steventon in 1814!

Jane Austen, if we are to judge by her tone at the end of *Emma*, regarded anything more elaborate as vulgar pretence.[4]

Jane's godfather, the Rev. Samuel Cooke, is known to have regretted the lack of music in Anglican churches, believing it to be one of the reasons for the greater attraction of Methodism. According to Mrs Trimmer, writing at the end of the eighteenth century, Psalms and Canticles were sung in cathedrals only; in parish churches they were said.[5] Parish clerks whose job it was to intone the responses often did it so badly as to be a laughing-stock. In villages such as Dummer, where an ancient charity had endowed a school, the children sometimes provided a choir to sing in the gallery at the back of the church, the congregation turning round to 'face the music'; but Jane Austen was obviously no enthusiast for hymn tunes, as none were to be found among her store of music.[6]

The austerity of the Anglican worship of the time, and of the surroundings in which it took place, may have contributed towards the restraint which Jane Austen felt in speaking and writing about religion. Obviously they did not have this effect on everybody but Jane was particularly susceptible to environment. During her early adult life she seldom mentioned religion, except when writing letters of condolence to bereaved relatives. Even then she expressed herself in remarkably stereotyped terms.[7] Only towards the end of her life, when she was overcome with gratitude for her family's affectionate support during her illness, was she able to overcome her inhibitions and write freely of God's goodness.[8] In the nineteenth century, religious novels were to become a popular genre, with heroes and heroines searching their souls relentlessly and spiritual mentors giving them advice in large doses. Jane

Austen, like the Augustan writers she admired, would have been amazed at such a development. Although she said herself that England had become more religious during the long wars against France, she was worried lest her readers should find *Mansfield Park* too serious and was particularly grateful to her relatives the Cookes for being among the first to say that they liked it.[9] In a lively letter to her nephew Edward, who was trying his hand at a novel, she mentioned the possibility of preaching in fiction as though it were a thoroughly comic idea: 'Uncle Henry writes very superior Sermons', she wrote. 'You and I must try to get hold of one or two, & put them into our Novels;-it would be a fine help to a volume.'[10] The nearest she ever came to any such device was in *Persuasion*, where it is thought that Captain Wentworth's reflections on the hazel-nut may have been derived from Julian of Norwich's *Revelations of Divine Love*, a work Jane Austen is unlikely to have read but which she may well have heard expounded from more than one pulpit. Significantly Wentworth, at the point where he adopts this preaching tone, is being portrayed as particularly didactic and overconfident.[11]

In spite of all this, Jane Austen was a deeply religious woman. It is unlikely that she ever thought of the morality which she advocated in her novels as anything other than an essential part of Christianity. She was no doubt aware that a number of formidable theorists of the time preferred to base morality on reason. To writers of the stamp of Rousseau, who wished to reform society morally without giving greater power to the church, it was convenient to argue that an individual achieves goodness not by following religious teaching but by living as a responsible member of a community, carrying out a proper role in the fundamental relationships of society such as the family, the workplace, the neighbourhood and the nation. Even John Locke thought that mere common sense was enough to convince people of the need to recognize each other's needs and rights. This approach was vigorously attacked by the Rev. Thomas Gisborne, an Evangelical writer whose work impressed Jane favourably once Cassandra had managed to persuade her to read it.[12] Not that she needed the guidance of any such writer on the matter, for she had derived her morality in the first place not from political theorists but from the catechism which she had learnt as a child and from the commandments which seventeenth-century tradition had caused to be painted on the walls of many of the churches she attended. In this context, honour to parents, respect for other people's property, honesty in word and deed and, on a more positive note, love for one's neighbour as for oneself were seen not as substitutes for religion but as expressions of it in daily life. Archbishop Secker in his *Lectures on the*

LECTURES

ON THE

CATECHISM

OF THE

CHURCH of ENGLAND:

WITH A

DISCOURSE

ON

CONFIRMATION.

By **THOMAS SECKER**, LL. D.
Late LORD ARCHBISHOP of CANTERBURY.

Published from the Original Manuscripts
By BEILBY PORTEUS, D. D. and GEORGE STINTON, D. D.
His Grace's Chaplains.

VOL. I.

DUBLIN:
Printed for J. EXSHAW, and J. WILLIAMS, Booksellers.
M,DCC,LXX.

A manual of religious instruction known to Jane Austen.
(*Dr Williams's Library*)

Catechism of the Church of England, a work known to Jane Austen, described 'the common duties of common life' as 'the greatest part of what our Maker expects of us'.[13] The very word 'neighbour', which Jane Austen so frequently used, had a characteristically biblical ring.

Having been brought up to regard the Old Testament as essential background to the Gospels, she would have known that Christ's ethical teaching sprang from the received body of ideas found in the ancient civilized world and especially in the Judaic tradition. After all, Christ said Himself that He came not to destroy the law but to fulfill it. What made Christianity revolutionary was its acknowledgement that, *pace* the Book of Proverbs, the good life does not necessarily bring rewards in the shape of honour and respect from one's fellow men (though George Austen, in a letter of advice to his young sailor son Francis, suggested that it would).[14] Thomas Sherlock, a mid eighteenth-century divine whose sermons Jane Austen said she 'preferred to almost any other', pointed out in one of his better known passages that God had sent His Son into the world not to show people how to be good, which they knew already, but to show that goodness was often rejected. Prior to Christ's coming, Sherlock argued, there could be no rational ground for believing that God required mankind to be virtuous, for as well as supplying men with reason He had given them freewill, and the result was that vice often flourished whilst virtue was trodden under foot. Christ, however, taught people that there is a life after death, in which such apparent injustices are put right – a life in which Christ Himself sits on the throne of judgement and metes out rewards and punishments in proportion to behaviour in this world.[15] Jane Austen was for the most part willing to leave the characters in her novels to this divinely appointed reckoning. John Dashwood and General Tilney are thwarted in some of their schemes but they continue on their acquisitive path; Mr Elliot remains the heir to Kellynch Hall; Wickham continues to leave gambling debts behind him wherever he goes. Only at the end of *Mansfield Park* is some sort of earthly punishment devised for the main offenders. It is hardly convincing.

The Evangelicals who appeared in the Church of England in Jane Austen's lifetime had a very different explanation for Christ's coming into the world. In their view His mission was to save sinners by bringing them to repentance, after which He would intercede and turn away the divine wrath. By showing that Christ's message could indeed reach the heart of many a hardened sinner, the Evangelicals revitalized a traditional chord in the beliefs of the Church of England, for it had been the duty of all Christians to spread the good news of Christ's coming ever since the risen Lord had told His disciples to go and teach all nations. That there was much need for the Gospel to be taught in the England of her day Jane Austen could have been only too well aware. She was certainly aware that godly principles are difficult to maintain and that every human being eventually needs forgiveness. It was perhaps with both these things in mind that she wrote to her niece Fanny in 1814:

> I am by no means convinced that we ought not all to be Evangelicals, & am at least persuaded that they who are so from Reason and Feeling, must be happiest & safest.

The recipient of the letter, who liked to discuss religion but who regarded Evangelicals (especially the overserious young man who was currently courting her favours) as unsophisticated and unacceptable in fashionable society, accused her aunt of having a different view of the Christian religion from her own. Jane Austen denied the charge: 'We only affix a different meaning to the world *Evangelical*', she replied.[16]

Jane Austen shared with the Evangelicals a belief that Christians should be up and doing in the world. The followers of Wilberforce threw themselves into the support of good causes, especially the abolition of the Slave Trade, a topic which Jane Austen allowed her heroine Fanny Price to pursue in *Mansfield Park*.[17] It has been suggested that in her last, unfinished, novel Jane Austen despaired of society around her,[18] but this seems unlikely in someone as proud of the Protestant tradition as Jane's letters to her brother Frank show her to have been. The detached air with which Charlotte Heywood viewed the materialistic society of Sanditon was natural in a newcomer; it was hardly likely to have lasted to the end of the novel. Jane Austen's heroines often need a crisis to bring out their moral fibre, and Charlotte seems destined to meet hers when the bubble of speculation on which the new seaside resort was founded bursts, as we are forewarned it will.[19] While it is true that Jane Austen's heroines often seem to withdraw into themselves when trouble assails them, they do so only in order to find strength to face life with greater courage. When Edmund Bertram finds Fanny Price in the East Room, he is wrong to think that she has gone there to escape from the problems caused by the amateur dramatics in progress downstairs: her private refuge in the old schoolroom is not only a place where she can pursue her own hobbies, but one in which she can get her disappointments and difficulties into perspective:

> She could go there after anything unpleasant below, and find immediate

consolation in some pursuit, or some train of thought at hand. Her plants, her books . . . her writing desk, and her works of charity and ingenuity, were all within her reach; or if indisposed for employment, if nothing but musing would do, she could scarcely see an object in that room which had not an interesting remembrance connected with it. Everything was a friend, or bore her thoughts to a friend; and though there had been sometimes much of suffering to her, – though her motives had been often misunderstood, her feelings disregarded, and her comprehension under-valued; though she had known the pains of tyranny, of ridicule, and neglect, yet almost every recurrence of either had led to something consolatory; her aunt Bertram had spoken for her, or Miss Lee had been encouraging, or what was yet more frequent or more dear – Edmund had been her champion and her friend: . . . and the whole was now so blended together, so harmonized by distance, that every former affliction had its charm.[20]

Even in bereavement, Jane Austen did not expect people to wallow in their distress; she presented the continual sighings of Mrs Musgrove for her boy killed at sea, and of Captain Benwick for his dead fiancée, as sheer self-indulgence.[21] When her own sister-in-law, Elizabeth, died at Godmersham she was afraid that her emotional brother Henry, in his sympathy for the bereaved Edward, would throw himself into a paroxysm of grief, though she wrote hopefully to Cassandra (perhaps with the intention of Henry seeing the letter), 'he will exert himself to be of use & comfort'. She herself at once took on the task of writing to relatives and friends and could hardly wait to take over from Mary at Steventon the care of Edward's two little boys until after the funeral. Unlike the Evangelicals, she did not expect people actually to rejoice at the translation of their nearest and dearest to a better world (she dreaded her Evangelical cousin Edward Cooper writing 'one of his letters of cruel comfort' to her brother); but she hoped that after a period of mourning they would be able to take up their added burdens with renewed vigour. 'Edward's loss is terrible, and must be felt as such', she told Cassandra:

and these are too early days indeed to think of moderation in grief, either in him or his afflicted daughter, but soon we may hope that our dear Fanny's sense of duty to that beloved father will rouse her to exertion. For his sake, and as the most acceptable proof of love to the spirit of her departed mother, she will try to be tranquil and resigned.[22]

For all her judicious appreciation of Evangelicalism in its more moderate forms, Jane Austen could state categorically to Cassandra in 1809 that she did not like the Evangelicals.[23] The more sententious and narrow-minded exponents of the creed certainly got her back up. Mere mention of her cousin Edward Cooper, who had once been a lively companion but had become more and more pompous as time went on, was calculated to bring out the worst in her. In 1801 she could hardly give him credit for writing cheerfully about the birth of his baby son: 'He dares not write otherwise to *me* . . .', she told Cassandra, 'but perhaps he might be obliged to purge himself from the guilt of writing Nonsense by filling his shoes with whole pease for a week afterwards.'[24] If Evangelicals lacked humour it was largely, in her view, because they had no understanding of human nature. She disliked the fourth book of sermons her cousin published because they were full of 'Regeneration' and 'Conversion', neither of which she believed her fellow human beings to be in need of.[25]

For fear lest the current emphasis on morality should lead people to believe that they could gain entry into heaven by good works, Evangelicals stressed the total depravity of human nature and the need to be 'born again' through the gift of the Holy Spirit. This was a view Jane Austen could not possibly accept. The undesirable characters in her novels are not so much born wicked as led astray. There is 'no positive ill-nature' in Julia and Maria Bertram; they are simply given the wrong sort of education. Willoughby had become thoughtless and selfish from 'too early an independence and its consequent habits of idleness, dissipation and luxury'.[26] Mrs Norris was even led into temptation by her own virtues:

> Having married on a narrower income than she had been used to look forward to, she had, from the first, fancied a very strict line of economy necessary; and what was begun as a matter of prudence, soon grew into a matter choice, as an object of that needful solicitude, which there were no children to supply. Had there been a family to provide for, Mrs Norris might never have saved her money; but having no care of that kind, there was nothing to impede her frugality.[27]

Jane Austen on several occasions came near to presenting idleness as the root of all evil – and idleness was something which could easily be avoided. It is wrong to think that she was looking forward to a new social dispensation in which everybody had a job: it would have been ludicrous in her day to suggest that Maria and Julia Bertram, let alone their lady mother, should enter paid employment. She merely believed that people should learn how to use their leisure time constructively, so that they did not become bored and hence open to temptation. She greatly admired sailors, not so much for the way they carried out their duties (about which we are told nothing) as for the way in which they occupied their time when on leave. Her brother Frank was always knotting fringes and turning silver, like Captain Harville, who though prevented by lameness from taking much exercize found constant employment indoors:

> He drew, he varnished, he carpentered, he glued; he made toys for the children, he fashioned new netting-needles and pins with improvements; and if everything else was done, sat down to his large fishing-net at one corner of the room.[28]

For women, an ability to paint, or sew, or play the piano can fulfil a useful purpose if engaged in for the genuine delight of self and others rather than for showing off. Thomas Gisborne recommended serious reading, an occupation in which Jane Austen expected all her friends to engage.[29] Above all, however, people should learn to think earnestly about life's responsibilities. Henry Crawford's trouble was that he had never done so.[30]

'Conversion' was another Evangelical requirement which Jane Austen could not regard as necessary. The characters in her novels frequently grow in moral stature as a result of developing their own potential rather than by undergoing some cataclysmic change. Jane Austen could not possibly have approved of a doctrine which divided people into sheep and goats, the saved and the damned, since she was constantly showing in her novels that there is both good and bad in everybody. According to Thomas Sherlock, even the repentant thief upon the Cross was unlikely to have experienced the sudden conversion so often attributed to him: the chances are that he had heard of Jesus some time before and the latter's teaching had begun to work on him.[31]

A balanced outlook on life was required by the natural religion under which Jane Austen had been brought up, for it was itself a middle way between the rationalism of the Deists and the irrationalism of the more extreme Evangelicals. Thomas Sherlock, Jane Austen's favourite sermon writer, was one of those who had fought to establish this position, arguing, like Joseph Butler before him, that reason gave support to enough of the teaching of the Bible for the rest to be taken on trust. Sherlock agreed with the Deists that the harmony of the universe bore witness to a Creator who was as wise as He was beneficent and that men would do well to obey His commandments.[32] In line with this reasoning, Fanny Price rhapsodized as she gazed out of a window on a clear moonlit night:

> Here's harmony! Here's repose! . . . When I look out on such a night as this, I

feel as if there could be neither wickedness nor sorrow in the world; and there
certainly would be less of both if the sublimity of Nature were more attended to,
and people were carried more out of themselves by contemplating such a
scene.[33]

Unfortunately, as Edmund Bertram points out, not everyone has been
taught the lessons of Nature. Mankind over the centuries has been
heedless and selfish, and wickedness and sorrow have perpetually dark-
ened the prospect. Not even Fanny could suppose that a more benevolent outlook would put an end to the suffering caused by tragedies such
as illness and bereavement, with which Jane Austen was not unac-
quainted although they do not feature largely in her novels. To cope
with both sinfulness and sorrow the traditional teaching of the church
drew attention to the divine intervention of God, who sent His Son into
the world to die for men's sins and to rise again that they might live. The
Deists denied that such intervention could be proved by reason, but
Thomas Sherlock thought otherwise. Was it likely that the God who had
had the power to create a perfect universe had lacked the power to
rescue it from error, he asked? Of course not:

All the mystery lies in this: that so high and great a person should condescend
to become man, and subject to death, for the sake of mankind. But does it
become us to quarrel with the kindness of our blessed Lord towards us, only
because it is greater than we can conceive? No, it becomes us to bless and adore
this exceeding love, by which we are saved from condemnation.

Sherlock concluded that:

To expect redemption from the Son of God, the resurrection of our bodies
from the same hand which at first created and formed them, are rational and
well-founded acts of faith.[34]

This meant equating the reasonable with the rational, as John Locke had
done. Deists rejected the connection, while Evangelicals complained that
it degraded the mysterious power of God. Orthodox Anglicans found
that it enabled them both to cling staunchly to their religion, at a time
when Christianity on the continent of Europe faltered, and to press its
ethical demands upon a generation none too willing to hear them. The
tracts of the S.P.C.K. revealed that the church was not diffident or
slumbering but firm in its faith and militant against the immorality of the
times.[35]

The letter of advice which the Rev. George Austen wrote to his son

Frank when the latter was leaving home to join the Navy reminded the boy first and foremost of his religious duties, before going on to spell out the moral precepts of behaviour befitting an officer and a gentleman.[36] The rest of the family doubtless received a similar training. George Austen clearly believed, along with such notable preachers of his time as Laurence Sterne, that the dictates of the Holy Spirit were so much in accordance with right reason as to be indistinguishable from the workings of the properly disciplined mind; but this did not mean that prayer could be abandoned and devotion neglected. The entire Christian tradition emphasized the need for God's grace to enable people to carry out the dictates of reason and conscience – to persist in their duty to their fellow men, to love their enemies and to sustain their faith in times of tribulation. Although Jane Austen seldom attributes such grace overtly to the heroines of her novels, there is no reason to suppose that she regarded them as achieving their admirable moral stance without it. Emma Woodhouse's opinion of Mr Weston shows us that Jane Austen did not think that personal affection could stretch beyond the sphere of intimate relations:[37] for our neighbours in general we need the kind of imaginative concern that the Prayer Book calls charity. Elinor Dashwood needs more than ordinary strength to seek the best for Lucy Steele when the latter is actively engaged in wrecking her happiness; Marianne Dashwood realizes that her own abysmal failure of spirits in similar circumstances demands atonement to God as well as amendment to her family and friends.[38] When Captain Benwick seems likely to be overcome by his sorrows, Anne Elliot advises him to seek consolation by reading the memoirs of worthy characters who had suffered. These, she says, will provide him with examples not only of moral fortitude but of 'religious endurances'.[39]

That Jane Austen believed religion necessary to make morality meaningful we can see from her description of Sotherton Court, where everything was ordered to perfection but where the disused chapel at the heart of the building made the whole complex dead and dispiriting.[40] To her mind, devotion to duty was inadequate without duty to God, even in wartime: whilst the general public went into raptures over the last words that Sir John Moore had whispered to Colonel Hudson after the successful retreat to Corunna ('You know, I always wished to die like this. It is a great satisfaction to know we have beaten the French'), Jane wrote disappointedly to Cassandra, 'I wish Sir John had united something of the Christian with the Hero in this death'.[41] Like many people, she expected a higher standard of behaviour from professed Christians than from others. She was duly shaken when she heard the news that a former neighbour at Steventon, Mrs Powlett, had deserted her husband and eloped with another man. 'I should not have suspected her of such a thing', she confessed to Cassandra. 'She staid the Sacrament, I remember, the last time that you & I did.'[42]

The sight of an old village church surrounded by mature trees and mellowing gravestones has often conjured up visions of a time when country people flocked obediently to services every Sunday. Available records suggest that if this idyllic state of affairs had ever existed it no longer pertained in Jane Austen's time and that, on the contrary, the habit of non-attendance had seized a hold in the countryside long before it became endemic in the towns.[43] Jane Austen tells us nothing about the labouring population in this respect. A chance remark in *Persuasion*, where it is assumed that Anne Elliot and Captain Wentworth would be attending the same church when they were both resident at Kellynch, suggests that she assumed the gentry attended.[44] Yet Parson Woodforde records in his diary many occasions on which the local squire and his family failed to appear at morning prayer – a significant failure in view of the close alliance between church and state that was believed to be essential for the well-being of both parties.

The idea that religion and society stood or fell together had been forcefully argued by Edmund Burke in relation to the French Revolution. In 1795 Bishop Richard Watson had written: 'When religion shall have lost its hold on men's consciences, government will lose its authority over their persons, and a state of barbarous anarchy will ensue.'[45] Jane Austen was accustomed to villages like Steventon and Chawton where the church and the manor house stood beside each other – the church sometimes inside the gates of the manor house, as at Newton Valence and Hurstbourne Park; but she knew also that many of the gentry were beginning to dislike such close proximity. Thus Maria Bertram, pointing out the advantages of Sotherton to the visiting party from Mansfield, says revealingly: 'I am glad the church is not so close to the Great House as often happens in old places. The annoyance of the bells must be terrible'.[46]

In Hannah More's works there is already the suggestion, popular in Victorian times, that it was the special role of women to make up for the growing godlessness of the male population – women being naturally more inclined to religion and having fewer temptations to combat. There is no evidence that Jane Austen supported this view. While it is true that her novels more often give a predominantly moral role to women than to men, this is probably because she was happier writing about women than about men and because her settings are the family and the neighbourhood, in both of which women played a prominent part. Even in such settings she did not overestimate their moral influence. In *Sense and Sensibility* the narrator comments that John Dashwood might have been a better man if he had married a woman who brought out his better characteristics rather than one who encouraged him in his worst; yet towards the end of the same novel Elinor tells Marianne categorically that she would have had no chance of reforming Willoughby if she had married him.[47] Jane Austen once pronounced marriage to be 'a great Improver', but the particular individual she was hoping to see improved on that occasion was the woman.[48] Among the members of her own family, Jane's moral and religious inspiration seems to have come in equal measure from her sister Cassandra and her brother Frank – the latter courteous, thoughtful, diligent and honest, and above all a devoted church-goer whenever he was not at sea. Shore-based for a time at Ramsgate he was known as 'the only officer who knelt in church'.[49]

For all her enthusiasm over the beauties of nature, which she once said must be, for her, one of the joys of Heaven, Jane Austen was not one of those who believed that God could be worshipped just as well by strolling around the countryside as by attending church. When Mary Crawford professes to prefer private devotions, Edmund Bertram opposes her on the grounds that the discipline of church-going is necessary to all but the most zealous worshippers and that the atmosphere of a church helps to keep the mind from wandering.[50] This did not mean that Jane Austen expected people always to enjoy going to church. The traditional emphasis among Anglicans was upon church-going as a duty rather than as a source of spiritual uplift. 'The Holy Communion, which it will be your duty henceforward to attend . . .' was typical of the tone adopted by the S.P.C.K.'s *Pastoral Advice to Young Persons before Confirmation*, and Jane obviously saw merit in it.[51]

She was not a stickler for attending church twice every Sunday but, whenever she missed an evening service (a morning service could be neglected only in appallingly bad weather), she took care to report to Cassandra that formal devotions had been held at home instead. These usually took the pattern of reading the liturgy set for Evening Prayer, followed sometimes by a sermon from one of the many collections available at the time. If children were staying, they were expected to join in, without any dampening of their spirits: 'In the evening we had the Psalms and Lessons, and a sermon at home', Jane reported when she was looking after her young nephews from Godmersham, 'but you will not expect to hear that they did not return to conundrums the moment it was over.'[52] In *Mansfield Park* we are given a homely glimpse of such devotions in the Bertram family, for it is on a Sunday evening, when Lady Bertram had heard 'an affecting sermon' and had 'cried herself to sleep' by the fire, that Edmund pours out his troubles to Fanny Price.[53]

There was an opportunity on such occasions for personal intercessions to be offered, culminating in the final repetition of the Lord's Prayer. Jane Austen, as acting head of the little female household at Chawton, was probably called upon to lead such intercessions whenever Cassandra was away from home, and three prayers, carefully composed by her (for she was no lover of extempore effusions) have survived among her published works (see Appendix, below, pp. 197-200).[54] They reveal a consciousness of the need for soul-searching which has sometimes been attributed to Evangelical influence; but it should be remembered that this was the traditional place for such exercizes. The opportunity would naturally appeal to someone convinced of the importance of self-knowledge as a basis from which to approach others. Thomas Sherlock himself might well have approved of the petition which ran:

> Teach us to understand the sinfulness of our own hearts, and bring to our knowledge every fault of temper and every evil habit which we have indulged in to the discomfort of our fellow creatures and the danger of our own souls . . .

Sherlock had categorized among the deadliest of sins those which the Psalmist called 'secret faults' (committed in ignorance, or from habit, or without realizing the consequence to others); but he had nevertheless assured his readers that they could be covered by some general petition such as the one provided in the Prayer Book for the forgiveness of 'manifold sins and wickedness', committed 'through negligence', and 'through weakness', as well as 'through our own deliberate fault'.[55] Jane Austen characteristically refrained from mentioning in embarrassing detail what she conceived to be her own particular faults, though she was clearly aware of the dangers inherent in her own shrewd assessment of the people around her and prayed earnestly for help in avoiding malice:

> Incline us, oh God . . . to be severe only in the examination of our own conduct, to consider our fellow-creatures with kindness, and to judge of all they say and do with that charity which we should desire from them ourselves.

On her deathbed she tried to make up for any uncharitableness she had shown towards her brother James's wife by saying to her, not quite truthfully: 'You have always been a kind sister to me, Mary.'[56]

Her restrained attitude to religion did not prevent her from feeling the presence of Christ in her life to the extent of being able to picture Him, in the way that she pictured the favourite characters in her novels. 'I have seen West's famous Painting, and prefer it to anything of the kind I ever saw before', she wrote to Martha Lloyd in September 1814.

> I do not know that it *is* reckoned superior to his 'Healing in the Temple,' but it has gratified *me* much more, and indeed is the first representation of our Saviour which ever at all contented me. 'His Rejection by the Elders' is the subject. I want to have You and Cassandra see it.[57]

Nor did her traditional Anglican beliefs preclude her from asking God, with a fervour equal to that of the Evangelicals, to 'quicken our sense of [His] mercy in the redemption of the world.' Her petition echoed the phraseology of the Book of Common Prayer, to which she was wholly devoted. Among the criticisms which she levelled at her cousin Edward Cooper was his enthusiasm for the British and Foreign Bible Society, an organization which Evangelicals, along with Dissenters, tended to support in preference to the more orthodox S.P.C.K. Whilst the Bible Society devoted itself wholly to spreading knowledge of the Scriptures, the S.P.C.K. promoted the Prayer Book as being of equal importance, even preferable in that private study of the Bible could lead to erroneous ideas as to what Anglicans should believe.[58] In *Mansfield Park* Jane Austen showed that she was aware of criticisms that were being made of the dreary manner in which the liturgy was intoned, and even that it contained 'redundancies' and 'repetitions'; but she apparently did not think that these attacks should be taken too seriously, for it was to the quick-witted but shallow-judging Henry Crawford that she attributes them.[59]

In a panegyric composed shortly after her death, Jane Austen's clergyman brother Henry described her as 'thoroughly religious and devout; fearful of giving offence to God, and incapable of feeling it towards any fellow creature'.[60] The final part of this judgement may be open to some doubt, but no biographer has seen cause to question the sincerity of her Christian faith, to which she constantly bore witness and from which she drew strength during her last, distressing illness. Discussion among critics has centred wholly upon the degree, if any, to which her religious convictions are manifested in her novels.[61] Whilst some, from the time of Archbishop Whateley onwards, have seen a specifically

Christian influence at work, others have vigorously denied that her moral stance in any way differed from that of an intelligent and sensitive rationalist. There is no evidence that she knew any such rationalists and she certainly did not portray any in her novels. Her fictional characters are either thoughtful and religious, or heedless and irreligious. The latter include Henry Crawford. When he has determined to marry Fanny Price, Jane Austen's comment to her readers is:

> Henry Crawford had too much sense not to feel the worth of good principles in a wife, though he was too little accustomed to serious reflection to know them by their proper name; but when he talked of her having such a steadiness and regularity of conduct, such a high notion of honour, and such an observance of decorum as might warrant any man in the fullest dependence on her faith and integrity, he expressed what was inspired by the knowledge of her being well principled *and religious*.[61]

Appendix

*Prayers Composed by Jane Austen**

I

Give us grace almighty father, so to pray, as to deserve to be heard, to address thee with our hearts, as with our lips. Thou art every where present, from thee no secret can be hid. May the knowledge of this teach us to fix our thoughts on thee, with reverence and devotion that we pray not in vain.

Look with mercy on the sins we have this day committed and in mercy make us feel them deeply, that our repentance may be sincere, & our resolution steadfast of endeavouring against the commission of such in future. Teach us to understand the sinfulness of our own hearts, and bring to our knowledge every fault of temper and every evil habit in which we have indulged to the discomfort of our fellow-creatures, and the danger of our own souls. May we now, and on each return of night, consider how the past day has been spent by us, what have been our prevailing thoughts, words and actions during it, and how far we can acquit ourselves of evil. Have we thought irreverently of thee, have we disobeyed thy commandments, have we neglected any known duty, or willingly given pain to any human being? Incline us to ask our hearts these questions oh! God, and save us from deceiving ourselves by pride or vanity.

Give us a thankful sense of the blessings in which we live, of the many comforts of our lot; that we may not deserve to lose them by discontent or indifference.

Be gracious to our necessities, and guard us, and all we love, from evil this night. May the sick and afflicted, be now, and ever thy care; and

* From *Minor Works*, pp. 453–57.

heartily do we pray for the safety of all that travel by land or by sea, for the comfort & protection of the orphan and widow and that thy pity may be shewn upon all captives and prisoners.

Above all other blessings oh! God, for ourselves and our fellow-creatures, we implore thee to quicken our sense of thy mercy in the redemption of the world, of the value of that holy religion in which we have been brought up, that we may not, by our own neglect, throw away the salvation thou hast given us, nor be Christians only in name. Hear us almighty God, for his sake who redeemed us, and taught us thus to pray. Our Father which art in heaven &c.

II

Almighty God! Look down with mercy on thy servants here assembled and accept the petitions now offered up unto thee. Pardon oh! God the offences of the past day. We are conscious of many frailties; we remember with shame and contrition, many evil thoughts and neglected duties; and we have perhaps sinned against thee and against our fellow-creatures in many instances of which we have no remembrance. Pardon oh God! whatever thou has seen amiss in us, and give us a stronger desire of resisting every evil inclination and weakening every habit of sin. Thou knowest the infirmity of our nature, and the temptations which sur-round us. Be thou merciful, oh heavenly Father! to creatures so formed and situated. We bless thee for every comfort of our past and present existence, for our health of body and of mind and for every other source of happiness which thou hast bountifully bestowed on us and with which we close this day, imploring their continuance from thy fatherly good-ness, with a more grateful sense of them, than they have hitherto excited. May the comforts of every day, be thankfully felt by us, may they prompt a willing obedience of thy commandments and a benevolent spirit toward every fellow-creature.

Have mercy oh gracious Father! upon all that are now suffering from whatever cause, that are in any circumstance of danger or distress. Give them patience under every affliction, strengthen, comfort and relieve them.

To thy goodness we commend ourselves this night beseeching thy protection of us through its darkness and dangers. We are helpless and dependent; graciously preserve us. For all whom we love and value, for every friend and connection, we equally pray; however divided and far asunder, we know that we are alike before thee, and under thine eye.

May we be equally united in thy faith and fear, in fervent devotion towards thee, and in thy merciful protection this night. Pardon oh Lord! the imperfections of these our prayers, and accept them through the mediation of our blessed saviour, in whose holy words, we further address thee; our Father &c.

III

Father of Heaven! whose goodness has brought us in safety to the close of this day, dispose our hearts in fervent prayer. Another day is now gone, and added to those, for which we were before accountable. Teach us almighty father, to consider this solemn truth, as we should do, that we may feel the importance of every day, and every hour as it passes, and earnestly strive to make a better use of what thy goodness may yet bestow on us, than we have done of the time past.

Give us grace to endeavour after a truly Christian spirit to seek to attain that temper and forbearance and patience of which our blessed saviour has set us the highest example; and which, while it prepares us for the spiritual happiness of the life to come, will secure to us the best enjoyment of what this world can give. Incline us oh God! to think humbly of ourselves, to be severe only in the examination of our own conduct, to consider our fellow-creatures with kindness, and to judge all they say and do with that charity which we would desire from them ourselves.

We thank thee with all our hearts for every gracious dispensation, for all the blessings that have attended our lives, for every hour of safety, health and peace, of domestic comfort and innocent enjoyment. We feel that we have been blessed far beyond any thing that we have deserved; and though we cannot but pray for a continuance of all these mercies, we acknowledge our unworthiness of them and implore thee to pardon the presumption of our desires.

Keep us oh! Heavenly Father from evil this night. Bring us in safety to the beginning of another day and grant that we may rise again with every serious and religious feeling which now directs us.

May thy mercy be extended over all mankind, bringing the ignorant to the knowledge of thy truth, awakening the impenitent, touching the hardened. Look with compassion upon the afflicted of every condition, assuage the pangs of disease, comfort the broken in spirit.

More particularly do we pray for the safety and welfare of our own family and friends wheresoever dispersed, beseeching thee to avert from them all material and lasting evil of body or mind; and may we by the assistance of thy holy spirit so conduct ourselves on earth as to secure an eternity of happiness with each other in thy heavenly kingdom. Grant this most merciful Father, for the sake of our blessed saviour in whose holy name and words we further address thee. Our Father which art in heaven &c.

Notes

Jane Austen's novels, letters and minor works are cited without her name first. The editions used are:

The Novels of Jane Austen: The Text Based on Collation of the Early Editions ed. R.W. Chapman (3rd edn, 5 vols, Oxford, 1923).

The Works of Jane Austen, vi, *Minor Works*, ed. R.W. Chapman (Oxford, 1954).

Jane Austen's Letters to her Sister Cassandra and Others, ed. R.W. Chapman (2nd edn, Oxford, 1952).

Preface

1. *Pride and Prejudice*, p. 342; *Letters*, no. 77, p. 300.
2. *Cornhill Magazine*, 973 (1947–48).
3. Peter Virgin, *The Church in an Age of Negligence: Ecclesiastical Structure and Problems of Reform, 1700–1840* (Cambridge, 1989), preface, p. iv.
4. *Minor Works*, pp. 432, 436, 438.
5. G.M. Young, *Victorian England: Portrait of an Age* (2nd edn, Oxford, 1953), pp. 22, 29, 33, 49, 59, 65, 84, 91, 102, 155, 166 n. 6.
6. Peter Laslett, 'The Wrong Way through the Telescope: A Note on Literary Evidence in Historical Sociology', *British Journal of Sociology* 27 (1976), pp. 321–22.

Chapter 1: Jane Austen's Clerical Connections

1. For the correspondence with Clarke, *Letters*, no. 113, p. 429; no. 113a, p. 430; no. 120, p. 444; no. 120a, p. 445.
2. *Minor Works*, pp. 428-30
3. David Cecil, *A Portrait of Jane Austen* (London, 1978), p. 79.
4. *Letters*, no. 18, p. 57.
5. Peter Virgin, *The Church in an Age of Negligence: Ecclesiastical Structure and Problems of Reform, 1700–1840* (Cambridge, 1989), p. 134.
6. W. Austen-Leigh et al., *Jane Austen: A Family Record* (London, 1989) p. 77.
7. *Minor Works*, p. 49.
8. *Letters*, no. 10, p. 23.

 9. Ibid., no. 55, p. 211.
10. Ibid., no. 12, p. 31; no. 28, p. 97.
11. Jane Austen Society, *Collected Reports, 1976–1985* (1989), p. 222.
12. Ibid., p. 224
13. *Letters*, no. 81, p. 317.
14. Ibid., no. 11, p. 29
15. Ibid., no. 1, p. 2; no. 10, p. 26; no. 27, p. 93; no. 29, p. 99; no. 2, p. 6; no. 13, p. 36.
16. Ibid., no. 29, p. 103.
17. On the relationship with Buller, ibid., no 25, p. 85; no. 39, p. 141; no. 43, pp. 150-51, 153; no. 44, p. 157.
18. Ibid., no. 44, p. 155; no. 69, p. 268. A glowing estimate of George Cooke appears in J.E. Austen-Leigh, *A Memoir of Jane Austen by her Nephew* (Oxford, 1926), p. 81.
19. An illustrated account appeared in J.P. Neale, *Views of the Seats of Noblemen and Gentlemen in England, Wales, Scotland and Ireland* (1st series. 6 vols, London, 1818–23), vi, n.p.
20. W. Austen-Leigh et al., *Jane Austen: A Family Record*, pp. 41-42.
21. For a reference to the earlier visit, *Letters*, no. 35, p. 123.
22. On the Leigh will, W. Austen-Leigh et al., *Jane Austen: A Family Record*, pp. 222-24.
23. *Letters*, no. 54, p. 207.
24. Ibid., no. 81, p. 316; no. 54, p. 207.
25. Ibid., no. 144, pp. 491–92; no. 81, p. 316. All James Leigh-Perrot's money (£24,000) went to his wife until her death, which occurred in 1836; thereafter £1,000 went to each of Mrs Austen's surviving children, the remainder to James Austen's son James Edward, who in consequence took the name Austen-Leigh.
26. R. Austen-Leigh, *Austen Papers, 1704–1856* (University Microfilms International, Ann Arbor, MI, 1980), pp. 244-47; *The Vyne* and *Stoneleigh Abbey* (National Trust Guides); *Mansfield Park*, pp. 85-90.
27. *Letters*, no. 66, p. 260: Jane Austen Society, *Report for 1987* (1988), p. 29.
28. *Letters*, no. 49, p. 181. On the house in Castle Square, J.E. Austen-Leigh, *A Memoir*, pp. 82-84.
29. *Letters*, nos 51-54, pp. 186-209.
30. James described Marlow in the *Loiterer*, no. 58, as the ideal college tutor.
31. On Moore, *Letters*, no. 49, p. 177; no. 52, pp. 193, 195; no. 53, pp. 200, 203; no. 69, p. 269; no. 89, p. 360-61.
32. Ibid., no. 72, p. 283.
33. Ibid., no. 75, p. 293.
34. Ibid., no, 75, p. 292.
35. C. Austen, *Reminiscences* (Jane Austen Society, 1986), p. 26.
36. *Letters*, no. 69, 271.
37. Ibid., no. 74, p. 289.
38. Ibid., no. 72, pp. 281-82.
39. On the Terry affair, Jane Austen Society, *Report for 1987*, pp. 21-28.
40. W. Austen-Leigh et al., *Jane Austen: A Family Record*, p. 195.
41. *Letters*, no. 84, p. 329.
42. Ibid., no. 106, p. 416.
43. Ibid., no. 86, p. 342.
44. Ibid., no. 84, p. 331; no. 85, p. 339.
45. Jane Austen Society, *Report for 1987*, pp. 11-13.
46. C. Austen, *Reminiscences*, p. 48.
47. *Letters*, no. 139, p. 476.

Chapter 2: Patronage

1. L.S. Sutherland and L.G. Mitchell, ed., *The History of the University of Oxford*, v, *The Eighteenth Century* (Oxford, 1986), pp. 263, 314.
2. G.D. Squibb, *Founder's Kin* (Oxford, 1972), pp. 1-3.
3. C. Austen, *Reminiscences of Caroline Austen* (Jane Austen Society, 1986), pp. 49-50.
4. *Pride and Prejudice*, p. 70.
5. R. Austen-Leigh, *Austen Papers, 1704–1856* (University Microfilms International, Ann Arbor, MI, 1980), p. 130; Sutherland and Mitchell, *History of University of Oxford*, v, p. 236; John Gascoigne, *Cambridge in the Age of Enlightenment* (Cambridge, 1989), p. 15.
6. Ford K. Brown, *Fathers of the Victorians: The Age of Wilberforce* (Cambridge, 1961), p. 33.
7. James Woodforde, *The Diary of a Country Parson, 1758–1802*, ed. John Beresford (Oxford, 1949), p. 116.
8. P. Virgin, *The Church in an Age of Negligence: Ecclesiastical Structure and Problems of Reform, 1700–1840* (Cambridge, 1989), pp. 134-37, 202.
9. *Letters*, no. 85, p. 339.
10. Gordon Rupp, *Religion in Oxford, 1688–1791* (Oxford, 1968), p. 495, writes of 'unseemly importunities'.
11. *Persuasion*, pp. 102-3.
12. Virgin, *Church in Age of Negligence*, pp. 141, 220.
13. Ibid., pp. 139-41.
14. W.R. Ward, *Georgian Oxford* (London, 1958), p. 7.
15. Woodforde, *Diary*, p. 100.
16. *Letters*, no. 105, p. 415.
17. Jane Austen Society, *Collected Reports, 1976–1985* (1989), p. 180.
18. Virgin, *Church in Age of Negligence*, pp. 172-73; *Northanger Abbey*, p. 13.
19. *Persuasion*, p. 217.
20. C. Austen, *Reminiscences*, pp. 18-19.
21. William Jones, *The Diary of the Rev. William Jones, 1771–1821*, ed. O.F. Christie (London, 1929), p. 147.
22. *Letters*, no. 89, p. 363; no. 90, p. 367.
23. Thomas Gisborne, *An Enquiry into the Duties of Men in the Higher and Middle Classes of Society* (5th edn, 2 vols, London, 1800), ii, pp. 3-4.
24. *Mansfield Park*, pp. 108-10.
25. Ibid., p. 109.
26. *Sense and Sensibility*. p. 295.
27. *Mansfield Park*, pp. 23-24; *Sense and Sensibility*, p. 295.
28. Virgin, *Church in Age of Negligence* (pp. 98-99, 194, 254) considers £150 a 'reasonable minimum', but Jane Austen seems to think that £300 hardly qualified as such.
29. G.F.A. Best, *Temporal Pillars: Queen Anne's Bounty, the Ecclesiastical Commissioners and the Church of England*, (Cambridge, 1964), pp. 13, 207-8.
30. Virgin, *Church in Age of Negligence*, p. 259.
31. C.K. Francis Brown, *A History of the English Clergy, 1800–1900* (London, 1953), p. 21.
32. *Letters*, no. 62, p. 241.
33. Virgin, *Church in Age of Negligence*, pp. 145, 194, 203, 259.
34. *Letters*, no. 30, p. 106.
35. *Pride and Prejudice*, p. 169.
36. Ibid., p. 383.

37. Jane Austen Society, *Collected Reports, 1976–85*, pp. 90-91; R. Austen-Leigh, *Austen Papers*, p. 288.
38. Virgin, *Church in Age of Negligence*, pp. 35-36.
39. On curates' stipends generally, ibid., pp. 222-31; and Best, *Temporal Pillars*, pp. 207-8.
40. Jones, *Diary*, pp. 147-48 (on p. 163 he refers to 'the drudgery of school').
41. *Letters.* no. 31, p. 112.
42. W. Austen-Leigh et al., *Jane Austen: A Family Record*, pp. 85, 88, 93-94.
43. *Sense and Sensibility.* pp. 276-77.
44. *Letters*, no. 14, pp. 39-40; no. 22, p. 70.
45. *Mansfield Park*, p. 24.
46. On Thomas Knight's will, see Jane Austen Society, *Report for 1987*, p. 11.
47. Rupp, *Religion in Oxford*, p. 495.
48. *Sense and Sensibility*, p. 197.
49. C.J. Abbey and J. Overton, *The English Church in the Eighteenth Century* (2 vols, London, 1878), ii, p. 13.
50. R.W. Chapman, 'Jane Austen's Friend, Mrs Barret', *Nineteenth-Century Fiction* (1949), p. 172.
51. *Mansfield Park*, pp. 247-48.
52. *Persuasion*, p. 78.
53. The 40 per cent estimate is from Virgin, *Church in Age of Negligence*, p. 200.
54. Ivor Morris, *Mr Collins Considered: Approaches to Jane Austen* (London, 1987), p. 64.
55. *Pride and Prejudice*, pp. 157, 163, 169.
56. Virgin, *Church in Age of Negligence*, p. 195.

Chapter 3: The Parson's Education

1. Jane Austen Society, *Collected Reports, 1966– 1975* (1977), pp. 9-12; W. Austen-Leigh et al., *Jane Austen: A Family Record* (London, 1989), p. 44.
2. *Northanger Abbey*, p. 64.
3. *Sense and Sensibility*, pp. 102-3.
4. Edward Gibbon, *The Memoirs of the Life of Edward Gibbon, by Himself* (London, 1990), pp. 50-62, 64-67.
5. *Mansfield Park*, p. 94.
6. *Letters*, no. 20, p. 64.
7. L.S. Sutherland and L.G. Mitchell, ed., *The History of the University of Oxford*, v, *The Eighteenth Century* (Oxford, 1968), pp. 3, 263, 360; John Gascoigne, *Cambridge in the Age of Enlightenment* (Cambridge, 1989), pp. 10, 21; Peter Virgin, *The Church in an Age of Negligence: Ecclesiastical Structure and Problems of Reform, 1700–1840* (Cambridge, 1989), pp. 134-37.
8. *Mansfield Park*, pp. 339-41.
9. Sutherland and Mitchell, *History of the University of Oxford*, v, pp. 470-75; D.A. Winstanley, *Early Victorian Cambridge* (Cambridge, 1940), pp. 149-54.
10. *Sense and Sensibility*, p. 275.
11. C.K. Francis Brown, *A History of the English Clergy, 1800–1900* (London, 1953), p. 243.
12. Virgin, *Church in Age of Negligence*, pp. 137-38; James Woodforde, *The Diary of a Country Parson, 1758–1802*, ed. John Beresford (Oxford, 1949), p. 15; *Mansfield Park*, p. 282.
13. *Letters*, no. 91, p. 374.
14. Sutherland and Mitchell, *History of University of Oxford*, v, pp. 470-75; Winstanley, *Early Victorian Cambridge*, pp. 155-56, 175; Gascoigne, *Cambridge in Age of Enlightenment*, pp. 9, 174-75.
15. J.E. Austen-Leigh, *A Memoir of Jane Austen* (Oxford, 1926), p. 11; Sutherland and Mitchell, *History of University of Oxford*, v, pp. 200, 242.
16. William Jones, *The Diary of the Rev. William Jones, 1771–1821*, ed. O.F. Christie (London, 1929), pp. 158-59.
17. William Cockburn, *Strictures on Clerical Education in the University of Cambridge* (London, 1809), pp. 4-6, 17.
18. Winstanley, *Early Victorian Cambridge*, pp. 168-69; Gascoigne, *Cambridge in Age of Enlightenment*, pp. 263- 68.
19. R. Austen-Leigh, *Austen Papers, 1704–1856* (University Microfilms International, Ann Arbor, MI, 1980), p. 133.
20. *Mansfield Park*, p. 88.
21. Sutherland and Mitchell, *History of University of Oxford*, v, pp. 431-33; Winstanley, *Early Victorian Cambridge*, pp. 83-85; Gascoigne, *Cambridge in Age of Enlightenment*, pp. 201-5.
22. Ibid., pp. 7-8, 21-22, 237-38; Sutherland and Mitchell, *History of University of Oxford*, v, p. 369.
23. *Mansfield Park*, p. 113.
24. Gascoigne, *Cambridge in Age of Enlightenment*, pp. 2, 7, 178-79.
25. *Letters*, no. 81, pp. 313-14.
26. Winstanley, *Early Victorian Cambridge*, p. 151.
27. Jones, *Diary*, p. 158.
28. *Mansfield Park*, pp. 92-93.

29. Winstanley, *Early Victorian Cambridge*, pp. 18-20; Gascoigne, *Cambridge in Age of Enlightenment*, pp. 249-56.
30. Sutherland and Mitchell, *History of University of Oxford*, v, p. 421; *Letters*, no. 75, p. 293.
31. J.E. Austen-Leigh, *A Memoir*, p. 10.
32. Gascoigne, *Cambridge in Age of Enlightenment*, p. 23; Virgin, *Church in Age of Negligence*, pp. 109-10, 255.
33. Sutherland and Mitchell, *History of University of Oxford*, v, p. 393.
34. Woodforde, *Diary*, pp. 21-23.
35. Benjamin Newton, *Diary of Benjamin Newton, Rector of Wath, 1816–1818*, ed. C.P. Fendall and E.A. Crutchley (Cambridge, 1933), pp. viii-xi, 2, 53, 149-51.
36. *Mansfield Park*, pp. 111-12.
37. Jones, *Diary*, pp. 111-12; *Mansfield Park*, p. 110.
38. Ford K. Brown, *Fathers of the Victorians: The Age of Wilberforce* (Cambridge, 1961), p. 36.
39. J.E. Austen-Leigh, *A Memoir*, p. 11.
40. *Northanger Abbey*, p. 3.
41. *Letters*, no. 31, p. 111.
42. *Letters*, no. 9, p. 2; no. 14, p. 38; *Northanger Abbey*, p. 107.
43. R. Austen-Leigh, *Austen Papers*, p. 132.
44. *Letters*, no. 42, p. 147.
45. *Persuasion*, p. 74; *Pride and Prejudice*, p. 71.
46. Jones, *Diary*, p. 76.

Chapter 4: The Parson's Income

1. Peter Virgin, *The Church in an Age of Negligence: Ecclesiastical Structure and Problems of Reform, 1700–1840* (Cambridge, 1989), p. 38.
2. *Pride and Prejudice*, p. 101.
3. *Sense and Sensibility*, p. 293.
4. On the complications at Cubbington, see Jane Austen Society, *Collected Reports, 1976–1985* (1989), p. 180.
5. *Sense and Sensibility*, p. 282.
6. W.R. Ward, 'The Tithe Question in England in the Early Nineteenth Century', *Journal of Ecclesiastical History*, 16 (1965), p. 68.
7. J.A. Venn, *Foundations of Agricultural Economics* (Cambridge, 1923), pp. 154-66.
8. *Letters*, no. 29, p. 103.
9. Ward, 'The Tithe Question', p. 70; idem, *Religion and Society in England, 1790–1850* (London, 1972) p. 9.
10. W.R. Le Fanu, *Queen Anne's Bounty* (London, 1921), pp. 51-55.
11. C.K. Francis Brown, *A History of the English Clergy, 1800–1900* (London, 1953), p. 18.
12. Ibid., pp. 17-18.
13. R. Austen-Leigh, *Austen Papers, 1705-1856* (University Microfilms International, Ann Arbor, MI, 1980), p. 29.
14. Gordon Rupp, *Religion in Oxford, 1688–1791* (Oxford, 1968), p. 494.
15. *Letters*, no. 13, p. 36; no. 12, p. 32; no. 18, p. 57.
16. Ibid., no. 13, pp. 35-36; no. 27, pp. 93-94.
17. E.g. *Mansfield Park*, p. 67.
18. *Letters*, no. 13, p. 36; *Pride and Prejudice*, p. 156.
19. William Cobbett, *Rural Rides* (Penguin edn, Harmondsworth, 1967), p. 106.
20. *Letters*, no. 24, p. 81.
21. Ibid., no. 18, p. 55.
22. *Mansfield Park*, p. 226.
23. John Skinner, *Journal of a Somerset Rector, 1803–1834*, ed. H. and P. Coombs (Bath, 1930), pp. 2, 62.
24. Virgin, *Church in Age of Negligence*, pp. 48-54.
25. Le Fanu, *Queen Anne's Bounty*, pp. 37, 43-44.
26. G.F.A. Best, *Temporal Pillars: Queen Anne's Bounty, the Ecclesiastical Commissioners and the Church of England* (Cambridge, 1964), pp. 207-8.
27. Edmund Burke, *Reflections on the Revolution in France*, in *The Works of the Right Honourable Edmund Burke* (2 vols, London 1834), i, pp. 426-43.
28. *Sense and Sensibility*, p. 283; *Northanger Abbey*, p. 226; *Mansfield Park*, pp. 3, 226.
29. Jane Austen Society, *Reports for 1987* (1988), pp. 12-13.
30. *Sense and Sensibility*, p. 292.
31. *Northanger Abbey*, pp. 135-36; *Mansfield Park*, p. 473.
32. *Sense and Sensibility*, p. 374; *Northanger Abbey*, p. 176; *Mansfield Park*, p. 31; *Emma*, p. 35; *Pride and Prejudice*, p. 169.
33. Ibid., p. 28
34. Ibid., p. 136.
35. Ibid., pp. 84, 105-6.
36. Virgin, *Church in Age of Negligence*, p. 110.
37. Ibid., pp. 110-11.
38. *Sense and Sensibility*, pp. 102, 298; *Persuasion*, p. 76.

Chapter 5: The Parson's Dwelling

1. John Woodforde, *Georgian Houses for All* (London, 1978), p. 77; B. Anthony Bax, *The English Parsonage* (London, 1964), p. 46.
2. *Letters*, no. 31, p. 111; W. Austen-Leigh et al., *Jane Austen: A Family Record* (London, 1989), p. 11.
3. Peter Virgin, *The Church in an Age of Negligence: Ecclesiastical Structure and Problems of Reform, 1700–1840* (Cambridge, 1989), pp. 146-47.
4. G.H. Tucker, *A Goodly Heritage: A History of Jane Austen's Family* (Manchester, 1983), p. 29; Jane Austen Society, *Collected Reports, 1976–1985* (1989), pp. 12-13.
5. Idem, *Report for 1987* (1988), p. 11.
6. Idem, *Collected Reports, 1976–1985*, pp. 245- 48; Tucker, *A Goodly Heritage*, pp. 29-30, 69; R.W. Chapman, *Jane Austen: Facts and Problems* (Oxford, 1948), pp. 20-22.
7. Bax, *The English Parsonage*, pp. 112-13.
8. C. Austen, *Reminiscences of Caroline Austen* (Jane Austen Society, 1986), pp. 56-57.
9. *Pride and Prejudice*, p. 213; R. Austen-Leigh, *Austen Papers, 1704–1856* (University Microfilms International, Ann Arbor, MI 1980), p. 175; J.E. Austen-Leigh, *A Memoir of Jane Austen by her Nephew* (Oxford, 1923), pp. 20-21, 38-39.
10. *Letters*, no. 10, p. 26.
11. Jane Austen Society, *Collected Reports, 1966–1975* (1977), p. 246; *Letters*, no. 36, p. 126.
12. Ibid., no. 18, p. 55,
13. Ibid, no. 13, pp. 34, 35; no. 9, pp. 20-21.
14. Ibid, no. 22, pp. 75-76; no. 25, pp. 82-83; no. 36, p. 126.
15. Constance Hill, *Jane Austen, her Homes and her Friends* (London, 1902), p. 71.
16. *Emma* p. 254; *Letters*, no. 1, p. 2.
17. Ibid., no. 89, p. 361; Maggie Lane, *Jane Austen's England* (London, 1986), p. 72.
18. *Sense and Sensibility*, p. 29.
19. John Skinner, *Journal of a Somerset Rector, 1803–34*, ed. H. and P. Coombs (Bath, 1930), p. vii.
20. Ibid., p. 24.
21. *Mansfield Park*, p. 65.
22. *Northanger Abbey*, pp. 176, 212-13.
23. W. Austen-Leigh et al., *Jane Austen: A Family Record*, p. 11; C. Austen, *Reminiscences* pp. 56-57.
24. *Pride and Prejudice*, p. 67.
25. Woodforde, *Georgian Houses*, p. 83; *Pride and Prejudice*, p. 155.
26. *Mansfield Park*, p. 57.
27. *Emma*, p. 83.
28. *Letters*, no. 139, p. 476.
29. *Pride and Prejudice*, p. 157; D.W. Smithers, *Jane Austen in Kent* (Westerham, 1982), pp. 41-51.
30. *Northanger Abbey*, p. 212.
31. *Mansfield Park*, pp. 241-44.
32. *Persuasion*, pp. 76, 85.
33. J.E. Austen-Leigh, *A Memoir*, p. 88.
34. *Letters*, note to p. 281.
35. C. Austen, *My Aunt Jane Austen: A Memoir* (new edn, Jane Austen Society, 1991), p. 4.
36. *Sense and Sensibility*, p. 108.
37. *Letters*, no. 130, p. 458.

38. J.E. Austen-Leigh, *A Memoir*, p. 85; *Letters*, no. 72, p. 281.
39. Ibid., no. 17, p. 50.
40. Lane, *Jane Austen's England*, p. 40.
41. *Mansfield Park*, p. 243.
42. W.R. Ward, 'The Tithe Question in England in the Early-Nineteenth Century', *Journal of Ecclesiastical History*, 16 (1965), p. 73.
43. William Cobbett, *Rural Rides* (Penguin edn, Harmondsworth, 1967), p. 396.
44. R. Austen-Leigh, *Austen Papers*, p. 273.
45. Mary Russell Mitford, *Our Village* (1st series, new edn, London, 1879), p. 8.
46. W.R. Le Fanu, *Queen Anne's Bounty* (London, 1921), p. 70.
47. *Mansfield Park*, p. 55.
48. *Letters*, no. 31, p. 111.
49. Ibid., no. 44, p. 159.
50. James Woodforde, *The Diary of a Country Parson, 1758–1802*, ed. John Beresford (Oxford, 1949), pp. 22, 24, 25.
51. Jane Austen Society, *Report for 1987* (1988), p. 42; R. Austen-Leigh, *Austen Papers*, p. 251.
52. *Persuasion*, p. 36.
53. *Emma*, p. 87.
54. Uvedale Price, *An Essay on the Picturesque* (London, 1794), pp. 403-9.
55. Anne Scott-James, *The Cottage Garden* (London, 1981), pp. 25-28, 35-36.
56. Richardson Wright, *The Story of Gardening* (London, 1934), p. 56.
57. *Mansfield Park*, pp. 53, 55-56.
58. Humphry Repton, *The Landscape Gardening and Landscape Architecture of the Late Humphry Repton, being his Entire Works on these Subjects*, ed. J.C. Loudon (new edn, London 1840), pp. 62-65, 90-94.
59. Ibid., p. 161; Clive Aslet, 'Stoneleigh Abbey, Warwickshire, ii', *Country Life*, 20 Dec. 1984; Mavis Batey, 'In Quest of Jane Austen's "Mr Repton"', *Garden History*, 5 (1977), pp. 19-29.
60. *Pride and Prejudice*, pp. 245, 253-54.
61. T.J. Wise and J.A. Symington, ed., *The Brontës: Their Lives, Friendships and Correspondence* (4 vols, Oxford, 1932), ii, p. 179 (Letter to George Henry Lewes, 12 Jan. 1848).
62. David C. Stuart, *Georgian Gardens* (London, 1979), p. 116.
63. F. de la Rochefoucauld, *A Frenchman in England, 1784*, ed. J. Marchand (Cambridge, 1933), pp. 45-46, 48.
64. Hill, *Jane Austen, her Homes and her Friends*, p. 71.
65. *Pride and Prejudice*, p. 165; Smithers, *Jane Austen in Kent*, pp. 45-47.
66. Cowper, William, 'The Task, Book I', *Cowper: Poetical Works*, ed. H.S. Milford (Oxford, 1967), pp. 129-45.
67. Jane Austen Society, *Collected Reports, 1966–1975*, pp. 245-48.
68. *Sense and Sensibility*, p. 374.
69. *Mansfield Park*, pp. 208-10.
70. Pamela Horn, *Life in a Country Town: Reading and Mary Russell Mitford, 1787–1855* (Abingdon, 1984), p. 6.
71. *Mansfield Park*, p. 72; *Letters*, no. 49, p. 178; no. 72, p. 281; no. 73, p. 237; J. E. Austen-Leigh, *A Memoir*, p. 85.
72. D. Jacques, *Georgian Gardens: The Reign of Nature* (London, 1983), p. 21.
73. *Mansfield Park*, pp. 322-23; *Sense and Sensibility*, pp. 305-6.
74. *Letters*, no. 72, p. 283.
75. *Emma*, p. 83; *Pride and Prejudice*, p. 155.
76. Robert Williams, 'Rural Economy and the Antique in the English Landscape Garden', *Journal of Garden History*, 7 (1987), p. 78.
77. R. Austen-Leigh, *Austen Papers*, p. 245.

78. *Letters*, no. 25, p. 86; Jane Austen Society, *Collected Reports, 1966–1975*, p. 246.
79. *Letters*, no. 23, pp. 76-77; no. 27, pp. 93-94; Woodforde, *Diary*, p. 177.
80. *Letters*, no. 74, p. 290.
81. *Mansfield Park*, pp. 54-55.
82. Dorothy Wordsworth, *Journals of Dorothy Wordsworth*, ed. Mary Moorman (Oxford, 1971), e.g. pp. 103, 106, 122, 123, 124, 127, 132, 134.
83. *Letters*, no. 62, p. 241.
84. *Northanger Abbey*, p. 214.
85. Cited by Woodforde, *Georgian Houses*, p. 80.
86. John Clare, 'The Parish', *The Poems of John Clare*, ed. J.W. Tibble (2 vols, London, 1935), i, pp. 542-69.
87. Jane Austen Society, *Reports for 1987*, p. 13.
88. *Letters* no. 44, p. 159.

Chapter 6: The Country Parish

1. James Austen, *Loiterer*, no. 21.
2. *Letters*, no. 10, p. 25.
3. The drawing is reproduced in *Letters*, facing p. 1.
4. J.E. Austen-Leigh, *A Memoir of Jane Austen by her Nephew* (Oxford, 1926), pp. 41-42.
5. Jane Austen Society, *Collected Reports* 1976–1985 (1989), p. 339.
6. *Letters*, no. 31, p. 110.
7. Ibid., no. 15, p. 46.
8. Ibid., no. 11, p. 30; no. 10, p. 25; no, 15, p. 45.
9. Victoria County History, *The County of Hampshire and the Isle of Wight* (6 vols, London, 1903–12), v, p. 560.
10. Constance Hill, *Jane Austen, her Homes and her Friends* (London, 1902), p. 63.
11. William Cobbett, *Rural Rides* (Penguin edn, Harmondsworth, 1967), p. 57.
12. *Sense and Sensibility*, p. 88.
13. *Letters*, no. 30, p. 104.
14. *Northanger Abbey*, p. 120.
15. V.J. Hunt, *Chawton 1841–81* (unpublished Ph.D. thesis, Portsmouth Polytechnic, 1986), pp. 5-7, 15-17.
16. *Letters*, no. 142, p. 489.
17. Ibid., no. 130, p. 458.
18. The picture is displayed at Jane Austen's House, Chawton.
19. F.C. and J. Rivington, ed., *The Clerical Guide* (1817; 2nd edn, 1822).
20. *Letters*, no. 78.1, pp. 504-5; no. 125, p. 450.
21. Gilbert White, *The Natural History of Selborne* (Harmondsworth, 1967), p. 17.
22. *Mansfield Park*, pp. 241-42.
23. *Northanger Abbey*, pp. 16, 232-33.
24. *Persuasion*, pp. 36, 102.
25. *Sense and Sensibility*, p. 197; *Northanger Abbey*, p. 212.
26. *Emma*, p. 7.
27. Ibid., pp. 83, 233.
28. Fanny Burney, *Selected Letters and Journals*, ed. Joyce Hemlow (Oxford, 1986), p. 58.
29. C.W. Chalklin, *The Provincial Towns of Georgian England* (London, 1974), pp. 4, 25, 317-18.
30. *Emma*, p. 68.
31. *Northanger Abbey*, p. 214.
32. *Pride and Prejudice* pp. 168, 170.
33. *Emma*, p. 66.
34. *Mansfield Park*, pp. 247-48.
35. *Northanger Abbey*, p. 209.
36. Anthony Russell, *The Country Parish* (London, 1980), p. 217.
37. *Letters*, no. 133, p. 464.
38. Ibid., no. 86, p. 344.
39. James Austen, *Loiterer*, no. 2; John Skinner, *Journal of a Somerset Rector, 1803–34*, ed. H. and P. Coombs (Bath, 1930), p. vii.
40. James Woodforde, *The Diary of a Country Parson, 1758–1802*, ed. John Beresford (Oxford, 1949), pp. 25, 35, 243.
41. Skinner, *Journal*, p. 42.
42. *Letters*, no. 142, p. 489.
43. *Mansfield Park*, p. 226.

44. *Pride and Prejudice*, p. 66.
45. *Mansfield Park*, pp. 339-40.
46. *Emma*, p. 75.
47. *Letters*, no. 64, p. 252.
48. William Jones, *The Diary of William Jones, 1771–1821*, ed. G.F. Christie (London, 1929), p. 176.
49. *Mansfield Park*, p. 92; *Letters*, no. 61, p. 238.
50. Ibid., no. 61, p. 238.
51. *Northanger Abbey*, p. 209.
52. Jones, *Diary*, p. 154.
53. Woodforde, *Diary*, p. 51.
54. *Mansfield Park*, pp. 92, 111.
55. Ibid., pp. 92-93.
56. *Letters*, no. 3, p. 7.
57. *Mansfield Park*, p. 58.
58. *Persuasion*, p. 78; *Sense and Sensibility*, p. 377.
59. *Emma*, pp. 111, 174-75, 455.
60. *Mansfield Park*, p. 111.
61. C. Austen, *My Aunt Jane Austen: A Memoir* (Jane Austen Society, 1991), pp. 8-9; George Crabbe, 'The Borough', *The Complete Poetical Works of George Crabbe*, ed. N. Dalrymple-Champneys and A. Pollard (3 vols, Oxford, 1988), i, pp. 338-470, lines 81-111.
62. *Pride and Prejudice*, p. 68; *Letters*, no. 6, p. 14.

Chapter 7: The Clergy and the Neighbourhood

1. *Sense and Sensibility*, p. 88; *Emma*, p. 191.
2. *Persuasion*, pp. 42-43.
3. *Letters*, no. 75, p. 294.
4. *Cornhill Magazine*, 973 (1947–48).
5. *Letters*, no. 72, p. 283; no. 73, p. 285; no. 74, p. 290; *Sense and Sensibility*, p. 30.
6. *Pride and Prejudice*, pp. 139, 255.
7. *Emma*, pp. 16, 303.
8. Ibid., p. 207.
9. *Pride and Prejudice*, p. 18; *Emma*, pp. 33, 360.
10. *Minor Works*, pp. 327-30, 335-36.
11. *Letters*, no. 24, pp. 79-80.
12. Ibid., no. 24, p. 80, no. 17, p. 52; no. 54, p. 205; no. 91, p. 373.
13. *Emma*, p. 165.
14. *Sense and Sensibility*, p. 103; *Pride and Prejudice*, p. 36.
15. *Emma*, pp. 92, 137, 183, 197, 214, 345; *Letters*, no. 98, p. 394.
16. John Skinner, *Journal of a Somerset Rector, 1803–34*, ed. H. and P. Coombs (Bath, 1903), p. 3.
17. *Pride and Prejudice*, pp. 66, 169.
18. William Jones, *The Diary of the Rev. William Jones, 1771–1821*, ed. O.F. Christie (London, 1929), p. 20.
19. *Sense and Sensibility*, p. 33.
20. *Letters*, no 12, p. 32; no. 15, p. 43; no. 18, p. 55; *Persuasion*, p. 39.
21. R. Austen-Leigh, *Austen Papers, 1704–1856* (University Microfilms International, Ann Arbor, 1980), p. 291; *Persuasion*, p. 43; Oliver Macdonagh, 'Highbury and Chawton: Social Convergence in *Emma*', *Historical Studies*, 18 (1978), pp. 42, 44-47.
22. T.J. Wise and J.A. Symington, ed., *The Brontës: Their Lives, Friendships and Correspondence* (4 vols, Oxford, 1932), ii, pp. 179-80.
23. Thomas Gisborne, *An Enquiry into the Duties of the Female Sex* (London, 1797), p. 206.
24. *Letters*, no. 87, p. 351; *Pride and Prejudice*, p. 35.
25. *Letters*, no. 27, p. 93.
26. *Sense and Sensibility*, p. 232; *Persuasion*, pp. 42-43; *Emma*, p. 219.
27. Ibid., p. 149.
28. *Letters*, no. 132, p. 462; no. 133, p. 464; *Pride and Prejudice*, p. 142.
29. Ibid., p. 76; Jane Austen Society, *Collected Reports, 1976–1985* (1989), p. 285.
30. *Letters*, no. 15, p. 43.
31. *Pride and Prejudice*, p. 87.
32. *Letters*, no. 2, p. 5.
33. James Austen, *Loiterer*, no. 21; *Letters*, no. 29, p. 99; no. 32, pp. 113, 117.
34. Ibid., no. 75, pp. 292-94; no. 78, p. 305.
35. *Northanger Abbey*, pp. 106-7, 111; *Sense and Sensibility*, pp. 96-98.
36. *Letters*, no. 14, p. 39.
37. *Sense and Sensibility*, p. 233.
38. Peter Virgin, *The Church in an Age of Negligence: Ecclesiastical Structure and Problems of Reform, 1700–1840* (Cambridge, 1989), pp. 110-12.
39. R.G. Thorne, ed., *History of Parliament: The House of Commons, 1790–1820* (5 vols, London, 1986), i, pp. 4-5, 9, 11, 121; iii, pp. 433-34.
40. Stephen Terry, *The Diaries of Dummer: Reminiscences of an Old Sportsman, Stephen Terry of Dummer* (London, 1934), p. 153.

41. *Letters*, no. 23, p. 75.
42. Ibid., no. 2, p. 6; no. 25, p. 82; R. Austen-Leigh, *Austen Papers*, pp. 257-58.
43. Terry, *Diaries*, pp. 39-41, 74-79; *Letters*, no. 24, p. 80.
44. Terry, *Diaries*, pp. 147-51.
45. Muriel Jaeger, *Before Victoria* (London, 1956), p. x.
46. James Austen, *Loiterer*, no. 21.
47. *Letters*, no. 116, p. 435.
48. Ibid., no. 85, p. 338; no. 86, p. 344; no. 87, p. 353; no. 88, p. 357.
49. James Woodforde, *The Diary of a Country Parson, 1758–1802*, ed. Mary Moorman (Oxford, 1971), p. 606; Skinner, *Journal*, p. 10.
50. The figures were communicated by Linda Colley in a paper entitled 'The Reach of the State: The Appeal of the Nation', read at the Anglo-American Conference of Historians, 1991.
51. Jane Austen Society, *Collected Reports, 1976–1985* (1989), p. 227.
52. Ibid., p. 211
53. *Letters*, no. 88, p. 356.
54. Ibid., no. 74.1, p. 501.
55. Ibid., no 13, p. 36.
56. Mary Austen wrote in her notebook on 25 Oct 1809, when her husband was rector of Steventon: 'Gave a dinner in Mr Digweed's barn, to all the poor of the parish.' C. Austen, *Reminiscences of Caroline Austen* (Jane Austen Society, 1986), p. 24.
57. *Emma*, p. 87.
58. *Pride and Prejudice*, p. 169.
59. Virgin, *Church in Age of Negligence*, pp. 117-18, 256.
60. *Emma*, p. 225.
61. Ibid., pp. 383, 465-66.
62. *Letters*, no. 18, pp. 55-56.
63. Woodforde, *Diary*, pp. 26-27, 33.

Chapter 8: The Parson's Wife

1. Park Honan, *Jane Austen: Her Life* (London, 1987), p. 12.
2. L.S. Sutherland and L.G. Mitchell, ed., *The History of the University of Oxford*, v, *The Eighteenth Century* (Oxford, 1986), p. 356.
3. *Emma*, p. 270.
4. *Letters*, no. 100, pp. 400-1.
5. *Emma*, pp. 290-291.
6. *Pride and Prejudice*, p. 140.
7. *Sense and Sensibility*, p. 36.
8. *Letters*, no. 11, p. 28.
9. *Emma*, p. 75.
10. Ibid., p. 181.
11. *Pride and Prejudice*. p. 106.
12. *Letters*, no. 61, p. 236.
13. *Emma*, p. 289.
14. *Letters*, no. 49, p. 177; no. 50, p. 185.
15. Ibid., no. 73, p. 286.
16. *Mansfield Park*, p. 28.
17. Ibid., p. 30.
18. W. Austen-Leigh et al., *Jane Austen: A Family Record* (London, 1989), p. 44.
19. *Emma*, p. 290.
20. *Mansfield Park*, p. 210.
21. *Pride and Prejudice*, pp. 122-23, 125.
22. *Letters*, no. 59, p. 226; no. 90, p. 367.
23. Ibid., no. 52, p. 193; no. 53, p. 203; no. 89, p. 361; *Pride and Prejudice*, p. 156.
24. *Letters*, no. 49, p. 177.
25. *Pride and Prejudice*, pp. 178-79.
26. James Woodforde, *The Diary of a Country Parson, 1758–1802*, ed. John Beresford (Oxford, 1949), p. 451.
27. William Jones, *The Diary of the Rev. William Jones, 1771-1821*, ed. O.F. Christie (London, 1929), p. 230.
28. *Emma*, pp. 41, 205-6.
29. *Letters*, no. 14, p. 39; no. 69, p. 267; no. 73, p. 284; no. 84, pp. 334-35.
30. Ibid., no. 29, pp. 101-2; no. 30, pp. 107-8; no. 36, p. 126; Jones, *Diary*, pp. 105-6.
31. Jane Austen Society, *Collected Reports, 1976–1985* (1989), p. 305.
32. *Emma*, pp. 155, 239.
33. Ibid., p. 375.
34. *Letters*, no. 75, p. 295.
35. Ibid., no. 43, p. 152.
36. Ibid., no. 78.1, pp. 504-5.
37. *Emma*, p. 66.
38. *Letters*, no. 14, p. 39.
39. *Northanger Abbey*, p. 174; *Letters*, no. 23, p. 75; no. 72, pp. 280-81; no. 88, p. 356.
40. *Mansfield Park*, p. 212.
41. Ibid., pp. 212-13.
42. *Letters*, no. 10, p. 25; no. 12, pp. 31, 36; no. 33, p. 119; *Emma*, p. 458.
43. Hannah More, *Coelebs in Search of a Wife*, in *The Works of Hannah More* (18 vols, London, 1818), ix, pp. 205-6.
44. Jones, *Diary*, pp. 78-79, 98, 103, 113.

45. W. Austen-Leigh et al., *Jane Austen: A Family Record*, p. 7; J.E. Austen-Leigh, *A Memoir of Jane Austen by her Nephew* (Oxford, 1926), pp. 5-7.
46. *Pride and Prejudice*, pp. 14-16, 108.
47. C. Austen, *Reminiscences of Caroline Austen* (Jane Austen Society, 1986), pp. 12-13; *Letters*, no. 48, p. 173.
48. Ibid., no. 44, p. 157; no. 118, p. 440.
49. Ibid., no. 4, p. 8.
50. *Sense and Sensibility*, p. 160.
51. *Persuasion*, p. 167.
52. Patrick Piggott, *The Innocent Diversion: A Study of Music in the Life and Writings of Jane Austen* (London, 1979), p. 7; *Letters*, no. 85, p. 339.
53. Ibid., no. 27, pp. 91-92.
54. Honan, *Jane Austen*, pp. 90-91.
55. *Pride and Prejudice*, pp. 105-6.
56. *Emma*, pp. 31, 41-2.
57. B. Anthony Bax, *The English Parsonage* (London, 1964), pp. 61-62.
58. Benjamin Newton, *The Diary of Benjamin Newton, Rector of Wath, 1816-1818*, ed. C.P. Fendall and E.A. Crutchley (Cambridge, 1933), p. 61.
59. J.E. Austen-Leigh, *A Memoir*, p. 39.
60. *Letters* no. 4, p. 10.
61. Ibid., no. 39, p. 142.
62. Jane Austen Society, *Report for 1988* (1989), p. 28; *Letters*, no. 17, p. 50; no. 23, p. 69; no. 32, p. 114; no. 33, p. 117.
63. Ibid., no. 13. p, 35.
64. Ibid., no. 32, p. 113.
65. Ibid., no. 62, p. 241.
66. Deirdre Le Faye, 'News from Chawton: A Letter from Mrs George Austen', *Review of English Studies*, new series, 38 (1987), pp. 364-65. The miniature of Elizabeth Austen by Cosway is reproduced in *Letters*, facing p. 216.
67. R. Austen-Leigh, *Austen Papers, 1704–1856* (University Microfilms International, Ann Arbor, MI, 1980), pp. 25, 29; *Letters*, no. 54, p. 207; no. 75, p. 296.
68. *Sense and Sensibility*, p. 375; *Pride and Prejudice*, p. 163; *Mansfield Park*, p. 41.
69. *Letters*, no. 137, p. 472.
70. *Mansfield Park*, p. 180; *Minor Works*, p. 532.
71. *Letters*, no. 6, p. 14; no. 30, p. 105; no. 32, p. 113.
72. Ibid., no. 30, p. 106; no. 31, pp. 111-12; no. 48, p. 173; no. 49, p. 181; no. 52, p. 193; no. 53, p. 202.
73. Ibid., no. 27, p. 91; no. 43, p. 151.
74. *Mansfield Park*, p. 469.
75. *Letters*, no. 27, p. 93; no. 30, p. 105; no. 32, p. 115.
76. R. Austen-Leigh, *Austen Papers*, p. 249.

Chapter 9: Manners and Morals

1. Edmund Burke, *Letters on a Regicide Peace*, no. i, in *The Works of the Right Honourable Edmund Burke* (2 vols, London, 1834), ii, p. 296.
2. John Skinner, *Journal of a Somerset Rector, 1803–34*, ed. H. and P. Coombs (Bath, 1930), p. 41.
3. Muriel Jaeger, *Before Victoria* (London, 1956), p. 16.
4. R.I. and S.W. Wilberforce, *The Life of William Wilberforce* (5 vols, London, 1838), i, pp. 285, 317; ii, p. 103; v, p. 169.
5. Hannah More, *Thoughts on the Importance of the Manners of the Great to General Society*, in *The Works of of Hannah More* (18 vols, London, 1818), vi, pp. 1-3; eadem, *Essay on St Paul* ibid., viii, pp. 344-46.
6. *Letters*, no. 65, p. 256; no. 66, p. 259; no. 73, p. 287.
7. Hannah More, *Manners of the Great* in *Works*, vi, p. 15.
8. *Persuasion*, pp. 140, 147.
9. *Emma*, pp. 319-20; James Austen, *Loiterer*, no. 39, p. 142.
10. *Letters*, no. 86, p. 343; no. 91, p. 370; *Emma*, pp. 270, 281.
11. *Mansfield Park*, p. 99.
12. Ibid., p. 463.
13. Ibid., pp. 391-92.
14. *Persuasion*, p. 68.
15. Ibid., pp. 74-75.
16. *Letters*, no. 82, pp. 322, 323.
17. Hannah More, *Coelebs in Search of a Wife*, in *Works*, ix, p. 189. Jane Austen was very interested in dress; see Penelope Byrde, *A Frivolous Distinction: Fashion and Needlework in the Works of Jane Austen* (Bath, 1979), p. 2.
18. *Northanger Abbey*, p. 24; *Letters*, no. 15, p. 45.
19. *Pride and Prejudice*, pp. 283-84, 287.
20. Hannah More, *Strictures on the Modern System of Female Education* (2 vols, London, 1799), ii, pp. 103-4.
21. *Northanger Abbey*, pp. 74-75; *Sense and Sensibility*, pp. 53-4.
22. *Letters*, no. 1, pp. 1-2; *Sense and Sensibility*, p. 53.
23. *Pride and Prejudice*, p. 183; *Mansfield Park*, p. 450.
24. Edmund Burke, *Reflections on the Revolution in France*, in *Works*, i, p. 414.
25. Ibid., i, p. 415.
26. *Mansfield Park*, p. 12.
27. *Letters*, no. 103, pp. 409-10; *Pride and Prejudice*, p. 369.
28. *Sense and Sensibility*, p. 333; *Pride and Prejudice*, p. 175.
29. *Mansfield Park*, pp. 462, 458-59.
30. *Sense and Sensibility*, p. 34; *Letters*, no. 141, p. 482.
31. *Mansfield Park*, p. 60; *Letters*, no. 137, p. 472.
32. Ibid., no. 141, p. 485.
33. Ibid., no. 49, p. 179.
34. *Northanger Abbey*, p. 72.
35. *Mansfield Park*, p. 47.
36. Hannah More, *Strictures*, i, pp. 66-68; ii, pp. 94-103; *Sense and Sensibility*, pp. 17-18, 48.
37. Ibid., p. 215.
38. *Pride and Prejudice*, p. 64. See also the opening words of the following chapter, p. 70: 'Mr Collins was not a sensible man.'
39. *Sense and Sensibility*, p. 94; *Mansfield Park*, p. 65.

40. *Pride and Prejudice*, p. 180.
41. *Sense and Sensibility*, p. 331; *Mansfield Park*, pp. 269, 350-51, 456.
42. Ibid., p. 19.
43. John Locke, *Second Treatise of Civil Government* ed. J.W. Gough (3rd edn, Oxford, 1976), chap. 2, para. 6.
44. *Northanger Abbey*, pp. 66-67, 200; *Sense and Sensibility*, p. 263.

Chapter 10: Morals and Society

1. William Wilberforce, *A Practical View of the Prevailing System of Professed Christians in the Higher and Middle Classes in this Country Contrasted with Real Christianity* (London, 1797), pp. 106-9.
2. P.B. Shelley, preface to 'The Revolt of Islam', *The Complete Works of Percy Bysshe Shelley*, ed. R. Ingpen and W.E. Peck (10 vols, London, 1965), i, p. 242.
3. *Letters*, no. 55, p. 212.
4. *Pride and Prejudice*, pp. 156, 161.
5. Ibid., pp. 144-45.
6. *Mansfield Park*, p. 324.
7. *Pride and Prejudice*, p. 378.
8. *Mansfield Park*, p. 3.
9. Ibid., p. 43.
10. *Letters*, no. 59, p. 229; no. 63, p. 247; no. 64, pp. 252-53.
11. *Minor Works*, p. 383.
12. Wilberforce, *A Practical View*, p. 109.
13. *Letters*, no. 14, p. 41; *Northanger Abbey*, pp. 175, 178-79, 182-85.
14. *Mansfield Park*, pp. 138, 139, 144, 145, 164, 165-66.
15. Ibid., pp. 53, 65, 82; Humphry Repton, *The Landscape Gardening and Landscape Architecture of the Late Humphry Repton, being his Entire Works on these Subjects*, ed. J.C. Loudon (new edn, London, 1840), pp. 63-64, 92-93, 336-37. (Repton wrote of 'taking down a few miserable cottages and rebuilding them as tenements, in a plain, uniform manner . . .')
16. *Persuasion*, pp. 146-50, 137-38, 148-50.
17. Louis Simond, *Journal of a Tour and Residence in Great Britain, 1810–11* (London, 1812), cited in Maggie Lane, *Jane Austen's England* (London, 1986), p. 73.
18. *Sense and Sensibility*, p. 194.
19. *Mansfield Park*, p. 115.
20. *Letters*, no. 36, pp. 127-28.
21. *Emma*, p. 130.
22. *Mansfield Park*, pp. 472-73.
23. *Persuasion*, pp. 38, 44.
24. *Letters*, no. 89, p. 361.
25. *Pride and Prejudice*, p. 239.
26. *Northanger Abbey*, p. 241.
27. *Pride and Prejudice*, p. 70.
28. *Mansfield Park*, pp. 19-20.
29. *Pride and Prejudice*, pp. 230-31, 299.
30. *Northanger Abbey*, pp. 247, 249-50.
31. *Persuasion*, pp. 217-18.
32. *Pride and Prejudice*, p. 135.
33. Ibid., p. 236.
34. *Sense and Sensibility*, p. 112.
35. *Mansfield Park*, p. 46.
36. *Emma*, p. 250.
37. *Pride and Prejudice*, p. 385.
38. *Letters*, no. 133, p. 465; no. 99.1, p. 508.
39. Leslie Melville, *The Life and Letters of William Cobbett in England and America* (2 vols, London, 1913), i, pp. 156-57.

40. Edmund Burke, *The Works of the Right Honourable Edmund Burke* (2 vols, London, 1834), i, p. 455.
41. *Spectator*, 131, 31 July 1711 (collected edn, London, 1850), p. 188.
42. *Letters*, no. 23, p. 75.
43. Ibid., no. 27, p. 92.
44. Ibid., no 75, p. 293; no. 101, p. 405-6.
45. Edmund Burke, *Letters on a Regicide Peace*, no. 1, in *The Works of the Right Honourable Edmund Burke* (2 vols, London, 1834), ii, p. 300.
46. *Letters*, no. 5, p. 12; no. 77, p. 300.
47. *Mansfield Park*, pp. 39, 200-1.
48. *Letters*, no. 74.1, p. 502.
49. *Pride and Prejudice*, p. 208; *Northanger Abbey*, p. 198.
50. *Emma*, pp. 358, 360.
51. *Letters*, no. 55, p. 211.
52. Ibid., no. 70, p. 276.
53. *Emma*, p. 149.
54. G.F.A. Best, *Temporal Pillars: Queen Anne's Bounty, the Ecclesiastical Commissioners and the Church of England* (Cambridge, 1964), p. 167.
55. Ibid., p. 168.
56. *Sense and Sensibility*, p. 226.
57. Ibid., p. 70; *Persuasion*, p. 13.
58. *Pride and Prejudice*, p. 310.
59. C. Austen, *Reminiscences of Caroline Austen* (Jane Austen Society, 1986), pp. 27-29.
60. *Persuasion*, p. 19.
61. *Emma*, p. 198.
62. *Persuasion*, pp. 73, 125.
63. Ibid., p. 85.
64. *Mansfield Park*, pp. 125, 182; R. Austen-Leigh, *Austen Papers, 1704–1856* (University Microfilms International, Ann Arbor, MI, 1980), p. 246.
65. Nikolaus Pevsner, 'The Architectural Setting of Jane Austen's Novels', *Journal of the Warburg and Courtauld Institutes*, 31 (1968), pp. 405-6.
66. *Persuasion*, p. 36; *Sense and Sensibility*, pp. 196-97.
67. *Letters*, no. 111, pp. 424-27; no. 116-18, pp. 433-41.
68. *Persuasion*, pp. 97-98.
69. *Letters*, no. 100, p. 461.
70. *Pride and Prejudice*, pp. 10, 387; *Mansfield Park*, p. 41.

Chapter 11: Worship and Belief

1. *Letters*, no. 89, p. 363; Jane Austen Society, *Collected Reports, 1966–1975* (1977), pp. 6-8.
2. Constance Hill, *Jane Austen, her Home and her Friends* (London, 1902), p. 119; James Woodforde, *The Diary of a Country Parson, 1758–1802*, ed. John Beresford (Oxford, 1949), p. 55; *Letters*, no. 36, p. 127; *Mansfield Park*, p. 408.
3. William Cobbett, *Rural Rides* (Penguin edn, Harmondsworth, 1967), p. 396.
4. C. Austen, *Reminiscences of Caroline Austen* (Jane Austen Society, 1986), pp. 39-40; *Emma*, p. 484.
5. W.K. Lowther Clarke, *Eighteenth-Century Piety* (London, 1944), p. 4.
6. Patrick Piggott, *The Innocent Diversion: A Study of Music in the Life and Writings of Jane Austen* (London, 1979), p. 144.
7. *Letters*, no. 8, p. 19; no. 40, pp. 143-45.
8. Ibid., no. 147, pp. 497-98.
9. Ibid., no. 96, p. 389; no. 99.1, p. 508.
10. Ibid., no. 134, p. 468.
11. *Persuasion*, p. 88; Jane Austen Society, *Collected Reports, 1976–1985* (1989), pp. 215-16.
12. Thomas Gisborne, *An Enquiry into the Duties of the Female Sex* (London, 1797), p. 42; *Letters*, no. 47, p. 169.
13. Gene Koppel, *The Religious Dimension of Jane Austen's Novels* (Ann Arbor, MI, 1988), p. 7.
14. John H. and Edith Hubback, *Jane Austen's Sailor Brothers* (London, 1906), pp. 16-20.
15. *Letters*, no. 101, p. 406; Thomas Sherlock, in V. Knox ed., *Family Lectures, or Domestic Divinity: Being a Copious Collection of Sermons* (London, 1791), i, pp. 295-96.
16. *Letters*, no. 103, p. 410; no. 106, p. 420.
17. *Mansfield Park*, p. 198.
18. A.M. Duckworth, *The Improvement of the Estate: A Study of Jane Austen's Novels* (Baltimore, 1971), pp. 218-29.
19. B.C. Southam, 'Sanditon, the Seventh Novel', in Juliet McMaster, ed., *Jane Austen's Achievement* (London, 1976), pp. 21-22.
20. *Mansfield Park*, pp. 152, 156.
21. *Persuasion*, p. 68, 97, 100-1.
22. *Letters*, no. 57, p. 220; no. 58, pp. 221-22.
23. Ibid., no. 65, p. 256.
24. Ibid., no. 32, p. 115.
25. Ibid., no. 113, p. 467.
26. *Mansfield Park*, p. 20; *Sense and Sensibility*, p. 331.
27. Ibid., p. 8.
28. *Persuasion*, p. 99.
29. Gisborne, *Duties of the Female Sex*, pp. 206-7.
30. *Mansfield Park* pp. 115, 350.
31. Knox, ed., *Family Lectures*, i, pp. 285-90.
32. Ibid., pp. 266-67.
33. *Mansfield Park*, p. 113.
34. Knox, ed., *Family Lectures*, i, p. 271.
35. W. Lowther Clarke, *Eighteenth-Century Piety*, p. 28.
36. Hubback, *Jane Austen's Sailor Brothers*, pp. 16- 20.
37. *Emma*, pp. 319-20.
38. *Sense and Sensibility*, p. 346.

39. *Persuasion*, p. 101.
40. *Mansfield Park*, p. 86.
41. *Letters*, no. 66, p. 261.
42. Ibid., no. 52, p. 197.
43. Peter Virgin, *The Church in an Age of Negligence: Ecclesiastical Structure and Problems of Reform, 1700–1840* (Cambridge, 1989), pp. 5-6.
44. *Persuasion*, p. 93.
45. E.R. Norman, *Church and Society in England, 1770– 1970* (Oxford, 1976), p. 17.
46. *Mansfield Park*, p. 82.
47. *Sense and Sensibility*, pp. 5, 351-52.
48. *Letters*, no. 60, p. 231.
49. Hubback, *Jane Austen's Sailor Brothers*, p. 114.
50. *Mansfield Park*, pp. 87-88.
51. W. Lowther Clarke, *Eighteenth-Century Piety*, p. 13.
52. *Letters*, no. 59, p. 227.
53. *Mansfield Park*, p. 453.
54. *Minor Works*, pp. 453-57.
55. Knox, ed., *Family Lectures*, i, pp. 276-80.
56. C. Austen, *My Aunt Jane Austen: A Memoir* (Jane Austen Society, 1991), p. 17.
57. *Letters*, no. 99.1, p. 507. For references to paintings which reminded her of characters in the novels, see ibid., no. 80, pp. 309-10.
58. Ibid., no. 133, p. 467; D.A. Winstanley, *Early Victorian Cambridge* (Cambridge, 1940), pp. 19-20.
59. *Mansfield Park*, p. 340.
50. *Northanger Abbey*, p. 8.
61. Koppel, *The Religious Dimension*, pp. 1, 125 n. 3; Duckworth, *Improvement of the Estate*, pp. 8, 26.
62. *Mansfield Park*, p. 294. The italics are the present author's.

Bibliography

1. Contemporary Works

Angus, W., *The Seats of the Nobility and Gentry in Great Britain and Wales* (London, 1787).

Austen, Caroline, *My Aunt Jane Austen: A Memoir* (new edn, Jane Austen Society, 1991)

—, *Reminiscences of Caroline Austen* (Jane Austen Society, 1986)

Austen, James, *The Loiterer* (Oxford, 1789–90).

Austen, Jane, *Jane Austen's Letters to her Sister Cassandra and Others*, ed. R.W. Chapman (Oxford, 1954).

—, *The Novels of Jane Austen: The Text Based on Collation of the Early Editions*, ed. R.W. Chapman (3rd edn, 5 vols, Oxford, 1954).

—, *The Works of Jane Austen*, vi, *Minor Works*, ed. R. W. Chapman (Oxford, 1954).

Austen-Leigh, J.E., *A Memoir of Jane Austen by her Nephew* (Oxford, 1926; from the 2nd edn, 1871).

—, *Recollections of the Early Days of the Vine Hunt* (London, 1865).

Austen-Leigh, R., *Austen Papers, 1704–1856* (University Microfilms International, Ann Arbor, MI, 1980).

Burke, Edmund, *The Works of the Right Honourable Edmund Burke* (2 vols, London, 1834).

Burney, Fanny, *Selected Letters and Journals*, ed. Joyce Hemlow (Oxford, 1986).

Clare, John, *The Poems of John Clare*, ed. J.W. Tibble (2 vols, London, 1935).

Cobbett, William, *Rural Rides* (Penguin edn, Harmondsworth, 1967).

Cockburn, William, *Strictures on Clerical Education in the University of Cambridge* (London, 1809).

Cooper, Rev. Edward, *Sermons* (2nd edn, London, 1805–6).

Cowper, William, *Cowper: Poetical Works*, ed. H.S. Milford (4th edn, Oxford, 1967).

Crabbe, George, *The Complete Poetical Works of George Crabbe*, ed. N. Dalrymple-Champneys and A. Pollard (3 vols, Oxford, 1988).

Edgeworth, Maria, *Belinda* (London, 1801.

—, *Practical Education* (London, 1798).

Fordyce, James, *The Character and Conduct of the Female Sex* (London, 1776).

—, *Sermons to Young Women* (London, 1766).

Gibbon, Edward, *The Memoirs of the Life of Edward Gibbon, by Himself*, ed. G.B. Hill (London, 1900).

Gilpin, William, *Three Essays on Picturesque Beauty* (London, 1792).

Gisborne , Thomas, *An Enquiry into the Duties of the Female Sex* (London, 1797).

—, *An Enquiry into the Duties of Men in the Higher and Middle Classes of Society* (5th edn, 2 vols, 1800).

Halfpenny, William, *Useful Architecture in Twenty-One New Designs for Country Parsonages, Farm Houses and Inns* (London, 1752).

Hodgson, Christopher, *An Account of the Augmentation of Small Livings by the Governors of the Bounty of Queen Anne* (London, 1826).

Jones, William, *The Diary of the Rev. William Jones, 1771–1821*, ed. O.F. Christie (London, 1929).

Knight, Richard Payne, *The Landscape* (London, 1794).

Knox, Vicesimus, ed., *Family Lectures, or Domestic Divinity: Being a Copious Collection of Sermons* (2 vols, London, 1791). (Vol. I includes extracts from the sermons of Thomas Sherlock).

Le Faye, Deirdre, 'Three Austen Family Letters', *Notes and Queries*, 230 (1985), pp. 329-35.

—, 'News from Chawton: A Letter from Mrs George Austen, *Review of English Studies*, new series, 38 (1987), pp. 364-68.

Locke, John, *An Essay Concerning Human Understanding*, ed. A.S. Pringle-Patterson (Oxford, 1934).

—, *Second Treatise of Civil Government*, ed. J.W. Gough (3rd edn, Oxford, 1976).

—, *Some Thoughts Concerning Education*, ed. J.W. and J.S. Yolton (Oxford, 1989).

Mitford, Mary Russell, *Our Village* (1st series, new edn, London, 1879).

More, Hannah, *The Works of Hannah More* (18 vols, London, 1818).

—, *Strictures on the Modern System of Female Education* (2 vols, London, 1799).

Neale, J.P., *Views of the Seats of Noblemen and Gentlemen in England, Wales, Scotland and Ireland* (1st series, 6 vols, London, 1818–23).

Newton, Benjamin, *The Diary of Benjamin Newton, Rector of Wath, 1816–18*, ed. C.P. Fendall and E.A. Crutchley (Cambridge, 1933).

Paley, William, *Evidences of Christianity* (London, 1794).

—, *Principles of Moral and Political Philosophy* (London, 1785).

Papworth, John B., *Rural Residences* (London, 1818).

Price, Uvedale, *An Essay on Architecture and Building* (Hereford, 1798).

—, *An Essay on Artificial Water* (Hereford, 1798).

—, *An Essay on the Picturesque* (London, 1794).

Repton, Humphry, *The Landscape Gardening and Landscape Architecture of the Late Humphry Repton, being his Entire Works on these Subjects*, ed. J.C. Loudon (new edn, London 1840).

Rivington, F.C. and J., ed., *The Clerical Guide* (1817; 2nd edn, 1822).

Rochefoucauld, François de la, *A Frenchman in England, 1784*, ed. J. Marchand (Cambridge, 1933).

Sandby, Paul, *Collection of 150 Select Views* (London, 1782).

Shelley, P.B., *The Complete Works of Percy Bysshe Shelley*, ed. R. Ingpen and W.E. Peck (10 vols, London, 1965).

Skinner, John, *Journal of a Somerset Rector, 1803–34*, ed. H. and P. Coombs (Bath, 1930).

Southey, Robert, *Letters from England, by Dom Manuel Alvarez Espriella*, ed. Jack Simmons (London, 1951).

Spectator, The (collected edn, London 1850).

Terry, Stephen, *The Diaries of Dummer: Reminiscences of an Old Sportsman, Stephen Terry of Dummer* (London, 1934).

Wakefield, Priscilla, *Reflections on the Present Condition of the Female Sex* (London, 1798).

Ware, Isaac, *Complete Body of Architecture* (London, 1756).

Watts, W., *The Seats of the Nobility and Gentry, in a Collection of the Most Interesting Picturesque Views* (London, 1779).

White, Gilbert, *The Natural History of Selborne* (Harmondsworth, 1987).

Wilberforce, R.I. and S.W., *The Life of William Wilberforce* (5 vols, London, 1838).

—, *Correspondence of William Wilberforce* (2 vols, London, 1840).

Wilberforce, William, *A Practical View of the Prevailing System of Professed Christians in the Higher and Middle Classes in this Country Contrasted with Real Christianity* (London, 1797).

Woodforde, James, *The Diary of a Country Parson, 1758–1802*, ed. John Beresford (Oxford, 1949).

Wordsworth, Dorothy, *Journals of Dorothy Wordsworth*, ed. Mary Moorman (Oxford, 1971).

2. SECONDARY WORKS

Abbey, C.J. and Overton, J., *The English Church in the Eighteenth Century* (2 vols, London 1878).

Addison, William, *Farmhouses in the English Landscape* (London, 1958).

Andrews, Malcolm, *The Search for the Picturesque: Landscape, Aesthetics and Tourism in Britain, 1760–1800* (London, 1988).

Aslet, Clive, 'Stoneleigh Abbey, Warwickshire, ii', *Country Life*, 20 Dec. 1984.

Austen-Leigh, Emma, *Jane Austen at Steventon* (London, 1937).

Austen-Leigh, M.A., *Personal Aspects of Jane Austen* (London, 1920).

Austen-Leigh, R.A., *Jane Austen and Southampton* (London, 1948).

Austen-Leigh, W. and Knight, M.G., *Chawton Manor and its Owners* (London, 1911).

Austen-Leigh, W. and R.A., and Le Faye, Deirdre, *Jane Austen: A Family Record* (London, 1989).

Baker, F., *William Grimshaw* (London, 1963).

Balfour, Lady, 'The Servants in Jane Austen', *Cornhill Magazine*, new series, 67 (1929), pp. 694-705.

Balleine, G.R., *A History of the Evangelical Party in the Church of England* (London, 1908).

Banfield, Ann, 'The Moral Landscape in *Mansfield Park*', *Nineteenth-Century Fiction* (1971), pp. 1-24.

Barrell, John, *The Dark Side of the Landscape* (London, 1980).

Batey, Mavis, 'In Quest of Jane Austen's "Mr Repton"', *Garden History*, 5 (1977), pp. 19-29.

—, 'Jane Austen at Stoneleigh Abbey', *Country Life*, 30 Dec., 1976.

Bax, B. Anthony, *The English Parsonage* (London, 1964).

Best, G.F.A., *Temporal Pillars: Queen Anne's Bounty, the Ecclesiastical Commissioners and the Church of England* (Cambridge, 1964).

Branton, C.L., 'The Ordinations in Jane Austen's Novels', *Nineteenth-Century Fiction*, 10 (1955–56), pp. 156-59.

Brown, C.K. Francis, *A History of the English Clergy, 1800–1900* (London, 1953).

Brown, Ford K., *Fathers of the Victorians: The Age of Wilberforce* (Cambridge, 1961).

Brown, R.J., *The English Country Cottage* (London, 1979).

Bush, Douglas, *Jane Austen* (New York, 1975).

Butler, Marilyn, *Jane Austen and the War of Ideas* (Oxford, 1975).

Byrde, Penelope, *A Frivolous Distinction: Fashion and Needlework in the Works of Jane Austen* (Bath, 1979).

Carnall, G., *Robert Southey and his Age* (Oxford, 1960).

Carpenter, E.F., *Thomas Sherlock* (London, 1936).

Cecil, [Lord] David, *A Portrait of Jane Austen* (London, 1978).

Chadwick, Owen, *The History of the Church: A Select Bibliography* (London, 1973).

Chalklin, C.W. *The Provincial Towns of Georgian England* (London, 1974).

Chapman, R.W., *Jane Austen: A Critical Bibliography* (Oxford, 1955).

—, *Jane Austen: Facts and Problems* (Oxford, 1948).

—, 'Jane Austen's Friend, Mrs Barret', *Nineteenth-Century Fiction* (1949), pp. 171-74.

Clarke, H.F., *The English Landscape Garden* (London, 1980).

Clarke, Basil F.L., *The Building of the Eighteenth-Century Church* (London, 1963).

Cook, Olive, *English Country Cottages and Farmhouses* (London, 1982).

Cooke, R.A., 'As Jane Austen Saw the Clergy', *Theology Today*, 18 (1961–62), pp. 41-50.

Cragg, G.R., *The Church in the Age of Reason* (London, 1962).

—, *Reason and Authority in the Eighteenth Century* (Cambridge, 1964).

Curtis, William, *History of Alton* (Winchester, 1896).

Davidoff, L. and Hall, C., *Family Fortunes: Men and Women of the English Middle Class, 1780–1850* (London, 1987).

Devlin, D., *Jane Austen and Education* (London, 1975).

Downes, Kerry, *The Georgian Cities of Britain* (Oxford, 1948).

Drew, Philip, 'Jane Austen and Bishop Butler', *Nineteenth-Century Fiction*, 35 (1980–81), pp. 127-49.

Duckworth, A.M., *The Improvement of the Estate: A Study of Jane Austen's Novels* (Baltimore, MD 1971).

Evans, Eric J., 'Some Reasons for the Growth of English Rural Anti-Clericalism', *Past and Present*, 66 (1975), pp. 84-109.

Evans, Mary, *Jane Austen and the State* (London, 1987).

Furneaux, Robin, *William Wilberforce* (London, 1974).

Garside, P.D., 'Jane Austen and Subscription Fiction', *British Journal of Eighteenth-Century Studies*, 10 (1981), pp. 175-88.

Gascoigne, John, *Cambridge in the Age of Enlightenment* (Cambridge, 1989).

George, M. Dorothy, *Catalogue of Political and Personal Satires in the British Museum*, vii, *1793–1800* (London, 1942).

Girouard, Mark, *Life in the English Country House* (London, 1978).

Gilson, David, *A Bibliography of Jane Austen* (London, 1982).

Grey, J. David, *The Handbook of Jane Austen* (London, 1986).

Hadfield, Miles, *A History of British Gardening* (London, 1989).

Hardy, Barbara, *A Reading of Jane Austen* (London, 1975).

Harris, Jocelyn, *Jane Austen's Art of Memory* (Cambridge, 1989).

Hart, A. Tindal, *The Country Priest in English History* (London, 1959).

—, *The Curate's Lot* (Newton Abbott, 1971).

—, *The Eighteenth-Century Country Parson* (Shrewsbury, 1935).

Hill, Constance, *Jane Austen, her Homes and her Friends* (London, 1902).

Honan, Park, *Jane Austen: Her Life* (London, 1987).

Horn, Pamela, *Life in a Country Town: Reading and Mary Russell Mitford, 1787–1855* (Abingdon, 1984).

Hubback, John H, and Edith, *Jane Austen's Sailor Brothers* (London, 1906).

Hunt, J.D., *Garden and Grove: The Italian Renaissance Garden in the English Imagination, 1600-1750* (London, 1986).

—, and Willis, P., ed., *The Genius of the Place: The English Landscape Garden, 1620–1820* (London, 1975).

Hunt, V.J., *Chawton, 1841–81* (unpublished Ph.D. thesis, Portsmouth Polytechnic, 1986).

Hussey, Christopher, *The Picturesque* (London, 1975).

—, 'Chawton House', *Country Life*, 9 Feb. 1945

—, 'Godmersham Park, Kent', *Country Life*, 23 Feb. 1945.

Hyams, Edward, *English Cottage Gardens* (London, 1970).

Hylson-Smith, K., *Evangelicals in the Church of England, 1734–1984* (Edinburgh, 1989).

Jackson, Michael, 'Jane Austen's View of the Clergy', *Theology* (1975), pp. 53-68.

Jacques, D., *Georgian Gardens: The Reign of Nature* (London, 1983).

Jaeger, Muriel, *Before Victoria* (London, 1956).

Jane Austen Society, *Collected Reports, 1949–1965* (1967).

—, *Collected Reports, 1966–1975* (1977).

—, *Collected Reports, 1976–1985* (1989).

—, Individual *Reports* annually from 1987.

Janowitz, Anne, *England's Ruins: Poetic Purpose and National Landscape* (Oxford, 1990).

Jenkins, Elizabeth, *Jane Austen: A Biography* (London, 1938).

Jones, H.M. and Cohen, I.B., *Science before Darwin* (London, 1963).

Kirkland, J.J., 'Jane Austen and Bonomi', *Notes and Queries*, 232 (1987), pp. 24-25.

Koppel, Gene, *The Religious Dimension of Jane Austen's Novels* (Ann Arbor, MI, 1988).

Lane, Maggie, *Jane Austen's England* (London, 1986).

—, *Jane Austen's Family through Five Generations* (London, 1984).

Lascelles, Mary, *Jane Austen and her Art* (Oxford, 1939).

Laski, Marghanita, *Jane Austen and her World* (London, 1969).

Laxton, Paul, ed., *The A to Z of Regency London* (London, 1985).

Le Fanu, W.R., *Queen Anne's Bounty* (London, 1921).

Lewis, C.S., 'A Note on Jane Austen', *Essays in Criticism*, 4 (1954), pp. 339-71.

Lockhead, Marion, 'Literature versus Celibacy', *Quarterly Review*, 294 (1956), pp. 207-17.

McClatchey, Diana, *Oxfordshire Clergymen, 1777–1869* (Oxford, 1960).

MacDonagh, Oliver, 'Highbury and Chawton: Social Convergence in *Emma*', *Historical Studies*, 18 (1978), pp. 37-51.

MacKinnon, F.D., 'Topography and Travel in Jane Austen's Novels', *Cornhill Magazine*, 59 (1925), pp. 184-99.

McMaster, Juliet, ed., *Jane Austen's Achievement* (London, 1976).

Malins, Edward, *English Landscaping and Literature, 1660–1840* (London, 1966).

Melville, Leslie, *Life and Letters of William Cobbett in England and America* (2 vols, London, 1913).

Mingay, G.E., *English Landed Society in the Eighteenth Century* (London, 1963).

Monaghan, David, '*Mansfield Park* and Evangelicalism: A Reassessment', *Nineteenth-Century Fiction*, 33 (1978–79), pp. 215-30.

—, ed. *Jane Austen in a Social Context* (London, 1981).

Morris, Ivor, *Mr Collins Considered: Approaches to Jane Austen* (London, 1987).

Mudie, R., *Hampshire* (3 vols, Winchester, 1833).

Mudrick, Marvin, *Jane Austen: Irony as Defense and Discovery* (Princeton, NJ, 1954).

Myer, V.G., *Jane Austen* (London, 1980).

Nardin, Jane, *Those Elegant Decorums: The Concept of Propriety in Jane Austen's Novels* (New York, 1973).

Norman, E.R., *Church and Society in England, 1770–1970* (Oxford, 1976).

Osborne, John W., *William Cobbett: His Thoughts and his Times* (London, 1966).

Ousley, Ian, *The Englishman's England: Taste, Travel and the Rise of Tourism* (Cambridge, 1990).

Pevsner, Nikolaus, 'The Architectural Setting of Jane Austen's Novels', *Journal of the Warburg and Courtauld Institutes*, 31 (1968), pp. 404-22.

—, and Wedgewood, H., *Warwickshire* (Buildings of England, London, 1966).

Phillips, Patricia, *The Scientific Lady: A Social History of Women's Scientific Interests, 1520–1918* (London, 1990).

Piggott, Patrick, *The Innocent Diversion: A Study of Music in the Life and Writings of Jane Austen* (London, 1977).

Platt, Colin, *The Parish Churches of Medieval England* (London, 1981).

Pollock, John, *Wilberforce* (London, 1977).

Prosser, G.F., *Select Illustrations of Hampshire* (London, 1833).

Purvis, J.S., *Dictionary of Ecclesiastical Terms* (London, 1962).

Ragg, Laura M., 'Jane Austen's Parks and Gardens', *Country Life*, 85 (1939), p. 632.

Rivington, S., *The History of Tonbridge School* (London, 1910).

Roth, Barry, *An Annotated Bibliography of Jane Austen Studies, 1973–83* (Charlottesville, VA, 1985).

—, and Weinsheimer, J., *An Annotated Bibliography of Jane Austen Studies, 1952–72* (Charlottesville, VA, 1973).

Rowley, T., *Villages in the Landscape* (London, 1978).

Rupp, Gordon, *Religion in Oxford, 1688–1791* (Oxford, 1968).

Russell, Anthony, *The Clerical Profession* (London, 1980).

—, *The Country Parish* (London, 1968).

Ryle, Gilbert, 'Jane Austen and the Moralists', *Critical Essays on Jane Austen*, ed. B.C. Southam (London, 1968), pp. 136-61.

Savidge, Alan, *The Parsonage in England: Its History and Architecture* (London, 1969).

Saville, Diana, *Walled Gardens: Their Planting and Design* (London, 1982).

Scott, Walter S., *White of Selborne* (new edn, Liss, 1985).

Scott-James, Anne, *The Cottage Garden* (London, 1981).

Smith, William, *A New and Compendious History of the County of Warwick* (Birmingham, 1830).

Smithers, David W., *Jane Austen in Kent* (Westerham, 1982).

Southam, B.C., *Jane Austen's Literary Manuscripts* (Oxford, 1964).

—, ed., *Critical Essays on Jane Austen* (London, 1968).

—, ed., *Jane Austen: The Critical Heritage*, i, *1811–70* (London, 1968); ii, *1870–1940* (London, 1987).

Squibb, G.D., *Founder's Kin* (Oxford, 1972).

Stephen, Leslie, *English Thought in the Eighteenth Century* (2 vols, London, 1963).

Stroud, D., *Capability Brown* (London, 1957).

—, *Humphry Repton* (London, 1962).

Stuart, David C., *Georgian Gardens* (London, 1979).

Sutherland, L.S. and Mitchell, L.G., ed. *The History of the University of Oxford*, v, *The Eighteenth Century* (Oxford, 1986).

Sykes, Norman, *Church and State in England in the Eighteenth Century* (London, 1934).

Tanner, Tony, *Jane Austen* (London, 1986).

Thomas, G., *William Cowper and the Eighteenth Century* (London, 1984).

Thompson, F.M.L., *English Landed Society in the Nineteenth Century* (London, 1963).

Thorne, R.G., ed., *History of Parliament: The House of Commons, 1790–1820* (5 vols, London, 1986).

Todd, Janet, ed., *New Perspectives* (New York, 1983).

Townsend, C., 'Miss Austen's Village and Ours', *Spectator*, 10 (1910), pp. 266-67.

Tucker, G.H., *A Goodly Heritage: A History of Jane Austen's Family* (Manchester, 1983).

Verey, D., *Gloucestershire* Buildings of England (London, 1970).

Venn, J.A., *Foundations of Agricultural Economics* (Cambridge, 1923).

Victoria County History, *The County of Hampshire and the Isle of Wight* (6 vols, London, 1903–12).

Virgin, Peter, *The Church in an Age of Negligence: Ecclesiastical Structure and Problems of Reform, 1700–1840* (Cambridge, 1989).

Watkin, David, *The Buildings of Britain: Regency* (London, 1982).

Ward, W.R., *Georgian Oxford* (London, 1958).

—, *Religion and Society in England, 1790–1850* (London, 1972).

—, 'The Tithe Question in England in the Early-Nineteenth Century', *Journal of Ecclesiastical History*, 16 (1965), pp. 67-81.

Watson, Winifred, *Jane Austen in London* (Alton, 1960).

Watt, M.H., *History of the Parson's Wife* (London, 1945).

Wellesley, [Lord] Gerald, 'Houses in Jane Austen's Novels', *Spectator*, 135 (1926), pp. 524-25.

White, R.J., *Life in Regency England* (London, 1963).

Willey, B., *The English Moralists* (London, 1965).

Williams, Robert, 'Rural Economy and the Antique in the English Landscape Garden', *Journal of Garden History*, 7 (1987), pp. 73-96.

Winstanley, D.A., *Early Victorian Cambridge* (Cambridge, 1940).

Wise, T.J. and Symington, J.A., ed., *The Brontës: Their Lives, Friendships and Correspondence* (4 vols, Oxford, 1932).

Woodforde, John, *Georgian Houses for All* (London, 1978).

Wright, Richardson, *The Story of Gardening* (London, 1934).

Young, G.M., *Victorian England: Portrait of an Age* (2nd edn, Oxford, 1953).

Index

(references to plates are in bold)

the above 6, 35

Corunna (Spain) 80, 190

Cosway, Richard (1740-1821), painter 138

Cowper, William (1731-1800), poet and Christian lay assistant at Olney 76, 79, 80, 83, 99, **16**

Cox, Mr, solicitor at Highbury *(Emma)* 91, 108

Crabbe, George (1754-1832), poet; curate (1781) at Aldeburgh; chaplain (1782-85) to Duke of Rutland; vicar (mostly non-resident) of Muston (1789-1814); vicar of Trowbridge (1814) 101, 180, **17**

Craven, Hon. Charles, Governor of South Carolina, Mary Austen's grandfather 137

—, William, Lord (1770-1825), 7th Baron and 1st Earl of the 2nd creation, 29, 31

—, William, Lord (d. 1791), 6th Earl 20, 26, 29, 129

Crawford, Henry *(Mansfield Park)* 70-71, 72, 90, 96, 139, 147, 148, 153, 157, 164-65, 168, 172, 186, 194, 195

—, Mary *(Mansfield Park)* 27, 32-33, 46, 50, 60, 69, 79, 98-101, 124, 125, 126, 132, 147, 153-54, 156, 157, 161, 167, 168

Croft, Admiral *(Persuasion)* 150, 175

—, Mrs *(Persuasion)* 150

Crook(e), 'young Mr' and '2nd Miss' 111

Cubbington (Warwicks.) 7, 25, 51

curates 21-22, 29-30, 50, 73-74, 86

Dalrymple, Dowager-Viscountess *(Persuasion)* 163

Darcy, Mr *(Pride and Prejudice)* ix, 29, 77, 106, 127, 152-53, 161, 168, 172

Dartford (Kent) 67

Darwin, Charles (1809-82), naturalist 42

Dashwood, Elinor *(Sense and Sensibility)* 57-58, 79, 125, 138-39, 140, 147, 151, 153, 156, 157, 167, 175, 190, 192

—, family *(Sense and Sensibility)* 103

—, John *(Sense and Sensibility)* 27-28, 160, 184, 192

—, Marianne *(Sense and Sensibility)* 80, 147, 151, 155, 156, 157, 164, 171, 175, 192

—, Mrs *(Sense and Sensibility)* 36, 68, 128

Dawkins, Betty, of Steventon 87

Dawlish (Devon) 9

Deane, Deane House (Hants.) 4, 7, 27, 28, 30, 31, 33, 45, 52, 61, 62, 69, 72, 87-88, 98, 103, 112, 113, 115, 131, 134, 137, 171, 175

Debary, Rev. Peter (1725-1814), vicar (1775) of Hurstbourne Tarrant 5

—, Rev. Peter (1764-1841), eldest son of the above; Trinity College, Cambridge; curate (1804) and vicar (1807) of Eversley 5, 88, 124

—, Ann, Mary, Susannah, Sarah, daughters of Rev. Peter Debary, vicar of Hurstbourne Tarrant 5

De Bourgh, Lady Catherine *(Pride and Prejudice)* 29, 33-34, 62, 109, 118, 122, 135

—, Sir Lewis *(Pride and Prejudice)* 69

De Feuillide, Comtesse Eliza (1761-1813), Jane Austen's cousin and (1797-1813) sister-in-law 4, 40, 47, 65, 137

Delaford *(Sense and Sensibility)* 32, 51, 57, 62, 91

D'Entraigues, Comte (1756-1812) 174

Dickens, Charles (1812-70), novelist xi

Digweed, family, of Steventon Manor (Hants.) 3, 86-87, 103, 113, 126

—, Harry (1771-1848), 2nd son and successor to Hugh Digweed as tenant of Steventon Manor 55, 86-87

—, Hugh (1738-98), tenant of Steventon Manor 86-87, 116

—, Rev. James (1774-1862), 3rd son of Hugh Digweed of Steventon Manor 3, 15, 86-87, 140

—, Mrs Jane, wife of Harry Digweed 113

—, William Francis, 4th son of Hugh Digweed of Steventon Manor 86-87

dilapidations 74

Disraeli, Benjamin (1804-81), Prime Minister (1868, 1874-80) xi

Donwell Abbey *(Emma)* 106, 122, 173, 176

Dorchester, Guy Carleton, Lord (1724-1808), and his wife, of Kempshott Park 107

Dove Cottage 82

Dummer (Hants.) 3, 16, 59, 88, 91, 103, 115, 181

Eastwell (Kent) 17

education 35-48, 132-34, 149, 152-53, 165, 187

Edward VI, King 135

Eliot, George (Marian Evans) (1819-80) xii

Elizabeth I, Queen 135-36

Elkstone (Gloucs.) 5, 7

Elliot, Anne *(Persuasion)* 22, 104, 148, 152, 157, 163, 175, 147, 160, 190, 191

—, Elizabeth *(Persuasion)* 148, 163

—, Mr William Walter *(Persuasion)* 49, 184

—, Sir Walter *(Persuasion)* 148, 163, 175

Elton, Rev. Mr *(Emma)* xi, 1, 37, 58-59, 70, 93, 96, 100, 118, 119, 122, 123, 130, 158, 165